# TALES FROM THE LIFE
# OF BRUCE WANNELL

# TALES FROM THE LIFE OF BRUCE WANNELL

ADVENTURER, LINGUIST, ORIENTALIST

Edited by

Barnaby Rogerson and Rose Baring

SICKLE MOON BOOKS

First published in 2020 by Sickle Moon Books, an imprint of
Eland Publishing Ltd, 61 Exmouth Market, London EC1R 4QL

ISBN: 978 1 900209 25 0

Front cover images: *Bruce in Afghanistan with his baz*;
*Bruce in the organ loft of the Église Saint-Michel, Cordes-sur-ciel*
(photo Andy Miller)

Back cover images: *Taxing Man* (photo John Batten);
*Bruce at Moghul tomb, Pakistan 1993* (photo Kate Quartano Brown);
*Bruce with a tour in Yemen 2008* (photo Richard Winter)

Inside cover images: *The Road from Rohtas* (photo Kate Quartano Brown);
*Bruce standing proud at the Abd'allah Ansari Shrine, Herat, Afghanistan*
(photo Andy Miller)

Text set in Great Britain by James Morris

Printed by Clays Ltd, Elcograf S.p.A

# CONTENTS

INTRODUCTION  9

CHRONOLOGY  21

A STUDENT OF LANGUAGE AND LIFE  29
A litter of *gourmands* *Julian Wannell*  31
Brown-haired and strikingly aesthetic *John Martin Robinson*  33
Picnics on the rooftop *Matthew Harragin*  35
Isis, but thousands of miles from Egypt *Neil Stratton*  38
An embarkation to Watteau-land *James Ramsay*  40
Over a low flame *Artemis Cooper*  43
Tax inspector *John Batten*  44
Random memories *Carla Gabrieli*  46

AFGHANISTAN AND PAKISTAN, 1985–98  49
Reading the Quran in Arabic in the early morning
 *Abdal Samad /David Summers*  51
A gift normally only bestowed on royalty *Jonathan L. Lee*  53
Kandahar, Afghanistan, April 1992 *John Butt*  56
Musical memories *Gordon Adam*  60
Neighbour in Pakistan *Brigitte Neubacher*  62
Inshallah *Lyse Doucet*  64
A life between adventure, Sufism and music *Ulrike Vestring*  66
Bound for Baluchistan *Frances Dodd*  68
A pianist and a cellist meet in Pakistan *Jean Gianfranceschi*  69
The most interesting year of my life *Elisabeth Rubi*  72
Speaking better than perfect French *Anthony Fitzherbert*  76
From Arcadia to the Hindu Kush *Kate Quartano Brown*  81
Two letters to Fynn Vergos *Bruce Wannell*  85

## A MODERN BATTUTA 95

Taliban marching powder   *Kevin Rushby* 97
Bruce: back into the blue   *Tim Mackintosh-Smith* 102
Cairo transformed   *Julian Reilly and Bojana Mojsov* 104
Bruce and Mahmoud   *Eric Stobbaerts and Adnan Ali* 106
Simon Everard Digby (1932–2010)   *Bruce Wannell* 109
Shaykh Abdu Rahim al-Bura'i, the Sufi   *Bruce Wannell* 116
The book that never was by the most interesting man
   in the world   *Nova Robinson* 126
Recollections: returning to Afghanistan   *Bruce Wannell* 130

## FREE-SCHOLAR, TRANSLATOR AND TEACHER 135

Bruce in Kabul   *Thomas Wide* 137
Timurid epitaphs, harpsichord and saffron   *Andy Miller* 142
A Sufi returns   *Fitzroy Morrissey* 145
… and then from his cape …   *Moin Mir* 147
Whenever our paths crossed   *Tahir Shah* 150
Bruce at Galle   *Razeen Sally* 152
Someone I needed in my life   *Richard McClary* 155
Editing Bruce   *Bijan Omrani* 157
Meet at Rustem Pasha   *Janet and Paul Starkey* 160
Lothians to Lahore   *Isabel Buchanan* 164
Speak to that gentleman over there   *Gianni Dubbini Venier* 166
Persian grammar   *Charlie Gammell* 171
Sour maids and other career advice   *Ben Cuddon* 172
'over the Kachikani glacier into Swat…'   *Nick Buchan* 174
Breakfast with Bruce   *Lydia Wilson* 176
A garden close to the tomb of Sa'di   *Robert Maxwell* 178
Persian cooking   *Bruce Wannell* 182
Sufi poetry for Amnesty   *Graham Henderson* 187
Rumi   *Alan Williams* 189
Designing books with Bruce   *Celia Ward* 192
A formidable but modest scholar   *Warwick Ball* 194

## AMATEUR MUSICIAN AND PROFESSIONAL GUEST 199

It began with Schubert's trout quintet at Isfahan
   *Norman MacSween* 201
Accompanying Bruce: piano wars   *Andrew Campbell-Tiech* 204
Journeys through life   *Christopher Sykes* 208
Bruce would call me '*umm-as-salon*'   *Dalu Jones* 211
Elusive, implausible   *Joe Roberts* 213
Bruce comes to the 'rescue'   *Lucinda Bredin* 215

Somewhere between Spitfire pilot and steampunk  *Peter Barker*  217
The call  *Julie Bland*  220
Italy with Bruce  *Helena Gerrish*  222
Bruce in Muscat  *Nicholas Armour*  224
Bruce has come and gone  *Ian Blois*  226
We'll take the Bruce route...  *Fiona Frame and Kai Price*  233
With Bruce for Hogarth at the Soane  *John Nicoll*  237
Hampi heroes  *George Michell and John Fritz*  240
An Italian memory  *Anthony Eyre*  242
A carpet bag of reference books  *Richard Lamborn*  244
Kamaa  *James Wannell*  246
Journey back to the violin  *Katherine Schofield*  251
Learning from a master at work  *Sina Fakhroddin Ghaffari*  257

DRAGOMAN BRUCE  263
Bruce the host  *Gwendolyn Leick*  265
His Flemish was camp, singing, poetic ...  *Sylvie Franquet*  268
Butter  *Rose Baring*  269
Bruce as dragoman  *Antony Wynn*  271
Reminding locals of good, forgotten traditions  *Reza Mir*  273
Before the gate of the legation  *Richard Lambert*  276
A stranger closer than a friend  *Dori Dana-Haeri*  278
With Bruce to the Hadramaut  *Sally Sampson*  279
The signature of the calligrapher  *Canan Alioğlu*  281
Bruce on tour  *Amelia Stewart*  283
Dragoman extraordinaire  *Warwick Ball*  286
Persian picnics  *Barnaby Rogerson*  292
From godfather to friend  *William and Alec Harragin*  299
If he was kidnapped...  *Heather Wannell*  301

LITERARY PARTNERSHIP  303
*William Dalrymple*  305

THREE FAREWELLS  331
Pots, pottering and *cintamani*  *Isabel Denyer*  333
Moscow, 1971  *George Lemos*  336
Bruce's house  *Nick Robinson*  342

AFTERWORD  345
Bruce's last performance  *Lisa Chaney*  347

# INTRODUCTION

Bruce Wannell was the greatest orientalist traveller of his generation: a Paddy Leigh Fermor of the East, a Kim for our own time. He lived in Iran through the revolution and worked for a decade in the North West Frontier during the Russian occupation of Afghanistan. Speaking Iranian and Afghan Persian with a dazzling, poetic fluency, he could also talk in Arabic, Pushtu, Urdu, Swahili, be amiable in Amharic, Spanish and Greek and could lecture fluently in French, Italian, English or German. Bruce could also sightread and transcribe the most complex Arabic calligraphy.

He had lived, not just travelled, through many of the lands of Islam and could reference their cultural artefacts against the artistic treasures of Europe. His curious combination of talents – linguist, musician, translator and teacher – were reflected in an international network of friendships with scholars, poets, aid-workers, archaeologists, diplomats, artists and writers. He was also a sponger of the first water, whose various achievements as a tyrannical house guest exceeded the collective literary tradition of Dickens's Skimpole, Evelyn Waugh's John Beaver or Olivia Manning's Prince Yakimov.

In the last fifteen years of his life, he combined all these skills and became the resident amanuensis of William Dalrymple, staying for months at a time in his house outside Delhi. Working together against a backdrop of tame goats, a brilliant cook, parrots, visiting fans, passing musicians (not to mention the presence of three Dalrymple children and their artist mother Olivia Fraser), they created four books about the Mughal Empire. It was a unique achievement, which combined fresh archival scholarship with a rollicking page-turning narrative, that both entertained and instructed a vast international readership, whilst subtly inoculating them with historical revisionism and scholastic multi-culturalism. In volume after volume – *White Mughals*, *The Last Mughal*, *Return of the King*, *The Anarchy* – William Dalrymple saluted the vital contribution of his scholar-house guest, who he acknowledged to be 'the best translator of eighteenth-century Persian' and 'probably my best friend in the world'. Bruce could be maddening. I remember William rather regretting paying him an advance (on which he immediately disappeared off to Ethiopia for months until lack of funds brought his return). Similarly, Bruce could be annoyed by the rock-star status of William in India, 'surrounded by sycophants until dawn.' Bruce was always wilful, spending months translating a Sufi poet fantasizing about being loved by a lion in the desert (knowing it was not likely to be of any use) but time after time made up for these 'diversions' by the most extraordinary discoveries, creating original translations of 'five Afghan histories in the book market in Kabul; the unused Mutiny Papers in Delhi and a bunch of first person eighteenth-century histories of late Mughal India.'

I think Malaysia and Indonesia were the only gaps left on Bruce's map of the Muslim world. His arena of greatest expertise was Iran and the old Empire of Persianate culture that surrounds it, such as Afghanistan, Central Asia, Pakistan and the principalities within Moghul India. He had a special facility for the deciphering of timeworn inscriptions, and an innate understanding of the influences that had inspired late medieval calligraphers: the interlayering of Persian, Turkic and Arabic literary and spiritual traditions and grammar, alongside local dialects. For Bruce knew at first hand the workings of a still intact traditional Muslim civilization: how a waspish poet, an enlightened mystic, a fawning historian or troop of musicians all fitted into the household of a ruler; how literature, for all the formal honour that it was given, in practice worked as little more than the prompt for a much more virile oral tradition; and how this recited language was itself interlaced with the giving and receiving of hospitality, of the civilized roles of food and music presided over by the host.

Aside from Dalrymple, he worked with a number of scholars to whom he would become a living legend. I witnessed a fund-raising evening organised by Amnesty International in an elegant City of London office, where he provided simultaneous translations from poet-exiles reciting in half-a-dozen languages. He had not even had time to change, for his plane had been delayed. It had caught fire leaving Kabul, where he had been teaching traditional calligraphy to young Afghan craftsmen, working to restore their city. On another occasion I accompanied him to a conference organised by the Ashmolean Museum in Oxford, around an exhibition of sacred and esoteric objects, and noticed over the day how he was greeted with special affection and respect by every single speaker and half of the audience. It was wonderful to see how well regarded and cherished Bruce was in this otherwise competitive academic world. In one way or another he had assisted them all in their researches, checking an inscription on site, working out a variant transcription or offering a fresh translation.

Bruce had converted to Islam as a young man on the North West Frontier. He had studied beside traditional Sunni scholars, taken up residence in the zaouia of hereditary Sufi scholars and throughout his life immersed himself in the rich literary tradition of Iranian poets and Shiite sacred texts. His work as a translator always fitted into this tradition of Islamic scholarship, where a succession of commentators, all working to understand a sacred tradition, form a golden chain. I began to think that the years of labour he put into translating the sacred cosmology of Imam Ali was never really designed to be finished but was a form of worship.

Within the world of Anglo-Islam, Bruce was saluted as a savant, a spiritually wise friend who was often called upon to help others in their quest for a fully lived life. In the end I think he believed more passionately in civilization than in any organised religion and was as interested in the commentators (be they Hafiz, Mozart, Rumi, Schubert, Ibn Arabi or Beethoven) as the Prophets and Kings. His essay on the references to paradise within the Quran (published by *Critical Muslim*), his selection of Sufi verse (published by Amnesty International), his translations in *Persian Poems* (with Robert Maxwell) are bookmarks on this long personal journey. He loved working with other minds, and I notice that all his published works were achieved in some sort of intellectual partnership. He was kind enough to give my biography of the Prophet Muhammad, and a later work on the first four Caliphs, a critical reading. The proofs came back not just corrected but ornamented with elegant spirals of calligraphy in coloured ink, which had themselves been annotated by later readings. I am not alone, indeed British writers on Islamic themes tend to divide into two factions: those who happily acknowledge their debt to Bruce, and those who bear the hidden scars of a Bruce book review.

Bruce had enthusiasm, he had stamina, he had knowledge, he had an ear and a delight for music, language and poetry. What he did not have was money or any interest in making it, let alone submitting to the slavery of a salary. He never owned a car, contributed to a pension fund or found himself burdened with a mortgage. As a young man straight out of university he taught English in foreign universities for five years, before working as a freelance translator-amateur musician-professional house guest in London for four years. For the next eight years (1985–1993) he was based in the North West Frontier of Pakistan: for the first two years as an administrator for Afghanaid, then as a freelance scriptwriter, translator and researcher into the complex internal politics of Afghanistan. When he left Pakistan, he accepted a commission from his friend, the publisher Nick Robinson, to write a travel book that would embrace the Islamic World, and travelled in Egypt, Syria, Sudan and the Yemen. The book was never published, for although he spent years on it, it became vast and he strangled it with footnoted scholarship that flickered between half-a-dozen scripts and a dozen languages. This failure must have been difficult to digest, but my wife did at least manage to extract, then edit and publish, a section from his Sudan travels. *The Independent* selected Bruce's essay to be serialised, which was a happy incident.

His home for the second half of his adult life was a narrow loft at the top of a terraced house in York owned by a housing trust. This cell would not have disgraced the vows of poverty of a hermit-scholar or a medieval medicant. It had no bed but was beautifully scented, with fragrances wafting out of his collection of Asian and African textiles, while the walls were entirely hidden by bulging shelves filled with a highly discerning library, three books deep. If you were lent one of these volumes, you invariably found several pages of Bruce's notes tucked into the back, plus references to other works and a photocopied article paper-clipped to an academic book review. I don't think there was a book in this loft that had not been properly read. There was certainly nothing second rate in that room. On a number of occasions young heroin addicts, his housemates, would break in and steal his books to sell in order to feed their addiction, but over the years the second-hand book dealers in York got to recognize Bruce's most valuable volumes and were able to return them. Bruce in his turn decided to feed the addicts, putting out food for them 'like the birds' and even visiting them in prison. He succeeded in his unlikely mission of civilising his English neighbours, furnishing the communal kitchen with Bokhara rugs and serving up delicious stews until the household became a model of its kind, winning prizes for best garden on a tight budget.

Bruce could sleep anywhere, and even when at home, simply wrapped himself up in a cloak and lay down on a hand-knotted woollen carpet from the mountains of Luristan. This habit of sleeping anywhere is one of the most enviable resources of a traveller, and makes a hotel of any cave, but it could also be alarming, for he might quite happily nod off while riding pillion on the back of a motorcycle. He knew nothing about engines or the mysteries of the gear box, which made him a very grateful and appreciative passenger, but also meant that all his friends had been 'wannelled' in their day. To be wannelled was to be coaxed into some wonderfully romantic quest – to identify some lost tomb of a legendary prince or some such thing – only to realise halfway through the journey that you were in fact being used as an unpaid chauffeur, conducting your guest safely to his next lodging. For one of the features of Bruce was that although he always appeared immaculately dressed, he travelled very light, never giving away his intentions by the size of his baggage. Other aspects of being 'wannelled' could be more fiscally alarming, like the time I was met at the door of a country hotel to be informed that 'all your other guests have already arrived Sir', or suddenly finding yourself in charge of the bill after a convivial lunch for six of Bruce's friends. But for a man of his slender means he was also extraordinarily generous with the little he had, giving away prized textiles and ceramics, though his favourite method of exchange was the gift of some carefully wrapped parcel of food, homemade or sourced from his travels: rock salt quarried from the Sahara, dried mulberries from Baltistan, pistachio nuts acquired in the covered souk of Aleppo, or some delicacy sourced from Leila's café-cum-shop in the East End, all assisted with detailed instructions on how they should be served. Like a nomad herdsman he could recognize when the ground needed a rest, and there were half a dozen houses in London where he placed himself by rotation. May they find their reward in the garden beyond.

Our office, in central London, would often be used as a bag drop, or as a base from which to extract a visa from an embassy, or for a teatime pause between lunch at someone else's club and the early evening lecture. He also loved to buy books from us before Christmas, leaving behind a Child & Co. cheque which would invariably bounce, so we ended up using them as bookmarks. I seem to remember that Bruce's Belgian grandfather had worked for a Catholic publishing house, and it became an important annual ritual picking up a book for his mother from a similar environment. We once made the mistake of trying to employ Bruce for a week, checking the accuracy of various translations within Fanny Parkes's Indian travel book. He would arrive very late, then make long, rather loud and piercing social calls, arranging meals and outings for himself over the next few days. After a lunch outing he would return, and then make a little textile nest for himself in the middle of the office floor and slumber. It was a period when we were employing half-a-dozen earnest apprentice publishers, who in the late afternoon he would feed with slices of polenta cake and bowls of rare tea. Just as they were leaving, he would finally settle down to work. It was fun, and good training for our young staff to meet a real traveller, walking around the office barefoot and wrapped in a shawl. But we made a resolution to hereafter cherish him as a friend and never to make the mistake of employing him again.

Bruce loved things that had been created with love and integrity, with authenticity and craft. He was seldom seen without some beautifully woven linen and silk scarf that had been picked up in an Eastern marketplace. He wore kaftans off the shoulder and a sarong with the balance and swagger of a native tribesman, though there was always something faintly offkey to his English wardrobe, as if Dick van Dyke was playing an Edwardian gentleman. Bruce also wore the slender moustache of a cad, the type which may once have been fashionable in the heyday of David Niven. The moustache did at least give some advance warning of the lethal amounts of charm that could be brought into play. Site guardians instructed to allow no-one near the archaeological trenches, bored security guards holding the key to the fortified gate of an embassy compound, body-built shaven-headed bouncers patrolling access to the palazzo would soon be reduced to conspiratorial giggles and become mere puppies in a Bruce escapade. One of his many successful social skills was an uncanny ear for identifying a regional accent and then talking about their homeland – be it Calabria, Baltistan or Khuzestan – with affectionate and intimate knowledge. He could also launch an artillery barrage of names, known, dropped or recently acquired, but pronounced with a flourish that connected the drawing rooms of Kensington with the courtyards of Khartoum, Sana'a, Venice, Aleppo, Isfahan and Beirut. But he was more, an aesthete on mission, much more interested in their gardens, libraries and pictures (not a social snob).

One of Bruce's survival tactics was to scent out a grand piano insufficiently used by its owners. He would infiltrate such a household as a gifted amateur musician, would begin to graciously accept trays of china tea, and by degrees advance to the status of pampered house guest. His delight in using the best silver and china, in sweeping out the floor of the neglected summer house in order to prepare an impromptu picnic, in boldly swimming in rivers and lakes, and in mixing lethally strong cocktails served at dusk on the lawn, would gradually bewitch the whole household. For he had the ability to teach people to enjoy what they were and what they already possessed. He also had a genius for appreciating real work, be it by musicians and cooks as good as himself, or much put upon cleaners and gardeners, whom he would charm and befriend. On several occasions in his life, he was the guest who came for the weekend but stayed for three years (George Lemos), six months (Susanne Drayson) or eighteen months (Juliet Crawley). I believe George had to sell his house in Islington in order to politely remove Bruce, who had somehow contrived for his piano to also be included in the household. Juliet Crawley appreciated his presence as a permanent house guest for she had been twice widowed and had two young children to bring up, as well as horses and dogs that needed care. But she became increasingly infuriated by his slow annexation of all the best furniture in the house, which Bruce spirited into his growing suite of rooms when she was off on a 'foreign mission'. Bruce once confessed to me that the thing he hated most was being put up in a bedroom filled with children's clothes and toys. It was a curious 'cuckoo-like' revelation, for I can think of at least four households where he became a beloved avuncular presence. I gather he was not such a popular presence with his two sisters-in-law but certainly proved to be an angel to his godson, who lost his mother just before going to prep school. In William's words 'I lost Mum but gained Bruce.' Bruce was planning the music for William's wedding well into his last week on earth, without really consulting the couple as to whether they wanted a whole service devoted to Brahms.

The greatest love of Bruce's life was his Belgian mother, followed by a handsome bearded Pashtun warrior, who was already married but managed to also cherish Bruce on the North West Frontier for a number of years. Listening to Bruce's memories of this friend, going through his martial exercises on the summit of a hill, framed by the peaks of the Hindu Kush, was like listening to Patroclus talking of his love for Achilles. Other affairs always paled in comparison with these two ideals of requited love though he had some spectacular successes, such as the secret policeman set to spy on his movements, whom he turned into a lover. As a teenage boy he had been seduced by one of the masters at Wellington, but looked back with affection on this man, who had introduced him to pleasures without any sense of shame. Bruce could quote the urgent, sensual, amoral poetry of Catullus with evident relish ('Just now I found a young boy stuffing his girl, I rose, naturally, and (with a nod to Venus), fell and transfixed him there with a good stiff prick, like his own.') I think when he quoted Simon Digby's preference for sex with men who were neither of his class nor of his nation, he was also speaking for himself. Bruce also had extraordinarily fine taste in female friendships, and made lifelong relationships with dozens of strong-minded, elegant, clever, capable and artistic women, which you will find out for yourself as you read this book. The intensity, longevity and importance of these loving friendships would not have been possible if he had settled down and committed to a single partner. And the way that he was cared for at the end of his life proved just how very strong those bonds were.

Bruce was the third child in a family of four, traditionally a place of comparative neglect for parental attention. As a child he managed to ascend a pedestal, through his brilliance as a musician and as a scholar. He won a set of straight A grades at Wellington, capped by a scholarship to Oxford. But by the time Bruce left university (including a year perfecting his French in Paris and a year his German in Berlin), a rift had opened between James Wannell and his effete, talented but lazy, sensual and homosexual son.

I am not capable of writing about Bruce's relationship with music but could recognize it as the central passion of his life. If Bruce had put this book together himself, the trunk of the narrative would have been based on a listing of sublime concerts, out of which stemmed all the secondary branches of his life – travel, friendships or work. I have however been fortunate enough to be carried along in the slipstream of Bruce's passion on many happy evenings, be it in a Turkmen yurt, before Kurdish shepherds, as opera guests at The Grange in Hampshire or in a jubilant Dalrymple-hosted picnic party at Garsington, in the baroque splendour of a Hawksmoor London church or an impromptu gathering arranged in some hospitable London drawing room. On each occasion, though transfixed with pleasure, excitement and emotion, I also realised that we existed on entirely different universes of musical comprehension. Fortunately, this book is enriched with dozens of essays from lifelong friends who fully shared his knowledge and his passionate engagement, and happily there are also some comic sketches and complaints which allow those as ignorant as myself to have a laugh at Bruce's gamesmanship on the keyboard. A friend of his warned me that 'Some musicians found him unbearable to play with. I am not that great, but I could not cope with his extremes of *rubato* – he probably felt I was too mechanical – and his complete indifference to whether the composer had marked a section PP or FF, but he was always improving and adapted amazingly well to arthritis in his fingers.'

If this book reveals nothing else, it shows the fundamental importance of music throughout his life, which kept him alive, passionate, competitive, minxy and interested to the very last. In the last week of his life, I had arranged a rather nice lunch laid out on the round table in the centre of our attic publishing office. I wanted to talk to Bruce about this book and so had forbidden him to sweep in any additional guests from the street and also got him to promise me that there would be no other conflicting dates in his diary that afternoon. Although pretty weak and clearly in considerable pain, Bruce rose to the challenge of these instructions, and halfway through the meal a beautiful Australian musician joined us, and before we could settle down to any editorial chat over coffee, I found myself helping him with his bags and navigating him to a hospitable London house to practise Brahms. So I never got the chance to check facts and dates, which I tentatively list below. They have not been footnoted by Bruce, but fortunately this book is a work in progress. We all hope for a proper biography of Bruce by Lisa Chaney informed by his letters and diaries. Now that he is no longer present to obfuscate the work of any editor, his Islamic Travels might even be published one day, in which case he will (at long last) be revealed to the world as the twentieth-century Ibn Battuta of the West. In the meantime the royalties from this book will help to support an annual Bruce Wannell Memorial Lecture in Persian Studies, to be held at the University of York, an idea championed by Richard McClary.

**Barnaby Rogerson**
Editor

# CHRONOLOGY

B ruce was **born on 25 August 1952** at Sandringham, a beach suburb of Melbourne, during his father's three-year experiment in emigration to Australia. Bruce's mother was Andrée Celine Moreau, one of two daughters of Luc and Jeanne Moreau. Bruce's father was William James Wannell, born 24 November 1916, one of the two children of Benjamin and Alice Wannell.

Andrée and Jim met at the end of the war and were married in Hamburg on 10 March, 1950.

Bruce was educated at Aldro prep school, Godalming, then Wellington College, Berkshire, where he achieved five A-graded A levels and a scholarship to Oxford. His family – which included a twin elder brother and sister, James and Corinne, and a younger brother, Julian – lived in Cyrene House, Surrey. Upon retirement the Wannell parents moved to an apartment in Oxton House, Kenton, Devon, and in their old age migrated to France to live beside their eldest son, James.

Bruce took a 'year off' to improve his German, then read French and German at **Oriel College, Oxford (1971–5)** which included another year of lotus eating, this time in Paris. No oriental element was yet apparent in the life of Persian Bruce apart from his study of Goethe's West-East Divan.

After university, Bruce taught English in **Italy, 1975–7**. Liceo Linguistico, Rome. James Ramsay sent me a flavour of these years. 'Bruce meeting me off the overnight train from Verona, and we walked unforgettably to his flat via Santa Maria Maggiore ... the *only way to admire 5th-century mosaics, I realise, is through clouds of incense on a sunny morning with a High Mass involving several cardinals in full swing (I wasn*'t churchy at the time, so have no idea what the Feast was) followed by breakfast in a superb little *pasticceria*. Bruce was adamant that it was not worth visiting the forum et al when one only had a few days: so we concentrated on early mosaics (one accessed via a most unpromising door on a boring street) and the baroque. To recover from neck-twisting adoration of Borromini we resorted one day to a totally charming and somehow affordable *trattoria*, with lunch slightly abruptly ended by an announcement that Bruce had to go to Voice of America to do his "culture slot". As we walked along I asked what he was going to talk about, and he said, "I thought I'd talk about eighteenth-century gentlemen's private libraries." "What do you know about THEM?" I asked. Bruce was vague.

"Oh well, of course... I'll be asking for your thoughts." The mixture of pasta, wine, and Borrominian perspectives made it impossible to think of how to get out of this bit of press-ganging. When he gave his talk it was clear he had in fact done some preparation – and talked about stamped leather bindings and the texture of old paper. Bruce's strategy for seeing the Sistine Chapel (this may no longer be possible) was of course to be at the head of the queue in the morning, then go straight to the Chapel – which you would have gloriously to yourself until the first tour had worked its way through. The strategy for our second visit was to visit other rooms first, then time arrival at the chapel just before closing time – so that visitors less brass-necked than Bruce (i.e. nearly everyone) would have left, and one could placate the infuriated staff with questions such as "Did they enjoy working in such a wonderful place, and had they noticed how Ghirlandaio and Botticelli both..." at which point the guard would be taken to the back of the chapel to appreciate whatever it might be – what was remarkable was that because Bruce asked them their opinion, a relationship would develop, and the mood became quite relaxed and positive. Friends of mine in Verona still remember Bruce as "the barefoot scholar".'

Then a **year in Germany, 1977–8**, teaching research presentation skills in English at Max Planck institute for Education Research. Berlin. I think this was the period when Bruce smashed his front teeth playing squash. Memories of this period were overwhelmed by the tragic death of his sister Corinne, twin to his elder brother James. Bruce remembered that his sister left behind two letters after her suicide and for the first time he 'watched the carapace of strength drain from the face of my father.'

**Two years in Isfahan, Iran, 1978–summer 1980** – teaching English and French at Isfahan University. Artemis Cooper seems to have provided Bruce with a useful personal introduction to Paul Gosht who invited him to teach English in Isfahan through the British Council. This happy task lasted for two years and seems to have been on a suitably ad hoc basis. Every third month, Bruce crossed a Persian frontier travelling into Afghanistan, Pakistan or India for a bit, then returned to the Iranian frontier to collect a fresh three-month tourist visa.

Bruce survived attempts to denounce him as a foreign agent, supported by all his students at Isfahan. But the violence of the revolution eventually caught up with him. In Isfahan he lodged in the house of Rev. Hassan Barnaba Dehqani-Tafti, the Anglican Bishop of Iran, Jerusalem and the Middle East. It was a family house, home to his four children: Shirin, Susanne, Goli and Bahram. The bishop was an intriguing character. He had been born to a poor Muslim family of slipper makers in the village of Taft but had been sent to a series of Anglican mission schools after the early death of his mother who had converted to Christianity. He formally converted as an eighteen-year-old, and his fluency in English made him a natural middleman during his period of military service (1943–5) which coincided with British military occupation. After studying for the priesthood he was ordained at Cambridge in 1949 and in 1952 married Margaret, the daughter of William Thompson, the English Bishop in Tehran whose job he took over in 1976. The revolutionary regime did not approve of either the bishop or the centuries-old network of Anglican schools and charities within Iran. The bishop was accused of corrupt practices and in October 1979 a gunman visited their house. The bishop narrowly escaped assassination in his bed (three bullet holes punctured his pillowcase) and his wife was wounded in the hand by another bullet, leaning over to protect him. The following year their only son, Bahram, who taught at the University in Tehran, and worked part time for NBC news, was abducted and killed, symbolically shot twice in the head outside the walls of Evin prison on 6 May 1980. Bruce helped Susanne (Bahram's colleague and closest friend) claim his body and escort it to the church in Isfahan. Bahram, who had been educated at Oxford and Harvard and taught economics, was aged just twenty-four.

It was time to go home.

Back in England Bruce sat the Civil Service exam, hoping for employment in the British Council or the Foreign Office, but was sent to Inland Revenue, Finsbury Park, north London. He didn't last long.

**Freelance translation work, 1981–5** This is the 'middle period' of Bruce as a professional house guest and amateur musician, largely based in London.

**Manager for Afghanaid. University Town, Peshawar, 1985–7** Specific projects included working within the refugee camps in Pakistan, creating employment for war widows and the fitting of prosthetic limbs for war casualties, but also providing convoys of cash to support war-damaged farming communities within Afghanistan, especially the farming hamlets of the upper Panjshir valley under the control of Ahmed Massoud. Bruce's fluency in Persian won him this job but after two years he had to return to London (to be cured at the Institute of Tropical Diseases) which gave the director, Romey Fullerton, the opportunity to replace him with Juliet Crawley. Despite this, Bruce remained a friend to Juliet, most especially evident after the assassination of her French husband, Dominique Vergos.

**Freelance consultant, monitoring aid projects in Afghanistan, for UN and other agencies, 1987–90** Bruce converted to Islam in this period, had himself circumcised, taught himself classical Arabic with which to read the Quran and lived like a local. He was a figure straight out of the Great Game, complete with his own horses, hawks and a knowledge of the best Afghan cooks and musicians. This period includes his celebrated journey, riding through North-Western Afghanistan (September 1989 to January 1990) working as the translator for Hugh Leach (an ex-Arabist from the Foreign Office), which included meetings with two of the most celebrated commanders of the Afghan resistance. Bruce considered Gulbuddin Hekmatyar to be evil personified but delighted in the company of Ahmed Massoud. Two years later he completed another major journey through Afghanistan (Ghur, Gharjestan, Chesht and Herat) inspecting and reporting on agricultural, educational and health projects. The letter he later wrote to Fynn Vergos, explaining the circumstances of his father's assassination, reveals just how familiar he was with all the complications of the North West Frontier in this period, thick with spies, researchers, journalists, diplomats and well-meaning aid workers.

**Researcher, script-writer and translator, Islamabad, Pakistan, 1990–93** Specifically a series of Pashtu and Dari 'soaps' for the BBC World Service ('sexed-up Archers for Afghanistan') which were designed as propaganda-light, a subtle attempt to marry Islamic culture to Western values.

**Travelling in the Middle East, 1993–5,** researching a book on Islamic culture for Nick Robinson of Constable but also immersing himself in life. Egypt, Syria, Sudan and Yemen and probably bits of North Africa, Caucasia and Turkey.

**Living in Healaugh, Tadcaster, Yorkshire, March 1997–summer 1998** Helping Juliet Crawley, now twice widowed, look after her two children (Fynn Vergos and Lettice Peck) while revising and adding to his travel book.

**Dragoman tour guide and guest lecturer, specialising in the Islamic world, 1997–2020** Initially Bruce worked for Martin Randall Travel which is without doubt the world's leading company for art, architecture, music and archaeology tours, complete with concerts and evening lectures. Later he also worked for Eastern Approaches run out of a cottage in the Scottish Borders by Warwick Ball, who had excavated in Iraq and Afghanistan before setting up a tour company that seemed to specialise in conflict zones. Bruce was at first rather dismissive of the 'paid' role of tour guide, but in the end he turned it into one of his passions and brought enchantment to hundreds of travellers. All the old social tricks of the ligger-guest: his ability to open doors, plot meals, arrange concerts and impromptu poetry readings, now merged with his brilliance as a linguist, his toughness as a traveller and his desire to teach, to 'open eyes'. He could flirt in all the languages of Europe and recite in half the dialects and tongues of the Middle East. He loved good food but could also survive off 'Taliban marching powder' – little handfuls of dried mulberries and walnuts. He was a fearless, interested, brave and kind host, except when it came to canned music, against which he waged perpetual war. As a tour guide he had two principal failings: an inability to suffer fools gladly and an indifference to time-keeping. Clients who wanted to tick off historic sites like a shopping list, leave their hotel at 9.00 a.m., lunch at 12.30 and be dropped back at their hotel at 5.30, would write impassioned letters of complaint to head office, denouncing the wilful and capricious Bruce Wannell. But six months later, many were booking onto a tour 'wherever Bruce is going.' After Warwick closed up shop in order to concentrate on Afghan studies, Bruce transferred his skills to Spiekermann Travel in the USA, which specialises in the Middle East.

His attic room in 46 Holgate Road held his books and tour-notes in between foreign travels and forays as a musical guest. I always thought of it as a bolt hole, but it became a real home. I showed an early draft of this to a mutual friend who wrote back with some corrections. 'I don't think you make clear that his room in York was in a Housing Association house, hence the drug and mental problems. An unsung part of Bruce's achievement in life, in my opinion, is the way he created a kind of almost therapeutic community there assisted by his neighbour Mark Speak ... that's possibly overstating it, but it was remarkable. Eventually the Housing Association would actually consult him on proposed new tenants, as they valued his role in creating a stable atmosphere.'

This was combined with several months (sometimes half the year) in Delhi, **working beside William Dalrymple 1999–2019**, translating original Indian documents and histories that had been written in Persian, which were used in the texts of *White Mughals*, *The Last Mughal*, *The Return of a King*, *The Anarchy*.

These strands of his life combined with his own freelance research and writing. The most distinctive products of this fruitful period include *Calligraphy and Epigraphy in Iran and Afghanistan* (2009) and *The Elite Burials of Herat and Kabul* (2013), topped up by translations of poetry (*Persian Poems* with Robert Maxwell), Sufi poetry (Amnesty International), articles on Iran, Pakistan and Afghanistan for the *Literature of Travel and Exploration: An Encyclopaedia*, a third of the text of the Odyssey Guide to Iran and book reviews in learned journals. Lectures delivered at Durham University, Goldsmiths College, Oxford University, Galle, the Institute of Ismaili Studies, Astene conferences and others. This body of work, annexed to the prodigious amount of original historical documents translated for William Dalrymple, was recognized with an Honorary Doctorate at York University, the year before he died.

# A STUDENT OF LANGUAGE
# AND LIFE

# A litter of *gourmands*

**Julian Wannell** *is Bruce's younger brother and currently lives in Cape Town with his wife, two children, two dogs and several guitars.*

My mother was an intelligent, witty, beautiful woman with a keen sense of ethics and a carnivorous, at times mischievous, sense of humour. She was a gifted musician, earning distinctions at pre-concert level in piano in Brussels in her late teens and continuing to play until arthritis in old age made it impossible. She then donated our fabulous family Steinway grand (on which we all cut our musical teeth, a wonderful gift of love to her from my father) to Bruce, who subsequently neglected it and allowed it to fall into a state of such disrepair as to render restoration economically unviable, yet the instrument almost unplayable.

My mother could adopt a persona of beatific quietude from time to time, preferring to live inside her thoughts. This could have been partially as a result of her being interested more by indoor pursuits, but also as she never learned to drive, relying always on others for transport outside of her home. Therefore, with my father frequently away and children at boarding school, she often had to amuse herself as best she could at home – and there was always enough to amuse her, as she had a voracious appetite for reading and loved to cook and make clothes, not to mention the hours she could while away with music.

There is an unlikely but true story of her turning up at Wellington with my father, an hour before Speech Day was due to start, in her brand new Mini (a birthday present from him). The idea was for my father to give her a driving lesson before the ceremonies commenced. Sadly, she crashed her new car straight into a huge boulder, decoratively placed on the perfectly edged lawn facing the main, imposing entrance to the heart of the school. That put a stop to her nascent driving career. She was not in any way a practical woman, needing assistance with anything much more complicated than a toaster – a trait she passed on in full to her middle son. When my parents moved to France and they both became frail – my father eventually bedridden with acute Alzheimer's – she gained notoriety for several times calling out the local fire brigade, at all hours, merely to change light bulbs etc.

She grew up in Brussels with a cook, so barely knew how to boil an egg when she got married. But as a wife and mother, and for a self-taught cook, her tastes and the products of her labour were wonderful. As a result, she produced a litter of *gourmands*! She had a keen eye for interior design and in later years, when children would come to visit from afar, her drawing room never looked the same as on the previous visit, restless as she was for fiddling with ornaments, furniture positioning and picture hanging. She was very loving and whilst she was neither sporty nor particularly outdoorsy, she contributed to us all receiving a rounded upbringing, with a very strong musical sensibility which we have all carried with us into adult life. Her beauty remained throughout her life, through sadness and joy, and she was always being complimented on her appearance – her children would glow with pride as their friends said she looked twenty years younger than the truth. Often wearing her own homemade clothes, she was normally very elegantly dressed. She was devoted to her husband and family and many of us only found their love letters from war time on the sad occasion of their deaths, only six months apart, but having lived a full life into their mid-nineties. When our father died, she surprised all of us with her pragmatic response and fortitude, revealing an inner strength which was admirable.

# Brown-haired and strikingly aesthetic
*Oxford, 1971*

**John Martin Robinson** *is a writer and architectural historian, and lives at Beckside House on the Lancashire–Westmorland Frontier, where Bruce was a regular visitor during his English perambulations, most recently at New Year 2020.*

B ruce became a friend at Oriel, Oxford, nearly fifty years ago. I was a graduate student there from 1970 onwards, and Bruce came up a year later, brown-haired and strikingly aesthetic, even then, in his pronunciation, mannerisms and general views. He was different from most Oriel undergraduates who tended to be a bit on the beefy side. Oriel was then (and remains) the rowing college par excellence, and the rowers set a tone of hearty hooliganism with regular revels in the quads (of a type which would currently be frowned upon) with the burning of boats on the lawns, or the theft of the bursars' red geraniums from the window boxes. They had their own table in the hall where they consumed their own hunk-building food: chunks of raw steak and that kind of thing, while the rest of us were served pies with bland fillings. To appreciate Bruce's full impact, he needs to be seen against that noisy backdrop, in his rooms in the Robinson Building in the second quad, exuding precise elegance and culture, definitely not a red-faced John Bull.

Bruce immediately set out to be the leader of the college aesthetes, admittedly a small group. He held regular poetry readings in the evenings and the sort of entertainments where you had to perform obscure short English plays, translating into French at sight as you went along. This was easier for Bruce to shine in, as he was bilingual, his mother being French-speaking Belgian, whereas some of us found our A-level French a little rusty. He was reading modern languages, and already developing the interests of his maturity in Persian poetry and Sufi mysticism.

These poetry and drama evenings were the understated end of Bruce's entertainments. He specialised in more ambitious fancy dress parties. One year he gave a *fête champêtre* which spilled over into the garden of the quad. It was made memorable by the inclusion of a real sheep which he had borrowed from a real shepherd encountered on a walk at Witham, near Oxford. I have forgotten how he managed to smuggle it into college past the observant NCO-type porter who could be very firm about that sort of thing, *Sir!*

Equally memorable was a Decadence Evening, where we all had to go as *fin-de-siècle* poets and read our works; Baudelaire and Verlaine as it were. Being ginger I went as Swinburne in a black velvet jacket, and even grew a little red beard to emphasise the authenticity (I am embarrassed to say that I so liked it, I kept the beard and the black velvet jacket for some time afterwards). Wine in large quantities (at discount from JCR) played a strong role in these entertainments and was part responsible for their light-hearted and hilarious character. Bruce, himself, was a great imbiber at that stage, which seems unlikely in retrospect, knowing of his later conversion to Islam. The after-effect of one such evening caused a small embarrassment. He had spilt a bottle of red wine all over his white shirt and sent it to the laundry without thinking. At the time Oxford was engulfed in a Ripper-type murder scare, and the laundry encountering a violently red-stained shirt, thought they must have the culprit and called the police. Bruce was surprised by a visitation from the constabulary. 'Oh no officer, not blood, just wine ... a perfectly ordinary little party, you understand: we were all dressed as Aubrey Beardsley, I in my best white shirt, and, yes, there was a sheep in the room, but.... just a glass of claret...'

Bruce always had a twinkly sense of humour which was one of his most endearing features. He was teasable, even about his family, which had its tragic side. Though he was close to his mother, he did not get on with his businessman father, and his older brother was 'ordinary'. I use that in the comparative sense in which I once heard Desmond Guinness describe his Mitford aunts: 'Well Unity was a Nazi, and Decca a Communist...but Debo was perfectly *ordinary*; she was a Tory!'

Coming from the Wuthering Heights myself – Lancashire, Scotland and the Wilds – I liked to tease Bruce about his living in Surrey which I thought 'suburban':

'Look at your address', I said, 'Cyrene House; on the way to Jerusalem is it?'

'Oh no', said Bruce. 'It was built in the 1930s by a local couple who named it after themselves. He was Cyril and she was Irene.'

# Picnics on the rooftop
## Oxford and Paris 1971–5

**Matthew Harragin** *met Bruce at Oxford, where they both read French and German at Oriel. They became close friends in their year abroad in Paris and shared a house on the Thames in their final year with Neil Stratton. Bruce was godfather to Matthew's son William.*

My first memory was the sound of his voice issuing from our French tutor's study. Bruce was early for once. I paused outside the door and heard this pretentious monologue, almost dowager like, which I assumed would be our tutor speaking. It was Bruce. My first impression was not overwhelming: long, thick, darkish hair; broad shoulders; slightly stout – too much Berlin Kartoffel in his gap year? I could see his sharp eyes taking me in. He was the open scholar, mine an incestuous closed one. I could see him grading me. My long hair and tan from working in a French port. Interesting. What was clear was that he had got the measure of the tutor, Arthur (I won't demean him with a surname). Arthur's French was execrable. Both of us were fluent. It was slightly embarrassing. Bruce decided at that moment not to waste valuable academic time writing essays for Arthur. To my knowledge he never wrote a single essay. Yes, he wrote notes. And from these notes and prodigious memory, he ad-libbed his essays to Arthur. We derived a system. I always read my essay first. Then if Arthur ever asked Bruce to repeat a line of his non-existent essay, I would interrupt with a red-herring question. It worked for our entire time at Oxford.

It didn't work with our brilliant German don, David Luke, who recognised Bruce's dilettantism as quickly as Bruce had nailed Arthur Crow (oops, sorry Arthur). David was the head German don in Christ Church, Oriel being too small, or poor, to afford one. So we would cross Oriel Square for shared tutorials in his modernist rooms. We were all impressed, if a little unsettled, by the stuffed viper that occupied a glass jar on top of his wardrobe. It seemed symbolic. For a time David even refused to teach Bruce, but in the end they saw eye to eye, perhaps through their shared love of Wagner. Bruce admired David's stripping down of German literature to key writers: Goethe (natch), Schiller, Kleist, Kafka, Mann, whom David translated very successfully, and Rilke. David became a good friend to us both and Bruce never forgot his outrageously mad performance of *Penthesilea* (Kleist) in the house that Bruce and I shared in our final year. Less successful was David's invitation for us to meet W. H. Auden. David had been instrumental in persuading Auden back to Christ Church, where he lived gratis in a sweet cottage within the college walls. David got Auden to invite us as two of his best (hardly) undergraduates. From the outset it didn't go well. I asked Auden for a match to light my cigarette. Auden had a hissy fit. Bruce settled back to enjoy the show. Auden prepared us two strong dry martinis and then proceeded to wheel out a few of his stock stories. He wasn't going to waste any creative juices on us. He had become time-obsessed and suddenly he realised he only had a quarter of an hour to slipper-shuffle to high table. He had just refilled our glasses and we were a bit surprised when he seized them and threw the contents down the sink. Bruce and I chuckled as we made our way back to Oriel. Bruce was not overawed by academic celebrity, particularly if it was running on empty. He had Pierre Boulez in his family after all.

Bruce was famous in Oriel for a *fête champêtre* that he gave complete with bright green artificial grass from the butcher in the covered market and a live lamb provided by my girlfriend, Lucy. Needless to say the lamb bleated throughout and watered the grass. Bruce loved the mix of artifice and reality, at least he did until some Downside heavies, obviously attracted by the sound of sheep, burst in and were sick all over Bruce's treasured bookcase. *Brideshead* Central.

In our third year we both went to Paris to teach in *lycées*. Again Bruce realised immediately that this was a waste of time and spent most of his teaching time travelling around France. He had a delightful *chambre de bonne* on the left bank and used to hold picnics, his favourite, on the rooftop. We would all follow his fearless exit through the window and lying with our backs on warm slate eat the deliciousness that he had bought from Jane McCaskie at Fauchon, looking across the river to the grey roof of Notre-Dame. How lucky were we? I still remember our departure from Paris. I had hired a deux chevaux and we crammed as many of our possessions in as we could, handing out the rest to our friends who had come to wave us off from Place Saint-Michel. We drove via Bruce's favourite Normandy monastery at Le Bec-Hellouin (picnic with white swans). At Calais we had to take all our possessions out of the car, which were stowed under a tarpaulin on the deck. We felt like refugees. Bruce loved it.

In our final year we shared a house with Neil Stratton by the river. The location was perfect. We had swapped the Seine for the Thames. Revising was impossible. In the mornings we would try to go to the modern languages library, but Bruce would fall asleep in the bath and by the time he arrived at George's in the covered market, I would have finished breakfast and be off to study, almost immediately falling asleep and dribbling over my textbooks. By the time Finals arrived, neither of us was really prepared. Bruce used to infuriate me by turning up to every exam twenty minutes late. I would hear the commotion at the back of the Examination Schools and know it was him. When I asked him why, he said he was too busy revising. He didn't care about degrees. It was knowledge that interested him.

Our last hurrah at Oxford was pure Bruce: a Venetian party with people arriving by punt. He had commissioned our good friend James Ramsay to write a masque for the occasion, which we performed mid-party. There were fireworks, champagne popping and laughter. And who can forget Bruce's laughter? Slightly camp, gurgling, encouraging, encompassing, inclusive, for it included everybody. It always would.

# Isis, but thousands of miles from Egypt

**Neil Stratton** *shared the downstairs flat in Isis House on Folly Bridge in Oxford with Bruce and Matthew Harragin in 1974–5, having just completed his first degree in zoology and started a research degree in developmental genetics. He subsequently put his years as an Oxford biologist to good use by moving to London and becoming a translator. He now lives in the Scottish Borders.*

I met Bruce over forty-five years ago because, perhaps like many of you reading this, I lived in a house on which his eye had fallen. My house, however, was no stately pile nor an exquisite Palladian gem. In fact, it wasn't even a house at all but a flat; a cold, damp flat tucked away behind a boatyard; a cold, damp flat on an island in a river that, though it styled itself Isis, was separated by thousands of miles and years from Ancient Egypt and Mesopotamia. What then could have drawn Bruce's eye to so workaday a dwelling?

In the summer of 1974 I found myself in sole possession of the ground-floor flat in Isis House but without the means to pay for it. I had moved in the previous autumn with two fellow students who were leaving that summer to get proper jobs whilst I, quite late in the summer term, found myself the recipient of a research scholarship that would allow me to live in penury but free from the drudgery of 9-to-5 for several more years. The flat, though cold and damp in winter, was idyllic in summer with riverside garden and mooring for punt. Did I take on a flat I couldn't afford or decamp to the Cowley Road? Messing about on the river trumped toadstools sprouting on walls and a hot water cylinder that struggled to fill the kitchen sink, let alone the bath. I took the plunge. Something or somebody was bound to turn up.

Sure enough, that August, just when Oxford was at its emptiest, somebody did turn up. I looked out of a window to see a strange figure standing in the garden. Unbeknownst to me, Bruce and his friend Matthew Harragin had just returned from teaching in Paris and now were in search of somewhere to live for their final year. I had a flat with two empty rooms. They were two wandering scholars with nowhere to rest their quill pens. It didn't take long to realize there was a deal to be done. And so it was.

What, however, perhaps makes my story a little different from your own experience of Bruce descending on your house is the fact that the stranger standing in my garden all those years ago was Matthew, not Bruce.

Bruce himself arrived with the start of the new term and there followed a year of madrigals, banquets cooked on nothing much bigger than a Baby Belling, interspersed with a modicum of work, though not necessarily of the sort Oriel's tutors would recognize; and then, as the days lengthened and warmed, evenings punting down the river to Iffley and the Isis Hotel.

All culminated in a *fête champêtre* conceived and staged by Bruce to celebrate mid summer and the end of finals. Guests (or at least some of them) in full Watteauesque attire and bearing invitations drawn by Kate Brown were punted across the river to steps at the foot of the garden. There followed a play written during the gaps between revising by the now Reverend Ramsay, dancing what we imagined to be minuets to music played by the house band and then fireworks at midnight.

So ended Bruce's Oxford apprenticeship for his life of travel and exploration.

# An embarkation to Watteau-land

**James Ramsay** *is an Anglican clergyman, living in north Norfolk. After a couple of years teaching English in Verona (Bruce was in Rome – serving as Ramsay's base in southern Italy and vice versa), he worked as a translator/interpreter in the UK. Ordained an Anglican priest in his thirties, he served in Oxford (the 'wrong' side of the ring road), Bucharest, and east London.*

A s the 'Baa!'ing in the back of the car became more vociferous, Bruce, ever the linguist, turned and 'Baa'd back. Quite a conversation ensued, the lamb's tone and timbre mimicked with enviable skill by my fellow first-year Modern Languages undergraduate.

We had collected the lamb from a battlemented manor house deep in the Berkshire Downs, and my ancient Morris Minor (little mushrooms growing in the window felts) rode the ups and downs of the long straight road like a ship at sea. 'Baa-aaa!' Was that the lamb or Bruce?

When setting out we had had in mind a Bo-Peep size lamb. The one John had loaned us was distinctly closer to slaughter age. 'How are we going to get it in?' I asked Bruce.

'I brought a blanket.'

Could anything be less problematic?

I drove up the narrow lane – long since closed to traffic – alongside Oriel and stopped by the small side gate. With sheepy endearments and soft scoldings Bruce swaddled the lamb in the blanket and bore it into College. The bleating, struggling bundle of tartan did not go unnoticed. 'We'll set the RSPCA onto you!' someone shouted. Bruce's precisely enunciated 'Don't be ridiculous' was not calculated to appease.

Having parked the car, I returned to help with preparations. Bruce had removed all furniture from his room against our forthcoming *fête champêtre*, and a Rex Whistlerish backdrop hung on the end wall. Disdaining a luxurious bed of straw in one corner, the lamb was trotting about on artificial grass borrowed from a greengrocer in the Covered

Market, seemingly happy with the cuddles and cooing of an already festively costumed shepherdess and an ivy-garlanded dryad.

The idea of an indoor *fête champêtre* had been inspired by the Watteau drawings in the Ashmolean and followed up in a vaguely Dadaist direction. I had knocked out a masque in mock eighteenth-century heroic couplets, with a part for every guest to read. The script kicked off with a stage direction: 'ENTER CHLOE with lamb'.

Bruce frowned. 'Where do we get a lamb from?'

Alarm bells began to ring. 'I thought a cuddly toy…'

'No, no! We must have a real lamb!'

A few days later we happened to be driving to visit I recall not what little-known garden or Lutyens house or folly that absolutely had to be visited (any car-owning friend of Bruce's was inveigled into acting as unpaid personal chauffeur), when miles from anywhere we picked up a hitchhiker carrying a Jack Russell terrier. He turned out to be a shepherd – still at agricultural college, hitching home from his farm placement. A little more probing (Bruce already at that age a deft wormer out of information from strangers), and it emerged that the shepherd was an old Etonian with a strong sense of the poetic. He would be only too delighted to lend us a lamb!

I should say this embarkation was, for me, from a different shore altogether. I was at Wadham, discovering Dostoevsky, Rimbaud, and *Angst*, late Beethoven and Mahler, Abstract Expressionism and the meaning of meaninglessness. Bruce's dandyism and precocity provided a kind of inverse ballast to such intensity. Karlheinz Stockhausen? Ah, but surely you know Reynaldo Hahn? Beckett, *d'accord*, but *mon cher*, you MUST read Crébillon *fils*.

Our *fête galante*, with Bruce's concealed record-player playing an LP of birdsong, and the lamb becoming increasingly interested in red wine, was doubtless very silly. Spoilt and 'entitled' we were. But our enactment of idyll was what might now be called a statement (do I hear a snort from up in the clouds?) against humourless functionalism, required forms of authenticity, self-congratulatory modernism. Under Bruce's baton – military rather than musical: not for nothing was he schooled at Wellington – the prevailing culture of Pink Floyd, pot and LSD, sport, and dogmatically non-Platonic sex was subverted (another snort?) by Rameau's *Les Indes galantes* and Watteau's shimmering world of vision and elusive realism in *L'Embarquement pour Cythère*.

To make the evening more surreal, Oriel was that night raucously burning a boat in the front quad, to celebrate being Head of the River.

Our lamb was the indisputable star of the masque and of the evening as a whole. Having become fond of muesli, its post-digestive deposits might have featured in one of Watteau's wonderful pastel nature studies, or these days have been sent for exhibition in Tate Modern – though Bruce would perhaps have found the game of conceptualisation nose-wrinkling.

The next morning a number of visitors came to verify the rumour that Wannell had a sheep in his rooms. But the RSPCA never turned up.

The return trip retained an idyllic quality. The lamb seemed at peace with the movement of the car, and Bruce's occasional 'Baa!'s struck an affectionate note. We deposited it back in the field, and it scampered off to join the rest of the flock. John invited us into the house to tell him and his mother how the party had gone, and we congratulated them on the beast's perfect manners. 'I'm afraid it had quite a bit of wine and muesli,' Bruce confessed.

John laughed. 'It'll give the meat extra flavour.'

Bruce and I felt hypocritically shocked.

As we walked out to the car the lamb saw us and rushed away from the flock towards us. Thoroughly sentimental, we bade adieu over the fence and tickled it behind the ears, which it had seemed to enjoy during the party.

Any self-respecting idyll must end with a shadow... a war plane tears out of the sky, crushing audibility, thrusting mere humans back into the earth to which they belong, before disappearing out of sight and earshot as suddenly as it had appeared. However, our disembarkation from that no-place of silliness, birdsong, and Rameau is unclear in my memory. Bruce presumably had to reorder his room. I threw myself into an enhanced excess of caffeine and metaphysics.

Oxford finished with a lavish *Fête Venitienne* with guests arriving by punt and a masque that had actually had some rehearsal.

In retrospect I see that the voyage we had embarked upon continued for nearly half a century, proceeding at first through other short car odysseys, sub-Dadaist absurdities and adventures, then through intermittent communications and meetings, conversations, ever new farewells, multiplied by the advent of internet and mobile phone, as gawky Gilles (Watteau's eloquently self-conscious Pierrot) was succeeded by other *galanteries*, more *mondain* attitudes, wider learning and greater self-knowledge and responsibilities.

Meanwhile at every stage, and as other cultural and linguistic reference points came to predominate, there remained the evanescent realism of a life in which music, nature, artifice, pleasure, sociability and danger defy reduction to spurious certainty and false comfort: a world that is both a memory and an impossible ideal, one in which, as we travelled, Bruce was always a most entertaining, if at times exasperating companion, and never less than adventurous guide and loyal friend.

# Over a low flame

**Artemis Cooper** *has written biographies of Elizabeth David, Elizabeth Jane Howard and Patrick Leigh Fermor, edited half a dozen collections of letters and created a collective portrait of the British in Cairo during the 1939–45 War. She was able to introduce Bruce to Paul Gotch, who had lived in Iran (Shiraz) between 1959–1966 during his long career within the British Council. Paul is a fitting character to have given the young Bruce a helping hand with introductions to find a teaching job in Iran. Paul had shared a house in Alexandria with Laurence Durrell and wrote* Three Caravan Cities *during the war. He was passionate about archaeology, a keen member of the Iran Society, and lectured on Swan Tours after he retired from the British Council in 1975. Paul Gotch taught Artemis how to make mayonnaise.*

Dear Barnaby and Rose,

This is a magnificent idea! I can't say I knew Bruce well, but every time I saw him (about once a decade) I wished I saw him more. I'm in Paris at the moment but I'll be back in Blighty soon. My most enduring memory is of Bruce when I first knew him. It involves no travel, except in so far as just being with Bruce was a sort of travelling. Anyway, he managed to persuade the house party (what house party? I've racked what's left of my brain but it's gone) to make Mrs Beeton's custard to go on our stewed damsons. So we duly took a dozen eggs and I don't know how many pints of milk and cream and pounds of sugar, and everything was going well till Bruce read out the next bit of the recipe: stir carefully over a low flame for two hours… Picture how we cursed him, as the stirring went on and on and on and we all wished we'd got a tin of Bird's and done it like everyone else. But that was Bruce for you: the authentic was always, always worth the trouble.

# Tax inspector
*London, 1981*

**John Batten** *is an old-school City man turned photographer, musicians' agent and jack-of-all-trades. Through his former colleague and dear friend George Lemos he first met Bruce in the early '80s.*

I first met Bruce when he was a Tax Inspector. He spotted my late father's hat. I snapped him wearing it. In the 1980s he suggested I accompany him to Afghanistan as his photographer but I foolishly declined, which means my travels with him comprised journeys of a different kind, where the mileposts were the books he gave me – the *Koran*, *The Mantle of the Prophet*, *Far Away and Long Ago*, *Persian Poems*, *The Anarchy*, *Dogs from A Sufi Point of View* – all suitably inscribed and treasured. Our actual travels – whether to an East End dive with naked girls and mirrored ceilings run by an acquaintance of mine, or to the V&A where he would spend over an hour explaining the story behind a carpet, or with the pianist Lara Melda to Garsington for Fantasio and Ewelme for the tomb of Chaucer's grand-daughter, Alice de la Pole – were invariably enriching in their different ways.

I was driving him down from York when we stopped at a motorway service area. I went inside to buy a sandwich, but when I returned I found to my shame he had bagged a table by the car park, laid a table cloth, set out glasses, napkins and plates, wine and victuals of a superior kind, all of which had been prepared for the drive and were lurking in his bag. He was, of course, immaculately dressed... alas, I have no photo of this extraordinary scene.

In the '80s, he sent letters from Afghanistan penned in a somewhat willowy style recounting tribal customs, experiences, horse races, processions of flagellants and so on, presumably posted later from Peshawar. I twice visited him in the St Pancras Hospital for Tropical Diseases where he languished with orange eyes and yellow skin. Later on he relaxed in my garden talking about life.

When he stayed in my flat in London shortly before he died he insisted, as he always did, on sleeping on the floor with no mattress. His visits over the years usually involved the polyglot coffee houses around Kings Cross and were typically enhanced by the staff's (and my own) astonishment at his absolute command of their different languages. He has left a huge hole in our lives...

# Random memories

**Carla Gabrieli** *was born in London in 1952; she is now retired, after teaching English literature at the University La Sapienza in Rome; she met Bruce for the first time in Rome in 1975.*

Ciao Brucie mio caro,

I still can't quite believe it. I can't even say I miss you, because I haven't accepted it yet.

Do you remember the first time we met? It was Matteo's idea. It was sometime in 1975. Maybe earlier, I am not good at dates. You two had started to chat while queueing for a concert at the Royal Festival Hall, and struck up a friendship. His English was quite fluent, you both loved music and art and beautiful objects and your fondness for Italy was already very strong. After a few months he 'sent' you to me in Rome. A few words on the phone 'my friend Bruce is coming to Rome; could you show him around' or maybe 'could you help him find a room'. And you arrived to the flat where I lived with Vittorio and Mariuma [my parents]. They took you to their hearts immediately and you became very much part of the family, endearing yourself to us all with your grace and intelligence. There was an upright piano at home, which I hardly ever used, and anyway I was no pianist, and you spent hours playing and practising. Mariuma especially loved to hear you, it reminded her of her father playing the piano at their house. She also much admired the very professional way you managed to slice roast beef; to create those perfectly symmetrical slices became your very special task.

I remember how, from the very beginning of our friendship, I alternated moments when I felt what a very special and lovable person you were, with moments when I had difficulty coping with your inclination to take it for granted that you would be welcomed, always, and at any time. I was ashamed of these strong oscillations. I was ashamed to feel at times irritated and almost invaded. After a few days in your company, your intensity and restless activity would drive me into a corner, leaving me tired and upset to the point that at times I would want to disappear or wish that you could disappear for a while. I have a feeling you somehow understood.

But you entranced me then and have ever since with your capacity to turn so many occasions into a *'festa'*, a leisurely *'festa'*, where time was not an issue, the only issue was beauty and enjoyment and intelligent *conversazione*, and sometimes even the latter was not necessary! What mattered was the present, the instant, and there was all the time in the world. Even if all we had for breakfast was bread and figs, the green figs had to be encased in a white linen cloth and placed in a glass bowl that would catch the light of the sun. There was music and poetry, the greatest loves of your life. And the innermost part of you, it seemed to me, emerged at its very richest when you could commune with all these beauties. The mask you sometimes wore and that would hold me apart, the persona that you had had to painstakingly create, in order, I imagined, to come to terms with importunate demons, would soften and relax. You could let go.

Then you found a room of your own in Trastevere. When I came to visit you once, you were wearing such an elegant silk dressing gown, or maybe robe would be the best word!

And at some point you went off to Iran. And then Peshawar. How broken you were when you told me of Bakhram's death and how you had had to, I seem to remember, keep vigil over his body.

Since 1975, thanks mostly, I must now admit, to your loyalty, our friendship has survived to this day. All these years, over forty years. It would still be here with us, if life or whoever there is, if there is anyone, hadn't suddenly decided that you should go elsewhere, leaving us, me, impoverished and flat. I was not as good as you were in protecting the preciousness of a friendship. The odd postcard, the Christmas greeting. You were never distant for long. And once, but just once, you actually admitted it had been hard to hold on. I am now more than thankful that you did.

There are single moments I hold dear.

That day in London. I had just arrived and felt like having a brief rest, but you whirled me off, my bedraggled self and my heavy suitcases, to what you said was a very special poetry reading in some improbable place. Was it Pimlico? The poetry reading turned out to be a precious experience. It was a small room with benches, maybe a church once upon a time. People just stood up and read their lines. I remember a very brief poem which moved me in particular. I still have the leaflet. Beverley Charles Rowe, 'From the Parthenon': 'A horse/from a temple/ sniffs the dark London air/ grieving for the smell of olives and /clear light'. And from there you dragged me off to some other very 'rare and unmissable' experience. How irritated I often was by what seemed to me at first a form of insensitivity. I always, almost always, ended up feeling grateful and enriched.

And that time in Venice, when you picked me up at Santa Lucia train station and announced a very intense programme: we would immediately be taking the vaporetto all the way to the island of Sant'Erasmo with the specific intent of gathering violet artichokes and cycling around the island and along the canals. The vaporetto wound its watery way around the islands of Burano, Murano, maybe Torcello, and landed us in lovely and remote Sant'Erasmo. Gianni Dubbini, who I met on that occasion for the first time, was with us. And it became such an enjoyable day, and then we had to rush back because there was yet another important concert, and then maybe a dinner with friends!

And the last time we shared a holiday? I couldn't know it would be the last. We spent a day in Florence together. May, June 2019? It was going to be once again a very full day. Breakfast at the café inside the ancient Farmacia of Santa Maria Novella, a Verrocchio exhibition and so on. Then things started slowing down.  First of all a visit to the beautifully decorated shop of the Farmacia itself, where we bought the oldest of the *eaux de cologne*, the so-called Acqua della Regina perfume, created for Caterina de' Medici in 1533. You loved the gently spicy combination of lavender, rosemary, bergamot, lemon and Acqua di Sicilia. So much so that when I came to see you in York in November 2019 you asked me to bring you a new bottle, as you had almost finished the previous one. And we spent more hours in the basilica of Santa Maria Novella than you had planned, discovering the Ghirlandaio frescoes and in particular the complex almost undecipherable scenes of Noah's Ark by Paolo Uccello which you felt drawn to and intrigued by.

And now, as you taught me to do in York, I have breakfast with brown bread and olive oil and za'atar.

tua Carlotta

# AFGHANISTAN AND PAKISTAN, 1985–98

# Reading the Quran in Arabic in the early morning

## Peshawar, North West Frontier, 1984 (memories of Bruce sent to Barnaby in a series of e-mails)

**Abdal Samad/David Summers**

I was living and working in Peshawar from 1984 to 1987. My job was running an office supporting widows and orphans. I got the job mainly due to my knowledge of the area and because I was a Pushtu speaker. Added to that I had to deal with a lot of Arabs, and fortunately I had also learnt that language. Originally, I am from Leicester but I travelled a lot in my teenage years as a hippie. I became a Muslim when I was nineteen in Swat in the North West Frontier Province of Pakistan.

You may know Abdal Rahman, an American who runs the American school in Marrakesh and has translated some books, or his friend Abdal Hadi, I can't remember their surnames but Abdal Hadi did his PhD on Ibn Abad of Ronda, just near where I am now.

Well both of them also became Muslims in Swat. Abdal Hadi stayed a while, learnt Pushtu, but then moved to Morocco. For a while they were part of a Sufi group there.

Myself I travelled from Swat and Kabul to Stockholm where I stayed for nine months working before returning to Leicester my hometown in 1972/73.

I stayed a few weeks then moved to Dewsbury where I stayed with Hafiz Patel, the head of the Tablighi Jumaah. I was there until '76 travelling each year for forty days in different countries. Sleeping in mosques travelling each weekend all over the UK. Early '72 or '73 I visited some English Muslims who were in a squat in London. I paid them a few visits and they came up to visit me. They all moved to Wood Dawling Hall outside Norwich. Their leader was Abdal Qadir/ Ian Dallas. They were all new to Islam, not having memorised much Quran, so I was asked to lead prayers as I had memorised a lot of it.

51

Then they got an old church hall and asked me to be the Imam, so I moved there.

One day in Peshawar in the mid 1980s I met Bruce at a UNHCR meeting, I think, and of course had a good chat with him. It's not often you meet a fellow countryman in that part of the world. He was very different from the normal NGO head or field director. He had, like myself, what some people may say, gone native. It was easy to spot the academics who talk and plan due to their PhDs but who have not sat much with the man in the street or refugee camp, who have few ties with the area in which they work. I used to attend similar meetings in Geneva, good people but remote from any refugee child or widow or experience of frontline war, killing, rape or poverty. Bruce was fluent in Farsi, said he had been in Iran. He was living not far from me in University Town, Peshawar. A very beautiful place to live, lots of gardens, trees and old colonial style houses.

He asked me if I could help him with Arabic reading of the Quran. I was lucky because I had studied it and had been an Imam in the Norwich mosque for several years. However I was working and started work about 8 a.m. each day, so we arranged to have sessions at about seven each morning. So I used to go on a bicycle to see him. For what he was studying it was the best time, early morning when the streets were empty. He was in an old villa with cushions. We sat on the floor. I went over the differences of pronunciation between Farsi, Urdu, Pushtu, and classical Arabic. Letters being the same but pronounced differently. I asked him if he knew about Haffs or Warsh because I had been studying calligraphy so I showed him one style of *alif* and another one. He had a Haffs Quran so we used that, simple, and I explained to him the dots and marks etc.

I can't remember what we read but he seemed familiar, just needed practice. I really enjoyed riding the bicycle early in the morning. When he told me he had been two years in Iran I am sure I brought up *Mathnawi* because it's one of my favourite books. Probably talked about carpets, another interest of mine.

He was a very knowledgeable and friendly guy and I am sorry to hear of his passing away. It's a good job we met when we did because nowadays, at seventy, I don't know if I could ride a bike like I did then. Allah bless him.

# A gift normally only bestowed on royalty
## Afghanistan, 1988

**Jonathan L. Lee** *is a British-born scholar specialising in the history and cultures of Afghanistan and the region. He has written numerous articles on the region and is the author of* The 'Ancient Supremacy': Bukhara, Afghanistan and the Battle for Balkh, 1731–1901 *(Brill, 1996) and* Afghanistan: a history from 1260 to the present *(Reaktion Books, 2018). From 1977–9 he was Fellow of the British Institute of Afghan Studies and is a Fellow of the British Institute of Persian Studies and of the Royal Asiatic Society. He now lives in New Zealand with his wife Kathy and their cat, Arwen.*

L ooking back through my files I discover that my friendship with Bruce dates back over thirty-five years. In 1984 I was struggling with a very difficult Persian text on the history of Ahmad Shah Durrani and I was searching for someone who might be able to help. Colleagues pointed me in the direction of Bruce, and sure enough within a matter of weeks of getting in touch with him, the text came back not just with a translation but with annotations and comments: a sign not just of Bruce's mastery of complex Persian literary styles, but of his profound engagement with Persian literature.

Later, in April 1988, we met in Peshawar. Bruce had just completed a monumental three-month journey through northern Afghanistan with the *mujahideen*, visiting places in the Turkistan mountains and the Gurziwan region which I had travelled through in 1977 and 1978. As always, Bruce was a mine of information as well as local gossip, including his usual scurrilous anecdotes. It was a joy to be able to talk about regions which I had also spent time in and to meet some of the commanders from the region. Bruce's contacts introduced me to a number of key individuals, old men who were custodians of the oral histories of Maimana and the Gurziwan region.

Bruce's travels, though, had led him to be disillusioned with the lawlessness of the Western-backed *mujahideen*, and in later subsequent letters he compared the bitter in-fighting between Jamiyat and Hizb-i Islami to the chaotic state of eighteenth-century Germany. Bruce also presciently noted that in a number of Western-funded *mujahidin* schools inside Afghanistan, the children were not just being incited to fight against the Soviet occupation of their country but were also indoctrinated with the belief that the real *jihad* was against the United States. No-one, though, at the time, seemed to take such a warning seriously.

Visiting Bruce in Peshawar became one of the highlights of my visits in the 1990s, a relief from the cantonised life of the expatriate community where so few spoke more than basic Persian, let alone Pushtu or Uzbeki. Even fewer had the kind of depth of understanding or engagement with Afghanistan's culture or the wider Persianate world that Bruce had.

Bruce hosted and was a frequent guest of many commanders from the Gurziwan region, as well as the Uzbek nationalist movement of Azad Beg, and Afghanistan's refugee literati. I introduced Bruce to my old Dari teacher from Kabul days and his family. He was already a well-known poet and writer, but he was also a master of Persian and Pushtu literature. For both of them such a friendship was important.

And can one ever forget Bruce's soirées with Herati musicians and poetry? One such event went on until 2.30 a.m. and since I could not get into my accommodation, I slept on the *tushak*s just as one would in any *mehman khana* in rural northern Afghanistan.

We continued our friendship after Bruce returned to the UK, meeting up every so often in York, Sheffield or London. Once in York Kathy and I attended another of Bruce's soirées. This time Bruce had met a Russian xylophone player busking in the street and despite the man being a complete stranger who spoke hardly any English, he invited him back to play at the event.

In July 2000, Bruce attended our wedding reception in the Derbyshire Peaks, arriving so late that he missed the actual wedding ceremony. Bruce, though, quickly imposed himself on the reception, talking in Persian to my old Persian teacher and mentor whom he had first met in Peshawar and whose family had finally been found asylum in the UK.

However, my most enduring memory of Bruce goes back to our Peshawar days and sums up the quintessence of his character. While Bruce was travelling by foot and horse through northern Afghanistan, a local commander gifted him a fully trained *baz*, or hunting falcon

– a gift normally only bestowed on royalty. Despite the arduous and dangerous nature of his expedition, Bruce emerged from Afghanistan with the *baz* on his wrist, complete with its hood, leash and even bells! Who else but Bruce would roll up with a falcon on his arm after such a journey, and who else could cite an appropriate Persian couplet or two to suit the occasion? The *baz* was something of a sensation for visitors to his house, sitting as it did calmly on its perch. I am not sure what happened to it. Maybe Bruce let it go when he left Pakistan?

We last met in early December 2018 at the BIPS lecture in London. Bruce, in his normal persuasive manner, had charmed me into gifting him a copy of my latest book. Sadly, we never managed to begin a project we had talked about for a few years, the reading of scores of Mughal and Timurid headstones that Warwick Ball and I had photographed in Kabul in 1981.

Yet despite his many talents – his musical ability, multilingual skills, and his depth of understanding of Islam and the Persianate world – it was always a mystery to me why Bruce never found a niche in academia or published any substantial body of work. He seemed content with his relatively meagre income as a tour guide or assisting others in their literary endeavours, a role for which I, and many others, are indebted. He was a free spirit, and perhaps, in the true sense of the word, a Romantic.

Early this January (2020), having heard of Bruce's terminal diagnosis, Kathy and I decided we would anyway send him our usual New Zealand calendar and include a letter thanking him for many years of friendship and citing a short poem by Hafiz. I don't know if he ever received the letter. I hope he did.

# Kandahar, Afghanistan, April 1992

**John Butt** *came as a hippie to the Pashtoon parts that straddle the border between Afghanistan and Pakistan in 1970. He became Muslim in the same year, going on to become a* talib – *a seeker of Islamic learning – noted as the first Westerner to graduate from Darul Uloom Deoband. Since then, he has been working as a journalist, broadcaster and storyteller, particularly through the medium of radio soap opera. He still lives in the Pashtoon parts of the world where he accepted Islam.*

The only trip I made with Bruce was to Kandahar in April 1992. In the course of that trip, and ever since, Bruce has been like an ethereal presence in my life – there, but not quite there.

The early Nineties, when I started working at the BBC, were heady days at the Corporation. Nowadays, with the emphasis on health and safety, the tendency is to protect staff from danger. In those days, the more dangerous the place and situation was, the more likely the BBC was to send you there.

That was how I set out for Kandahar in the spring of 1992. The government of Dr Najibullah was fast losing control of its former strongholds. Provincial headquarters were falling one by one to anti-government forces. Kandahar was about to fall. I was working with the BBC Pashto service at the time. They asked me to go and cover the fall of the southern Afghan city of Kandahar.

How Bruce fell in with me, on that trip to Kandahar, I am not sure. I had met him once before. It was when he had been head of Afghanaid in Peshawar in the mid-Eighties. Afghanaid was one of the organisations set up to assist Afghan refugees. I am sure writing funding proposals and reports – management even – such as one had to do as head of an aid organisation like Afghanaid, would not have been Bruce's calling. He was enamoured of Afghan music and culture, born of his love of Persian language and literature. That was what brought him to Afghanistan.

It was indeed a musical evening that brought me one evening to Bruce's Afghanaid office, next to the railway line in Peshawar's

University Town. My friend Abdal Samad took me to the function. Abdal Samad was working in one of the aid agencies, and kept in contact with Afghanaid. Bruce had called some Afghan musicians together, and they were playing for the attendant guests. It was not really the type of Afghan music that I was used to. This was Persian music, much more refined compared to the more raucous Pashto music that I had become accustomed to over the years.

It was Abdal Samad who maintained contact with Bruce in the coming months. Abdal Samad and I had become Muslim in the same year – 1970 – and in the same place – the Swat valley in northern Pakistan. We were both 'Pashtoon' Muslims, both from England. I was still switching between Swat and Peshawar at the time we met Bruce. In any case, it was probably Abdal Samad rather than me who was better disposed to take up on a request that Bruce had.

Bruce asked Abdal Samad to come and help him with his recitation of the Quran. Before work every morning, Abdal Samad would take a cycle ride to Bruce's place. The two Englishmen would conduct a discreet 'Quran'al-Fajr' (Al-Quran, 17:78) session every morning. I say discreet, since I only found out very recently about these Quran sessions. Neither Abdal Samad, nor Bruce, told me about them.

Neither did I know at the time about Bruce's prodigious grasp of the Persian language. I only found out about that when we were both sitting with the outgoing Governor of Kandahar province, General Mohammad Akram in the spring of 1992, and Bruce was interviewing him. Bruce's pure, pristine, cultured Persian amazed both me and the governor. The Governor could hardly summon up a reply, so aghast was he at Bruce's Persian. It was as though he was ashamed to speak his own Afghan Persian in the presence of such an accomplished linguist.

Next year, in 1993, Bruce was doing some work for the BBC Pashto service on some drama scripts. I was not apprised exactly of the work he was doing. The big job as far as Pashto – and indeed Persian – radio drama for Afghanistan was concerned was coming up though. That was to bring '*The Archers* to Afghanistan'. As it happened, I was given that job.

So it was that I made it back to Peshawar, still the epicentre of all relief activities related to Afghanistan, as founding editor of what was to become known as *New Home, New Life*. Along with the head of the BBC Pashto service Gordon Adam, I felt obliged to pay a courtesy call on the British High Commissioner to Pakistan, Sir Nicholas Barrington. Sir Nicholas was indignant, and not very diplomatic. To my face he said that he thought Bruce should have got the job, not me. 'No one knows Afghan village life as well as Bruce,' he noted. That may have been true, but as Sir Nicholas should have known, management never was, and never would have been, Bruce's forte. I have never been particularly good at delivering a report to donors on time. Bruce would have been a disaster.

Still, Bruce remained this fleeting presence in my life, as I ran the *New Home, New Life* ship through the Nineties. He was living in Islamabad, close to the house of the BBC Islamabad correspondent Lyse Doucet. Sometimes I met him in Lyse's house. Our friendship really blossomed, though, in the second decade of the new millennium. Whenever Bruce came to Kabul, the first thing he would do would be to ring me up and invite me over to lunch. He would be working with Jolyon Leslie, usually at the Aga Khan Foundation. We met once in Delhi, when Bruce took me over to the Nizamuddin shrine, where he was well known to the shrine-keepers. 'One of the finest examples of Tughlaq architecture,' he remarked to me on the Nizamuddin mosque. Bruce was indeed the best judge of such matters.

My last meeting with Bruce was in my English hometown of Cambridge. True to his love of the finer things of life, Bruce had come down from York to visit the Fitzwilliam Museum. I was visiting the dentist, opposite the Fitzwilliam on Trumpington Road. 'I do hope the dentist treated you kindly,' Bruce texted me.

Which brings me to the two points that are a cause of particular remorse to me, following Bruce's parting from this world. One is that, despite all the things we had in common, and despite our frequent meetings and the evident warm feelings between us, I never really cultivated Bruce's friendship. We never really benefited from each other as much as we could have done.

There are countless ways I could have benefited from Bruce's encyclopaedic knowledge, in particular from his love of Persian poetry, a passion of mine also. But speaking as a Muslim, and a more traditional Islamic scholar than Bruce, though I am also somewhat unconventional in my Islamic scholarship, I feel I could have mentored him more as far as his Islamic faith was concerned.

Despite him brushing up his recitation of the Quran, and despite him being known to friends as Bruce – sometimes Feruz (Turquoise) – Aziz, I never saw Bruce as a practising Muslim. I saw him as a modern-day Sir Richard Burton-type figure, enamoured and fascinated with the Muslim world, but not actually a Muslim.

So when Bruce told me that he had 'woken up one morning, and lost his faith', I did not know what to say. I could have said to him that everyone had doubts from time to time, but this should provide even more impetus to settle into one's daily Islamic routine. I could have told him it doesn't matter what you are – agnostic, atheist, whatever – just go through the motions and you will come out of the experience as a Muslim in your own mould. I could have said to him that everyone's faith fluctuates – even that of the Companions of the Holy Prophet – but that should not be a reason to abandon one's faith altogether; in fact, it can be a source of strengthening of one's faith. I could have related to Bruce any number of Hadith from the chapters on evil promptings – *al-wasa'is* – or temptation.

I could and should have done, but I didn't and now Bruce is gone and I will not get a chance.

# Musical memories

**Gordon Adam** *was a journalist and development worker working on Afghanistan and Pakistan for thirty years. He was head of the BBC's Pashto Service from 1986 to 1994.*

Two music-related memories of Bruce stand out for me: one – in the late 1980s in Peshawar when I arranged to meet him early (for me) one summer's morning. I went round to his very humble mud-brick dwelling on the outskirts of University Town, and he emerged bleary eyed from a room reeking of stale chars (cannabis) with a couple of equally tired looking Afghan lads. He looked happy with life: 'Gordon, dear friend, welcome'. He introduced me to his friends: 'We have been up all night listening to music – starting with Palestrina and then all of Beethoven's symphonies. They loved them, it is amazing how really great music crosses cultural boundaries'. I was never sure how much the chars contributed to the overall sense of enjoyment!

The second was about three years ago, staying together with Bruce on the small inner Hebridean island of Lismore. Coming back from a walk, Bruce passed a young man, clearly a tourist, clutching some sheet music. They said hello, and Bruce asked: 'Are you a musician?' The man said yes, he was a baritone, at music college. 'What's the music?' 'Diechterliebe, by Schumann', he responded. Bruce was over the moon: 'I love Diechterliebe, let's find a piano and we can run through it'. So it was, an hour later, I went into the kitchen of the crofters next door Duncan and Anne, who were looking slightly stunned as this amazing sound emerged from the sitting room – a high baritone, accompanied at full throttle by Bruce shouting not-so-occasional advice on interpretation. 'I've never heard anything like it', Anne – who was the church organist – murmured. Over the next few days, Bruce returned to her piano, and typically, spent some of that time playing duets with Anne.

I was at the receiving end of his musical advice just once, at Bruce's memorable sixtieth birthday party in Ullapool, not far from where I live, which included a wonderfully diverse jamming session from Western classical and baroque sonatas to Persian and Afghan traditional songs. On a couple of occasions during my time at the BBC I tried tapping into Bruce's literary creativity. But it was not easy: broadcasters write to deadlines, a concept which Bruce seemed unaware of, or perhaps didn't approve of. On one occasion he was contributing to a live broadcast linking studios in London and Peshawar marking some significant event – a difficult technical challenge in the early 1990s. It was almost derailed because Bruce's article was so late. It only went on air because I made a frantic phone call from London to a mutual friend and Afghan scholar asking him to stand over Bruce until it was completed, and then personally deliver it to my harassed colleague, Dr Akbar, who was presenting the show.

As others know far better than me, Bruce's scholarship was extraordinarily wide ranging. I only experienced this once, in a formal sense. It was in Kabul, possibly at the office of the Afghan Research and Evaluation Unit, where he spoke fluently for an hour with the help of a few slides, on Islamic grave inscriptions. It is a very niche field, but his enthusiasm and enormous understanding of the topic made this a gripping event. He was, as many will agree, 'one of a kind'.

# Neighbour in Pakistan
## Islamabad, 1990

**Brigitte Neubacher** *spent nine years in Manhattan (1981–90): jazz clubs, Miles Davis, Sting, Gil Evans Orchestra, and Javier Perez de Cuellar; then eleven years in Afghanistan and Pakistan (1990–2001). At long last and ever since mainly back home in Vienna, Austria.*

Once upon a time, in the early 1990s, I decided I'd had enough of Manhattan, after almost ten years.

Arriving in Islamabad in early May 1990, I was shocked: no jazz clubs, no women in the streets. Where are the women? Busy at home, I was told.

Near my new home on a dead-end street in F-7/2, Islamabad, huge marihuana plants. Where am I? Tiny bags in Manhattan cost a fortune not long ago. The smell was overpowering.

My first encounter with the East: two friends, an Iranian female, an Afghan male (slightly overweight) came to visit me in my always 'open door' home.

They came with a book: HAFEZ. Ah… Persian text, Persian writing.

The two taught me how to read Hafez. Just open the book and choose a page at random.

So I did. Hafez told me that a Turkish guy, who had just left me (correct), that I should forget him. Perfect advice. So I did.

Soon after my arrival in Pakistan I also met you. You, living almost across the street.

Bruce, I decided, you would be the perfect person to teach me Persian, so I could read Hafez by myself. We had one Persian lesson. Thank you Bruce for your patience.

I was ignorant, naive and enjoyed discovering the world East of Manhattan and Europe – being Austrian by birth.

Thank you Bruce for lovely concerts in your elegant home, all of us sitting on Afghan cushions and kelims. My legs and knees got used to that also.

Music, Hafez, and a bit of Persian. Thank you Bruce.

Great pity that after you had presented a lecture about the Prophet (PBUH) including an image of the Prophet (PBUH), you had to suddenly leave Pakistan. Missed you then. Miss you now. And miss your knowledge, wisdom, curiosity and adventurism.

# Inshallah
## *Islamabad, 1992*

**Lyse Doucet** *is the BBC's Chief International Correspondent. She lived in Pakistan and Afghanistan from 1988 to 1993, where she was the BBC's correspondent, and spent many memorable moments with Bruce during that time, and beyond. 'I sadly missed his funeral in February because I was in Doha covering the signing of the Afghan Taliban/US deal. I thought Bruce would forgive me.'*

Many remember Bruce as the house guest of all house guests. I remember him as my neighbour. In the early 1990s, Bruce's abode was a short quick walk across a small square of a park tucked into our leafy neighbourhood of Islamabad. By day, with this quiet city's sunshine streaming through the windows, we'd share lunch sitting crosslegged on a chik mat or Afghan carpet – everyone including the cook eating together. By night, traditional music often filled the rooms, or the buzz of intense debate, wine discreetly served in earthenware jugs.

One of my most abiding memories is how Bruce would often slip into a bubble, engrossed in discussion on some esoteric subject or another with one intellectual or another. There was one man, whose name I forget, but whom I can still visualise with Bruce at Islamabad receptions – from arrival to departure, to and from the buffet table, enveloped in intense conversation. I'd tease that they should leave their bubble for a bit. They never would. Why would they?

Bruce wasn't just my neighbour. He was my first Persian language teacher. We'd sit on his patio miniature, on rattan chairs, Bruce chuckling as he crooned 'Non, je ne regrette rien,' rolling his Edith Piaf r's with delighted exaggeration. Our lessons took on an added urgency when President Rafsanjani of Iran visited Pakistan. This was my rare chance to approach him directly, with an official letter, to ask about opening a BBC office in Tehran. I recently found that little spiel, written in pencil, with dark accent marks to highlight the correct pronunciation.

We rehearsed, I memorised. And then threaded my way through Iranian and Pakistani bodyguards to plant myself in front of a bemused but smiling President. Wannell words flowed.

'What did he say?' Bruce demanded with his endearing enthusiasm. I understood all of it, I proudly told my teacher. What was the President's reply? Inshallah.

We laughed – a lot, for a long time.

# A life between adventure, Sufism and music

**Ulrike Vestring** *studied law in Berlin, Grenoble and Bonn. With her husband Alfred she lived at German embassies in Lebanon, Yemen, Madagascar, in Paris, Vienna, Saudi Arabia, and Pakistan. All along, music has been her favourite pastime.*

To me, Bruce was like two persons, different but somehow complementary. In each, traces of the other shone through.

Whenever he came to the house, our head bearer Gul Zaman, a proud Pathan from Pakistan's northern areas, would bring in a cup of tea, while we talked, trying to live up to our guest's elegant English. Along with his pleasant manners Bruce could have learned it in a nineteenth-century style nursery. When he sat down at the piano, he turned into his musical self. To accompany my modest recorder playing for a baroque sonata, he used the tiny harpsichord we had brought from Paris. Our small band of music lovers carried the instrument wherever it suited us. Once, on an Easter morning, we even had it on the terrace outside, where our three cranes and the chickens we kept joined the audience.

The other Bruce however was deeply steeped in South Asian culture. On his research trips he ignored hardships and travelled extremely light. He explored the Indus delta by dhow, discovering almost unknown archaeological sites and traces of pre-Islamic civilisations.

Whether he was Muslim I never knew. But he certainly was devoted to the great Persian mystic Jalaluddin Rumi. Bruce invited us to his small house for evenings of music and poetry. When we had settled down onto straw mats covering the floor, Bruce opened our minds to Sufi music played by musicians from Afghanistan who had somehow made it to the relative safety of Islamabad.

Bruce often left town without notice. We were worried when we heard that he had gone to Afghanistan, in the summer of 1994. In Kabul, then all but deserted by foreigners, our friend met Irene Salimi, a German lady married to an Afghan. She was in charge of the German embassy compound, safeguarding the office, the residence and the beautiful gardens from plunder and stray bombs. She kept the Afghan staff busy cleaning, dusting and polishing. And saw to it that at the end of each month, gardeners, cooks and sweepers received their salaries.

When Bruce discovered that at the residence, a beautiful grand piano had survived, he persuaded Mrs Irene to throw a 'concert-cum-dinner'. Amidst chaos and fighting in the city, there was Bruce, dressed in a freshly ironed white shirt over ample black trousers local style, playing Bach's Italian concerto from memory.

What a privilege to have known this exceptional human being who spent a lifetime wandering between Orient and Occident.

# Bound for Baluchistan

**Frances Dodd** *met Bruce in Islamabad in the early 1990s, when her father was head of the Fulbright Foundation there. Bruce appeared one day at the British High Commission to assist the visiting Dr Annemarie Schimmel, an authority on Sufi traditions, in delivering her lecture. He was soon a fixture in town, promoting a flowering of musical collaborations and fine performances. Frances is now a violist and librarian in Vancouver, British Columbia.*

I really thought I'd somehow see Bruce again, after Pakistan. Our last meeting was in Islamabad – we parted at the door, he bound for the Baluchistan coast by train in the company of an Afghan youth, aiming to ride a dhow, as far as I can remember. Yet he introduced me to some of the finest music ever, including the Bach sonatas which I have just played over Christmas. Such fun was had while he was in town, including a royal welcome and musical receptions at the German and Italian embassies, plus a mad evening of Strauss waltzes hosted by my parents. And how could one forget his series of evening concerts for Afghan musician refugees, performing the ragas of Rumi, lyrics of which he circulated in translation (still stored somewhere in my files). What an amazing time, now lost to us all for mortality's sake. But, death be not proud! Or so I say to myself, for he lives on in our memories. Many thanks for your accounts. I can just picture him encouraging you all towards a second performance.

# A pianist and a cellist meet in Pakistan
*Islamabad, 1991*

**Jean Gianfranceschi**

It was with a great sense of trepidation that I moved house and home from Washington D.C. to Pakistan in 1991. Newly wed to a U.S. diplomat, I left behind my legal career and a very satisfying avocation as amateur cellist, with projects such as performing all of Beethoven's string quartets (with a former member of the Boston Symphony Orchestra).

How did all this loss result in a transformation into the happiest and most adventurous chapter of my life? People, and first and foremost among them – Bruce Wannell.

Soon after my arrival, I was still unpacking boxes, when unannounced, a certain blue-green-eyed British gentleman of elegant speech and appearance appeared at my door, introducing himself as a pianist. He had gotten word that I was a cellist and he proposed we play together. I said that would be great, and yes, let's do that one day once I've had a chance to settle in, we decide on what to play, work up our parts a bit, etc. etc. But no, Bruce said we should play right then, today, now. Luckily I had shipped my grandmother's piano from the U.S. and so, after a bit more feeble argument on my part, play we did! (I never stopped arguing with Bruce, but I never won any arguments!)

And thus began the saga of a musical partnership that spanned three decades – stretching across Asia to England and Continental Europe. We played often for pleasure – the three Bach Gamba Sonatas, Beethoven sonatas, French songs by Fauré and Massenet, Handel sonatas (with fellow-cellist and long-time Swiss friend Elisabeth Rubi – who was a constant presence at that time in Pakistan, and in on many of the Bruce adventures) and more.

Despite my constant haranguing, Bruce never practiced all that much (he lacked a piano, after all) but his incredible talent and innate musicality carried the day, and playing with him was some of the most

69

satisfying playing I've ever done. Bruce always had something to say, musically. Something that came from the heart.

Bruce was a great one for organising concerts and other adventures. He inveigled many a European ambassador to host (and participate in, in the case of the German Ambassadors's wife, Ulrike Vestring) elegant luncheons and dinners to showcase the musical talents of the expat community. I was far from the only participant – Bruce dug up everyone of musical talent in the community and enlisted them on our pursuits. A particularly memorable occasion was on New Year's Day in the early '90s at the Vestrings' (the German Ambassador's) lovely residence in Islamabad. We figured no one would be available on New Year's Eve, due to various celebrations, so Bruce selected a suitably late start time for the next morning. And sure enough we had a big turnout. I had a little squabble with Bruce about whether we should play inside (my choice – where there was an enormous, suitable reception hall) or outside on the patio overlooking the garden – Bruce's choice. As always, Bruce won, and we played outside, setting the harpsichord under the arching fronds of a Poinsettia tree bedecked with enormous crimson flowers, overlooking the undulating, tree-studded, emerald lawn with strutting peacocks. It was a sunshiny day – shirtsleeve weather – and the result was enchanting. My ill-found fears of chilly breezes blowing the music away, bad acoustics, etc. were forgotten. It was a perfect and memorable start to the New Year.

Not all concerts were as successful. My friend Elisabeth will tell you about an ill-fated concert/dinner I organised at our home in Peshawar that was supposed to feature Bruce.... who somehow got side-tracked in Khwazakhela and ended up a no-show. This led to my falling into a snit, a short-lived rupture, which was mended only when Elisabeth prepared a rösti dinner and invited us both, to engineer a reconciliation. Elisabeth and I still laugh about it every time we meet.

There were many other adventures with Bruce. Our friendship started with music, but quickly branched out to include travels and other experiences, such as following a stream from Islamabad up into the Margalla Hills (the foothills of the Himalayas), scrambling up some rocks and through the trees to discover a beautiful, totally secluded, turquoise pool. I still have the image of Bruce diving in, headfirst, from a towering rock formation into those cool, clear waters. I have another image in my head of a crosslegged Bruce, sitting meditatively atop the dome of an abandoned Buddhist stupa in a remote meadow where we had gone for a walk and a picnic....

Then there was the time Elisabeth, my husband Rob and I found ourselves in Lahore with Bruce and we ended up crashing an elegant party for Basant – the kite-flying celebration – but I think Elisabeth will tell you about that. It was the only time in my life I met Imran Khan, current PM of Pakistan, but then known as a handsome cricket star.

After Pakistan, despite years of other tours in the U.S., Madagascar and Belgium, I never lost touch with Bruce. He was someone who always remembered and cared for his friends, and his postcards from exotic locales turned up with regularity. When we moved to Paris, I saw him more often and we played together each time. My husband and I visited him in York, where he showed the beauties of his adopted town, brought out the carpets and candles into his lovely garden for a party, organised a musical concert at a friend's house (where we trotted out our favorite repertoire from our Pakistan days), and took us on a long ramble in the Yorkshire dales.

I never knew when Bruce would turn up (and I still didn't know *after* he told me when he was going to turn up) but I could always count on him to turn up eventually, and to really BE there for me when he did turn up, and to turn daily life into an adventure! My husband Rob and I will miss him, and remember him with love.

# The most interesting year of my life
## *Peshawar, 1989*

**Elisabeth Rubi's** *parents were immersed in art, spirituality and travelling, so she learned yoga from her father and learned to lay out the Chinese oracle as a child. After finishing her studies in biology she took an overland trip to Nepal but when she arrived in Herat she felt she had finally arrived home. She became a musician, dividing her time between teaching and chamber concerts but in 1987 decided to go back to the university to study Islamic science, languages and comparative religion. Her professor said she could write her thesis in Pakistan and Afghanistan, which is where she met Bruce. She lived as a music teacher in Switzerland but used her four months of annual holiday to live in Peshawar, from 1992 to 2015. She travelled all over Pakistan and much of Afghanistan, writing about holy places, making pictures and meeting interesting people. She is now retired from teaching music and runs a small boutique of eastern textiles called Gauhar Shad.*

It was in '89 when I first heard of Bruce. We were travelling in the north of Pakistan, in the Swat Valley. In Kalam, strolling through the bazaar I heard Swiss-German spoken and those Swiss, working for Swiss Development Corporation, invited us to their house.

They worked on a potato project and during our discussion they asked what we were doing in that part of the world. I explained to them my interest in Islamic culture – Sufi music, architecture, literature, art in any form and that I was on research for my studies over there. Oh, then you must get to know one person, who is interested in exactly the same topics, it's Bruce Wannell, we do not have his address but you will sure find him in Peshawar. He visits us from time to time, to organise his unforgettable culture evenings even in the rough mountains of the Hindukush. They said he lately came to make a lecture about Heinrich Heine and Rainer Maria Rilke.

Going down to Peshawar I thought it would be nice to meet this interesting mysterious man, but Peshawar has several million inhabitants, so it was unlikely to meet people like that by chance.

Some days later we visited our beloved carpet dealer in Khyber Bazaar. We were sitting there looking at the wonderful Afghan carpets when a man stormed in, in a beige shalwar qameez, wild hair, not looking at us at all and he started a very vivid talk with our carpet friend Sufi, whose name was Sufi but he also was one. I did not pay much attention as they discussed in Farsi a personal issue and I thought he was a local Afghan.

Sitting there and drinking tea I suddenly had the feeling I should ask him if he had an idea where we could find Bruce Wannell. He gave me a short glance and then said, I am Bruce! We were so puzzled, hard to believe.

Two incredible coincidences. First we heard in Hunza from a German tourist that if we would like to meet one of the best carpet dealers we should go for breakfast to the Khyber Hotel in Peshawar to meet a French man called Farooq and he would bring us to that person. So we ended up in Sufi's shop and the second coincidence was to meet by chance the only Swiss living in Swat to tell us to meet Bruce.

Bruce invited us for breakfast next morning in his room in University Town at 7 a.m. As we had never been in that part of Peshawar it was quite hard to find him. When we finally arrived it was a real Bruce setting. In a wonderful *chapan* he was sitting on cushions like a king, in a wonderful decorated room being already busy with two Afghans: to one he gave a French lesson and for the second he wrote a letter for a law case. The house was rented from Frederic Roussel who later put the NGO Acted in place and lived nearby in the so-called White House.

After tea, the next guest stormed into the room, a French lady, Chantal Lobato, a journalist writing about Afghanistan too, ex-wife of writer Olivier Roy. She had just come back with her *mujahideen* friends from visiting Ahmad Shah Masoud in the Panchir Valley and told us how the famous Mujahed was doing in his mountain fortress. What an interesting start of my long and intense friendship with Bruce. A few month later I felt somehow tired from my normal life in Switzerland and dear Bruce had the solution. He said why do you not come to live in Peshawar so you can study Farsi and relax in that extremely interesting city.

So I packed up my things, even the cello came with me and I landed in University Town, where I rented a wonderful house and spent the most interesting year of my life. My house partner was Wali Seraj, nephew of King Amanullah, an incredibly intelligent and interesting man, even a prince. I learned so much from him too when he told me about his life at the royal court.

Once in Peshawar, Bruce introduced me to all the people who were in Peshawar working somehow for Afghanistan: Alain de Bures, Frederic Roussel, Olivier Rousselle, Bernt Glatzer, others in Islamabad,

Brigitte Neubacher, Adam Nayyar, Doris Buddenberg, Philippe Labreveux, many diplomats and as the BBC office was next to Bruce's flat we met also Lyse Doucet.

He instructed me how to behave, where to dress locally, where European, what I should avoid writing of (military, ISI, drugs). He gave me all the info on where I should call for a visit to the best pool in a garden in Peshawar, where I could find pianos, where the Mirs of Mastuj or Chitral had their residence in Peshawar to get information and invitations if going up there. Then he introduced me to many Afghan and Pakistani musicians, like the nephews of Sarahang, the Afghan Amir Jan, Salimat Ali Khan and his sons Sharafat and Shafaqat, Sabz Ali.

And as he later moved to Islamabad, when he came to visit Peshawar he always lived in my house. He even harvested the oranges in the garden, took them to Islamabad in a taxi and came back with jars of marmalade.

He could have lived in much more elegant houses, like the White House with lots of servants, cooks, cars etc, but he said, you know when I want to recite the Quran in the morning I feel better with you than with other friends. And in the years '92–'93 we played together in all the places having a piano, in Peshawar and Islamabad. Very nice our music rehearsals and concerts in Pascal Maubert's house, in the German Embassy with Ambassador Vestring, in Anthony Fitzherbert's, in our friend's house the American diplomat Gianfranceschi in Peshawar, in the American Club etc. As I am a cellist and he was a very good pianist we gave so many concerts, many also with the other cellist Jean, the American diplomat's wife, it was a real joy. I gave lots of concerts with classical professional pianists in Switzerland who might have been better technically but what I liked with Bruce was his energy and joy when playing. He had a big problem to work long enough on a piece. One day he said to me playing in Maubert's house, let's try the Brahms Sonata. I said Bruce we will play Beethoven in the concert tonight, so please let's practise that. Then on another concert day he said let's go to the bazaar to look for nice textiles and carpets. I said you know when I play in the evening I need to practise before and no carpet hunting.

Only one evening we were very angry with him, as my friend Jean mentions in her writings. We invited half Peshawar for a music evening, with an Afghan music group too, a big dinner following and at 6 p.m. Bruce called, sorry I am in Khwazakhela, about six hours rough road trip up north, I will not make it, could you please tell everybody to go home and come back next day. So we made it a cello duet evening. It went quite well, we said we do not need that man and Jean refused to talk to him for some time before we were good friends again.

We travelled a lot together. I remember a special trip to Indus Kohistan.

I needed some photos of the wooden mosques of that region and we started up to Besham on the Indus. We arrived much too late, with no provision only a little water and started to climb the incredible steep hill in one of the most dangerous areas of Pakistan. Soon it got dark, I could not follow Bruce, he ran off and left me back in an area where behind every rock an armed local was hiding with a Kalashnikov, wondering what that white lady was doing here. Our Pashtun friend dragged me up the hill, in a very gentle way and reaching our goal in the middle of the night we could sleep in the village Hujra, meeting point of the men, in a village called Quley. We lay down realising that the beds were completely full of bed bugs, it was horrible. I looked to Bruce, who was sitting straight up in a white shalwar qameez and I asked him, how can you cope with that disaster. Very loudly he said what wonderful air up here, I enjoy a lot, this wonderful breeze. I could have killed him.

If I needed some information for my studies Bruce could help. I said I would like to work on the main Herati Sufi saint Abdullah Ansari (eleventh century). He said: there are two people in the world who can give you the information – Bo Uthas in Stockholm or Serge de Beaurecueil, the Dominican monk in Paris. And really he took me to meet that extraordinary person in his monastery in the Faubourg St Honoré in Paris.

Unforgettable the evenings we created in Islamabad. Bruce prepared a poem of Rumi, Hafez or Saadi and wrote it down in Farsi, with an English translation. Then he read it to the guests and let Sharif Ghazal and his group put it into music. It helped us better understand how Afghan music was functioning.

After Pakistan we met in London, York, Switzerland, Paris, for concerts, for literature evenings, all these happenings I will miss a lot. One dinner I still remember in London. Bruce was staying in a wonderful house and said to me a very high up of the English Intelligence will come for dinner. What do you think if we make just a rich cheese plate, a good wine and dessert. So we went to the cheese shop and he said, could you buy the cheese, I have just £4 left. So I bought the cheese and we went back to the flat, where the walls were plastered with real Turner paintings. Incredible, even with no money Bruce managed to keep some elegance and standards.

I spoke with Bruce in German. He is the only English man I know who spoke German without any English accent.

After our first visit with Bruce in University Town, I ended up renting a house 50m from that room and stayed there around twenty-five years.

I am so grateful for those incredible circumstances that let us meet. It made my life more colourful. Thanks Bruce, I miss you a lot.

# Speaking better than perfect French
## Peshawar, 1988

**Anthony Fitzherbert** *is a practical agriculturalist who has had a long working relationship with the countries of the Near and Middle East and Central Asia which includes close associations with Iran, Turkey, Afghanistan, Pakistan and the Central Asian Republics and continues. He lives with his wife Anne in a small village in Cumbria where they have had a house south of Kendal for thirty-five years. At eighty-one he is semi-retired. Their two daughters and grandchildren live nearby.*

My first encounter with Bruce was in late 1988 in Peshawar at a meeting with that personification of French linguistic nationalism Alain de Bure, in the office of the French NGO MADERA. Bruce's was already a name to conjure with in that world of aid, arms and opium, spooks, spies, sinners, saints and Sufis. By the time we met, he was already a legend among the dramatis personae on the Peshawar stage where he had been based for the previous two years, interspersed with mysterious forays into the remoter corners of the Hindu Kush. He had already publicly converted to Islam, eschewing life in the 'farangi' (European) ghetto of University Town for the more exotic social delights of the bazaar. Earning a precarious living with short commissions from UN Agencies and the aid fraternity, he had already become a byword in the musical demi-monde of that frontier town.

Speaking better than perfect French as well as Persian, Bruce had a special affinity with the French NGOs, whose idiosyncratic political rivalries matched those of the Afghans in their complexity. I was at that time based in Rome with the Food & Agriculture Organisation of the UN as the desk officer responsible for both Afghanistan and Pakistan, on a field mission to start planning the rehabilitation of Afghanistan's agriculture. It was hoped that this could start once the Soviet military forces had left the country in February 1989, as recently agreed in Geneva. I was in Peshawar on reconnaissance, endeavouring to find out who among the international NGOs already working across the Afghan frontier were involved in agriculture and related subjects. I had already been across the frontier myself to see the situation at first hand in two provinces – Kunar and Paktika.

MADERA were working in the Kunar valley and Nuristan, involved with issues involving forestry, horticulture, irrigation and livestock. We quickly established a common bond as each of us (Bruce, Alain and myself) had lived and worked in Iran before the revolution of 1979. With my spoken French never having left the 'schoolroom' and Alain refusing to speak English as a matter of nationalist principle, our meeting was conducted in Persian, the one language we had in common! Bruce occasionally intervened where translation and interpretation was needed. We made friends instantly and it lasted.

Later the following year (1989), after the Soviets had left Afghanistan, I was posted out to Pakistan to set up and manage the FAO's agricultural rehabilitation programme and we established offices in Islamabad, Peshawar and Quetta. I continued to see Bruce on my regular visits to Peshawar and across the frontier, where he enriched my life with useful introductions, information and insights. Then, in 1992, when his life was threatened by certain intolerant *jihadis*, he moved his base from Peshawar to Islamabad, where I was living with my wife and two daughters. We saw him on a more regular basis.

We were living on the top floor of a house belonging to a charming lady – Hania Begum – who occupied the ground floor. Hania, from a distinguished N.W. Frontier family, was the widow of a general much decorated for his gallantry in the campaigns in Burma and elsewhere in the Second World War. She absolutely doted on Bruce, not only for his ability to quote verses from the Pushtu and Persian poets, but for having become a Muslim of the '*Sufi*' variety she admired. Across the street from us lived a highly cultured Pakistani family who possessed a nice piano. With his sixth sense for such things, this was soon located by Bruce who charmed its owners into allowing him to play whenever he wished. This he did to our great pleasure, with the windows always wide open so that the strains of Mozart and Schubert, beautifully played, wafted across the road.

Indeed Bruce had an unfailing nose, not only for pianos that he considered worthy of playing, but for other musicians to play with – pianists, violinists, cellists and flautists. As well as organising musical events in his own lodgings, Bruce was adept at locating suitable private houses whose inhabitants, both international and Pakistani, considered it a privilege to be asked to host these musical evenings arranged for carefully selected audiences.

These evenings were not confined to solos, duets, quintets and quartets gathered to play pieces drawn from the great Western composers. Bruce's interest and taste was truly catholic, embracing oriental as well as Western music. So these soirées were just as likely to be devoted to Afghan *ghazals* and Punjabi Sufi music as to Beethoven. I remember, as in a surreal dream, one extraordinary evening with gypsy musicians that included a mesmerising and bewitching girl dancing in a haze of *charis* (cannabis) smoke.

There was another memorable evening organised round a farewell party given for departing friends by Juliette von Seibold on the roof of her top-floor flat in north Islamabad looking up to the Margalla Hills. Juliette had painted the flat roof white for the occasion. The musical entertainment was organised by Bruce who had covered the roof with carpets, qilims and cushions. The musicians were Afghan, their leading *rubab* player a former heroin addict whom Bruce was reputed to have 'rescued' – called (I think) Ustaad Amir Jan.

Juliette has reminded me that the guests, including several ambassadors, were feasted on roast lamb with rice and *khir* followed by cardamom pudding. Anne and I came with our two daughters (Emily and Virginia), home for the holidays from their boarding school in England. They will never forget that evening. The stillness of the star-filled night, with distant, soundless monsoon lightning playing over the hills. The strangeness of the *ghazals*. The whiffs of *charis*, inspiring the musicians to even greater feats of musical and vocal skill, drifting across the carpets on the night breeze and two small girls tugging on my arm whispering – '*Daddy! Daddy! What IS that funny smelling smoke?*'

I think Bruce was happy in Islamabad. Although he loved his adventures into the interior of Afghanistan, despite sickness and danger, the brittle edgy life of Peshawar had become too dangerous for him. In Islamabad he could relax. There were friends who had horses that he could ride. The mountains were close at hand where like a leprechaun he would lead unwitting (and witting) friends on goat-like scrambles up tumbling waterfalls in the Margalla hills.

Later after we had returned to Cumbria, to our house south of Kendal, and Bruce had settled in York, we continued to see him periodically. As our visitors' book shows he would usually come and stay a night or two at least once a year, usually on the excuse of some local event like the 'Pot Fest' at Hutton in the Forest. He had other friends, like Bobbie and Betsy Bell in Settle, who lived not far from us with whom he also stayed and made music with likeminded, musically talented friends.

Usually he would give us notice of his arrival, but the first occasion, not long after he had settled in York, was an exception. We had been out all day. Returning home as dusk and rain were falling we found a note on our doorstep from Bruce to say that he had walked over from Barbon (in the Vale of Lune), where he was staying with his old Oxford friend, the architectural historian John Martin Robinson. Armed with our address and a map he had decided to call on us. Finding us out for the day he had spent the afternoon chatting, drinking tea and eating cake with our nextdoor neighbours, whose general knowledge of the more exotic parts of the world outside the north of England was negligible. They were completely captivated! His note said that he had got tired of waiting so was walking back to Barbon. This was about eight miles by road and night was falling. My wife (Anne) and I immediately jumped in our car, finally catching up with Bruce a good five miles down the road striding through the Rigmaden woods in the gathering dusk, his old-fashioned macintosh flapping in the wind. We picked him up and took him home for more tea and a dram of whisky, before delivering him back to his friend in Barbon.

Through most of these latter years I was still doing work that took me back to Central Asia and the Middle East, so we always had much to talk about and tales to exchange. Postcards would arrive from far-flung locations with exotic names in the Himalayas, Africa or India, written in his beautiful handwriting addressed to all our family, having sometimes been many weeks on the way. He was by this time spending much time in India doing translation work for Willie Dalrymple to whom, as a cousin of mine, I had been able to introduce him.

Bruce always had great natural empathy for the young, which I have seen demonstrated on a number of occasions. He had always been fond of our daughters, whom he first met as schoolgirls in Pakistan and he never failed to ask after them.

Our younger daughter, Virginia, remembers with pleasure an occasion some years ago, when she was working in London, being telephoned by Bruce, out of the blue, inviting her out for breakfast! A truly memorable breakfast chosen with the greatest care from a selection of delis of good name. Bruce himself selected the ingredients with enormous gastronomic skill, much time being spent on choosing exactly the right kind of smoked salmon and other appropriate ingredients to go with it. It was indeed a breakfast experience to *remember*!

I know that Bruce gained a reputation for taking full and sometimes over-full advantage of his friends' hospitality, but in truth he never abused ours and never once overstayed his welcome. Perhaps our piano did not come up to his high standards and so he was never tempted to linger? Certainly it was usually in great need of being tuned! But it was not just that.

Sadly it was not possible for us to see Bruce in the months and weeks before he died although we kept in touch and spoke on the telephone. He was certainly not without his faults but despite all Bruce was a very dear friend who brought colour to our lives and we will miss him greatly.

Bruce – Requiescat in Pace.

# From Arcadia to the Hindu Kush

**Kate Quartano Brown** *met Bruce at Oxford in 1971, and later trained as a singer in Austria. Finding that soubrette sopranos were two-a-penny and all of them better at networking, she turned to directing. She carved a small but respectable niche in baroque opera (notably the works of Pope Clement IX) and was the first woman to direct Handel at the festivals of Halle and Goettingen. She also directed new work, including the premiere of Jonathan Dove's* Tobias and the Angel. *Then she married and now cultivates websites and gardens.*

A fine spring evening in Oxford. Oriel College has bumped its way to being Head of the River and the front quadrangle is lit by flames as the bellowing hearties burn their boat, while in a room in a more secluded quad a lamb gambols on artificial grass, pausing now and then to share a bunch of grapes with Pan and an assembly of minor deities. All the movable furniture (except for the piano) has been shoved out of the room, and Daphnis has painted entrancing sketches of Arcadia on lengths of canvas that hide the more prosaic bookshelves. I am Melpomene in a black veil. We picnic on the plastic grass, cadged from a stall-holder in the Covered Market, and recite Dionysos' sadly not immortal couplets on the Triumph of Contemplation (James Ramsay aka Dionysos has more on the Lamb elsewhere). It was a moment even Evelyn Waugh might have thought too extravagant, but an early example of Bruce's capacity to create his own defiant aesthetic out of nothing on a budget of irresistible charm and total refusal to allow dissent. He was well cast as Pan.

After Oxford there was the ill-fated attempt to become respectable. I went to see him in the tax office at Finsbury Park, up a concrete stair to a bleak grey room filled with filing cabinets, and Bruce behind a large empty desk with a copy of 'Teach Yourself Accounting' opened in front of him. I am not at all sure whether he ever read much of it. There was always something more interesting to do. Many years later, when he was staying in Nick Robinson's flat in Shepherd Market in order to write a book, I gave him a laptop, no internet, just a nice efficient word-processor. Several months later he rang to ask how to turn it on. I am glad he never persevered with accounting, but I do wish he had written that book. He was such a magnificent letter-writer, it would have been splendid to have had something more permanent.

The letters and postcards came from anywhere from the Hebrides to the Himalayas. One came from Germany recounting hitchhiking encounters – one day he was picked up by a countess and invited to her Schloss, the next by some Baader-Meinhof groupies, plotting bombs as he pretended to sleep on a fur pelt in the corner. Another letter described events in Tehran during the revolution: 'On my way back from a rehearsal of the Messiah, I narrowly avoided a rioting mob at the end of the street...'

Bruce is woven in and out of almost fifty years of friendship, and nearly always with music. He played when I sang for my great-aunt's funeral, and when I sang for Corinne's. We massacred Schubert and drank dazzling wine at George Lemos's house, we sang canzonets in Oxford and in Islamabad, and also in Olga's café high in the Dolomites – she was very polite about the canzonets, and then asked for something that everyone knew so I began '*Mi chiamano Mimi*' and the entire café, all fervent patrons of the arena in Verona, joined in. We performed the *Lamento della Ninfa* for someone's house concert, we had a lovely time with the *Shepherd on the Rock* at another (the clarinet played by Andrew Lyle, who himself succumbed to cancer two years ago), we made music for ourselves in friends' houses, we went to concerts and regrettably indulged in unrelenting and unashamedly elitist criticism.

In 1993 a show I had been engaged to do in May was cancelled at short notice, and the next day a tax refund cheque arrived in the post. The obvious thing to do with this unexpected opportunity was to accept Bruce's invitation to go out to Pakistan for a few weeks. Luckily I kept a diary – it's not that I don't remember most of it, it was epic, but that I sometimes need to convince myself that it all really happened.

There was a long walk in the Murree Hills, with a Chitrali Prince and the Wolf (an exiled Afghan, devoted to Bruce), where we dodged bolts of lightning and nervous lodgekeepers with guns, and the unwelcome attentions of foresters too long away from their wives. The Prince was a notable asset at that point. There was an excursion to Peshawar to meet old friends, retired generals more British than the British, to buy things in the bazaars and visit a Mughal tomb at dawn. In Islamabad there were afternoons of Mosel wine and Telemann at embassies, Purcell in churches, tea and gossip with expatriate Britons, Germans, French, Swedes, Americans. There were heated political discussions and peaceful visits to Sufi saints. And there were all the exiled Afghans, bringing poetry and music and dance into the night and frequently at breakfast.

This extraordinary visit ended with a trip to Nanga Parbat with a group of Bruce's Islamabad friends, camping on summer pastures beside the Raikot stream (now a resort with chalets, then a few tents and a campfire). We went walking, slowly at that altitude, down towards Tato, where the summer huts have porches like little wooden Greek temples. One of our company claimed descent from Alexander the Great, and was very keen on pointing such things out. Another walk took us up towards Bayal Camp, on the way to Base Camp. Behind us, the Hindu Kush stretched along the northern sky, in front of us the threatening bulk of Nanga Parbat, and from time to time vertical clouds, massive avalanches, formed on its white slopes. We watched them, resting on huge erratic boulders in the sun as Bruce read Rumi, Khayyam and Hafiz aloud, translating as he went, discussing the power of poetry to transcend language barriers through its music.

We had flown up to Gilgit but bad weather (and a bully of an airport policeman called Hyacinth who would not be bribed with poetry) forced us to take the road back down, an overnight journey by bus: shadowy settlements lit by gas lamps, the headlights illuminating sudden blazes of green from a waterfall, night bazaars selling hot tea and smuggled Chinese goods, Venus glowing over terraced paddyfields, the deafening crowds of Rawalpindi, and home to find more musicians in the middle of a wild jam session.

Eating out with Bruce was always memorable, whether lunch at the Gavroche (he identified spices in the sauce on the leeks and asked the waiter to find out whether he was right. The answer came back that the chef had used Veeraswamy's curry powder and was not particularly bothered) or tea at the Wolseley (he asked for anchovy toast. The charming Serbian waiter was completely foxed by this and we ended up with a silver dish of anchovies and another of butter, together with a toast rack. It was fine).

Our last lunch, in December of last year, was altogether less amusing, but shot through with the light of an old, intermittent, but deeply loyal and true friendship. One of the last conversations we had was about the expression and cultivation of love. Bruce made an art of it. His gifts were many and unexpected: a cup rescued from a skip, a vivid kilim, several hats and a sumptuous scarf, an astonishingly beautiful box of wood and metal marquetry (a wedding present – he arrived late, the plane from Tehran had been delayed, he stayed on, nearly the last to go), a little bowl of lapis lazuli. They anchor him in my life, but my enduring memories of him are nearly all of him on his way somewhere else, whether off to Yorkshire or the Yemen, or simply journeying in his mind, as in the photograph of him sitting on top of the Mughal tomb outside Peshawar at dawn, with the mountains of the Khyber Pass in the blue distance behind him.

# Two Letters to Fynn Vergos

*Both letters were printed in JULIET: A LIFE IN MEMORIES, edited by Georgiana Campbell and published by Sickle Moon Books, part of Eland, in 2017.*

Dear Fynn,

It was a pleasure to see you and your sister this evening. As we discussed, I will here note down my memories of your father Dominique Vergos and the circumstances of his death in Peshawar, Pakistan.

Afghanaid was very short of money and in order to help with domestic expenses, rooms were let out to visiting journalists. Robert Cranborne of the Afghanaid committee in London was sending out the newly invented transmitting equipment for testing to get news rapidly from the field to broadcasters. Among other journalist guests – Peter Jouvenal, Julian Gearing – we also hosted your future stepfather Rory Peck. There was no office vehicle then, so I hired two brothers, Saber and Naser of the Tsuluzai clan of Kama, Ningrahar, Afghanistan to bring their rickshaws every morning to transport anyone who needed their services.

When Juliet (then Crawley) came out to help me after one of my bouts of amoebic dysentery and jaundice, Naser and Saber were promoted to drive the office vehicles which by that time had been purchased. They quickly became devoted to your mother, whose generosity and dignity won their respect. These Pushtuns were members of the Hizb-e Islami party of Gulbuddin Hekmatyar, and had strong rivalry with the Panjshiri Tajiks who also helped run the office, who belonged to the Jami'at Islami party of Burhaneddin Rabbani. Juliet was ambitious and quickly wanted to run the office in her own way and preserve her own independence, though she was not so good at balancing ethnic and political rivalries within the office. Our committee in London was divided between liberal aid worker types (Elisabeth Winter) and more hawkish elements (Romey Fullerton), so we often received marching orders that were quite contradictory.

During the course of my second trip into Afghanistan, this time with the *mujahideen* of the Mahaz Melli party of Pir Gailani, to the base of Amin Wardak in Wardak, in 1986, I met your father who was travelling west towards Qandahar to see Mullah Madat, a tall, handsome and charismatic teacher who was the original founder of the Taliban. Dominique was travelling independently and taught me how to assess a *mujahideen* camp – cleanliness, order, efficiency etc. He told me of the longer periods he had spent observing such places as the Russian airbase at Shindand in the west of the country. He also told me that if he worked for three months, he expected to be able to play for the remaining nine months! I invited him to come and stay at Afghanaid when we both returned to Peshawar. I believe this was how he met your mother. Dominique had been a fashion photographer and was a dashing figure whose raffishness – and especially whose demanding taste in what an elegant woman should be – soon had a profound effect on Juliet.

After their marriage and honeymoon in the Maldives, they rented a house with a garden in University Town, not far from the American Club. Soon it filled up with a large cage of green parakeets on the back terrace, a small camel, and a *kuchi* dog with a cropped tail, which you played with as a child. Your father started working at the Swedish Committee for Afghanistan, under the liberal ex-journalist Anders Faenge, where he was commissioned to build up a database on military resistance commanders in Afghanistan, and was increasingly critical of the behaviour of Gulbuddin Hekmatyar's Hezb-e Islami. At the same time he was increasingly frustrated and often became drunk at the American Club, which led to fights with your mother, with bruises for her and scratches for him, and frequent bursts of Kalashnikov gunfire in the yard to let off steam at night. The local gossip, which had connected Dominique originally with the CIA, now concentrated on how long this situation could go on, and my Pushtun friends, the brothers Naser and Saber, expressed serious concern for your mother's safety.

I had meanwhile left Afghanaid after less than two years, had travelled independently across Afghanistan on horseback in the summer of 1987, and returned to Peshawar to select and train a team of Afghan monitors for the American medical NGO 'Freedom Medicine'. I was living down the railway line in an enclosed courtyard house in an area not yet lived in by Europeans. Shortly afterwards, I had to go and stay with a Pakistani general, Jehanzeb Afridi, when my life and that of my servants was threatened by Hezb-e Islami after I had publicly criticised their robbery of one of our medical supply caravans destined for Shi'i Hazaras.

On the evening of your father's death, I had had some Shinwari musicians from the east of Afghanistan perform in my guest room, and we had just finished and gone to bed when at about 2 a.m. there was banging at the gates, and Naser was let in, shouting that 'That fool Dominique has gone and killed himself' and insisting that I come immediately. We drove to University Town and I found your mother sobbing uncontrollably over the corpse of her husband, which had been lifted onto the charpoy in the *chowkidar*'s room at the back of the garage. She managed to tell me that the body had been slumped across the door and that she had had to push with all her strength to force her way in after she heard shots fired and Dominique did not come back after one of their rows: she had been reading her Old Testament in bed to calm down. She was in such a state – great gut-wrenching groans and sobs; I was worried and went to fetch the Catholic priest to calm her. Later she told me that that night she had had a miscarriage as a result.

By the time we came back, Dr Philippe Truze, who worked with a medical NGO, had also arrived. He very calmly and efficiently pointed out the clean bullet-hole at the base of your father's skull and the smashed bone of the forehead where the bullet had emerged, and said that it was impossible that Dominique had killed himself. Rigor mortis had begun to set in, if I remember rightly – the body was difficult to move. The Pakistan police then arrived, loudly proclaiming that it was a clear case of suicide. We then looked more carefully at the wall of the *chowkidar*'s room and found brain and bone matter splattered over and above the door – your father was tall and had almost certainly been held against the door, face to the door, after some struggle, and shot by whoever had overpowered him. I found a lot of fresh cracked paint fragments on the flowers growing outside below the one small window of the *chowkidar*'s room, which was almost certainly the only way the murderers could have got out. And murderers – plural – because one man could almost certainly not have overpowered your father, even drunk – and certainly not Naser's weedy young nephew who had recently started as the night *chowkidar*, and who was later conveniently blamed for the murder.

We carried on searching and found fresh bullet holes in the brickwork at the far end of the garage yard, in a straight line from the *chowkidar*'s room, through the garage itself where an older brown jeep was parked – its lower mudguards had also been recently perforated and another car parked in the drive: it seems that a shot or two was fired from the *chowkidar*'s room to entice your father into the room where he was killed – he was not a man to run from gunshots, especially when angry.

The American Consulate insisted on hosting the memorial service for Dominique in their garden, though he had never officially or publicly worked for them; Juliet asked me to choose texts and music for the occasion. It may, possibly, have been out of respect and affection for your mother that the Americans made this gesture, who was herself, perhaps, by that time already working for them.

Some time later, Commander Abdul Haq brokered a reconciliation between your mother and the family of the young *chowkidar* accused of the murder – it was necessary to reach some face-saving conclusion if she wanted to continue living and working in Peshawar. A *jirga* was held and a sheep sacrificed. I'm not sure if blood money was paid (probably not – your mother grandly forgave the young man, who was very probably innocent of the actual murder, though may well have been intimidated into covering for the murderers, or letting them into his room) but she settled down to life as a young widow in the same house.

The rumour of suicide was still circulating, as was another, more vicious rumour that Juliet had killed her husband herself – both absurd and patently untrue. Dr Truze's examination of the corpse also put paid to the rumour that the young *chowkidar*, panicked by Dominique's aggressive behaviour when drunk, had fired in self-defence – that would have led to bullet wounds in the front, not the back of the head.

My interpretation takes into account the context of other incidents and murders that happened at this time of critics of Hezb-e Islami – for instance, that of Professor Sayyed Bahauddin Majruh, who wrote newsletters critical of Hezb-e Islami and was murdered at the door of his house-cum-office; or of Andy Skrypsowiak, who was murdered in Nuristan en route to visit Ahmad Shah Massoud, Gulbuddin Hekmatyar's one-time colleague and now inveterate rival (the murderers were rewarded by Hezb-e Islami with fast cars that they drove with impunity around Peshawar). My close friend Wahid of Tagao, who ran the best martial arts club in Peshawar and was a quite remarkable karate and tai-chi practitioner, was repeatedly subjected to pressure to carry out assassinations for Hezb-e Islami. He assured me that no murder was carried out unless previously vetted and passed by the Pakistani ISI – he claimed that he managed diplomatically to resist such pressure – but many may well have taken the reward and trusted the unofficial cloak of protection and secrecy.

My interpretation is that Dominique's new work for the Swedish Committee (left-liberal in its Western staff, but among its Afghan staff penetrated by Hezb-e Islami spies as well as Maoists, Pushtun nationalists etc) certainly irritated and alarmed the Hezb-e Islami, who were the favoured party of the Pakistani ISI and of the American CIA. The funding and overall direction may have come from that source at the top, but delegation down to grassroots, plus ruthless manipulation by Gulbuddin with his well-honed terrorist instincts and training, meant that Hezb-e Islami was virtually unchallenged on the ground. The Americans did not want to see this reality. When Alastair Crooke sent a confidential report to the London FCO criticising the CIA's over-reliance on Hezb-e Islami, he was summoned to explain himself not to London but to Washington: not long after he left the service. I remember interpreting for Hugh Leach's confidential FCO research on Islamist movements worldwide during his Pakistan tour, and the unpleasantness of sitting so close to Gulbuddin, a really chilling monster. The decision to murder your father probably had the tacit approval, or assurance of indifference, of the Americans, who apparently had stopped employing Dominique, and probably disapproved of his extensive knowledge of Afghan commanders and Hezb-e Islami's appalling record of betrayal and murder being put on the database of a neutral and potentially critical organisation such as the Swedish Committee for Afghanistan. This may have been an added cause of his increasing frustration and turning to drink and domestic violence. The Pakistani ISI almost certainly allowed the murder, hence the prearranged propaganda that it was suicide: Naser, the police and the subsequent rumours all point in that direction. It must have been more or less facilitated by Naser and his nephew, probably out of their genuine worry about your mother's safety, and out of obedience to the party's orders. At the very least, they conveniently got out of the way while the murder was perpetrated, and Naser came to fetch me with the prearranged story of suicide. Not very long after, he had a serious nervous breakdown and his nerves never recovered even after he emigrated to Sweden. The fact that the young *chowkidar* did not run away – he could easily have gone back to his home area of Kama just over the border near Jalalabad – indicates that he had been given assurances of protection if he took the blame.

My dear Fynn, I hope this can help clarify what remains a murky story, and allow you to come to some sort of closure with the loss of your father when you were so young. I have not referred to diaries of the time, only to what I remember: some images are very vivid, others blurred; I have tried to indicate which, and also to separate presentation of facts from rumours heard and interpretations constructed.

With love and best wishes for 2011,
Bruce Wannell

**Second letter**
(*written in York after your phone call from military duty in Northern Ireland*)

Dear Fynn,

Once again you have asked me to write about your family, this time about your mother, whose memory remains vivid, though the memories float like disconnected images as the strict framework of time past grows vaguer.

I first met your mother in 1986 when reporting back from Peshawar to the offices of Afghanaid on an upper floor of a building in Cecil Court, London. She was sitting at a desk near the door, the first person encountered on entering the office; under the desk lurked her diminutive terrier, Thatcher. Juliet was relaxed and humorous, dressed in camel-brown colours – I remember her laughter which she often used to disarm new acquaintances. She had recently come down from Edinburgh University, and had broken off a relationship with a fellow-student from Devon. She was working for the steely Romey Fullerton, who had recently introduced me to Peshawar.

The Afghanaid field office in Peshawar occupied a rented villa in a garden in Gulmohar Road along the railway line. The line ran only to the Khyber Pass. Train traffic was infrequent. When your mother came out to assist me during one of my illnesses, the railway line formed the perfect exit for her large whitish-grey horse to reach the emptier sandy areas where she could gallop at will. That horse, as difficult and temperamental as the men your mother liked, was the first significant purchase she made on arriving in Pakistan. The Panjshiri Tajik family who brokered the deal were soon lavishing hospitality on her, in a traditional Afghan bid to exercise influence: I had employed the brothers Hasham and Quddus as office orderlies, but soon they were answering only to Juliet, and were lording it over the Pushtun brothers Naser and Saber from Kama near Jalalabad. In the early days when Afghanaid had little money, I had employed these brothers to provide us with motor-rickshaws, our only transport. Later, when American money started rolling in, they graduated onto jeeps and Pajeros – though they occasionally were nostalgic for their rickshaws and once took me to an outlying Sufi shrine for a noisy all-night ceremony, attended by hordes of other rickshaw drivers.

Your mother was a good horsewoman, and her skill impressed the *mujahideen* commanders, especially those from the north of Afghanistan who would sponsor *buzkashi* games, when we were allowed to push our horses into the scrum to watch the sand-filled calf-carcass pulled by the mounted players at close quarters. Once, we met the large burly Uzbek commander Pahlawan Hafiz who challenged your mother to ride an angry horse which reared and kicked: she refused to be thrown, and Pahlawan became her devoted admirer, even allowing her to scold him for the appallingly dingy conditions in which he kept his wives, noticeably worse than his horses' stables and diet! I meanwhile had not covered myself in glory, allowing the grey to bolt with me one early morning when Juliet was unable to exercise him, and Quddus watched laughing helplessly as I whizzed by, scattering gravel and almost knocking over refugee market stalls on the outskirts of University Town.

The number of horses grew: your mother soon had five, and Peshawar's summer climate, often approaching fifty degrees Celsius and with high humidity, was not kind to them. So, one year, your mother asked me and Frederic Roussel to accompany her and her Arab groom and a stocky Panjshiri dwarf to cooler hill-country where the horses could be left for the hot season. I suggested Swiss friends who were running a forestry project in northern Swat. The horses and grooms were duly sent up and we followed a few days later. From there we rode through the largely trackless forests of Tal-Lamutai in Dir, with villagers bringing us bowls of yoghurt as we passed. Frederic shouted at the horses with such vigour and authority that my pony, distracted by some distant mare on heat, and who was totally ignoring my attempts to keep him in control, forthwith returned to obedience; your mother always looked self-possessed, sitting on the charpoy string-beds while I made conversation in Pushtu when we stayed at little forts, where the sons of our hosts gave us welcome leg-massages in the evening; and so on to the ever-hospitable anglophile Chitrali princes over the Lowari Pass, which we crossed on the day of Eid. When we reached the first of the *shahzadas*, a bottle of whisky was accepted and we were able to camp in the orchard by the river.

In Chitral town we went riding on narrow paths along the river with a handsome young French couple, at breakneck speed, then stopped to watch the polo: every goal was celebrated with a fanfare from the drums and oboe-like instruments with a piercing reedy noise. At the end, the leader of the winning team performed a slow, Pyrrhic dance as he left the polo-ground. Juliet had to get back to Peshawar by plane, Frederic was going off in another direction and I was due to take the five horses and two grooms on to the village of Pasti on the slopes of the highest mountain in Chitral, Tirich Mir. Frederic entrusted his saddlebags to Juliet to take back to Peshawar. The next we heard, she was being held in custody and questioned by airport security: Frederic had forgotten to tell her that the saddlebags contained his loaded pistol.

She was holding her own when my French doctor friend arrived, telling the security officer not to be so childish: luckily the doctor played polo with the officer, so Juliet was able to board the plane – rather late – and resume her office work in Peshawar.

Your mother had never fallen into the trap of wearing cheap Pakistani *shalwar kameez*, almost the uniform of the American missionary girls and Mennonites. She remained resolutely English in her dress and manner – but she was also sensitive to the culture of the Afghans, and earned their respect by generosity, tact and trust. This sometimes seemed like bravura. Saber needed to borrow money: the family was always falling into further feuds with disaffected or disreputable cousins. Juliet gave it to him out of her own funds, never asking for any guarantee of repayment in writing or for any witness to the transaction. 'Elle avait de la classe', as the French would say. Once your father Dominique's influence grew, she also had style – daring little black dresses worn to evening parties, with bold jewellery. From the moment she arrived in Peshawar, she made it obvious that she was not taking orders and was fully intent on following her own agenda. Once she had helped remove me from the organisation, she gave me a splendid farewell party on the lawns at Gulmohar Road, where musicians played and I danced with my anthropologist friend Benedicte and our Afghan friends praised the *kabutar-bazi*. In the end she didn't take over my job; a rather dull, but safe, character took over and bureaucracy took hold.

I stayed with an Afghan family in town, then moved into a low whitewashed courtyard hotel. Juliet and Dominique moved into a house in University Town where the deep terrace sheltered a large cage of green parakeets and a fluffy, cuddly, nomad puppy whose tail had been cropped. In the garden another gift from nomad *mujahideen* commanders, a small camel, was one of your playthings – but you have probably forgotten that. I benefited from leaving the aid agency with its school-uniform and tent-making programmes for war-wounded refugees, and went to train Afghan monitors to travel in-country to evaluate civilian aid given to communities free from Russian communist control. Juliet worked more and more with the Americans, Dominique eventually with the Swedish Committee for Afghanistan, as a result of which he was murdered: but that I have described in my other letter to you.

We next met in London, when I returned from three years in Africa. She invited me to Yorkshire, where since her second bereavement and the loss of her eye to cancer, she was enjoying the hospitality of her brother-in-law in a row of cottages at Healaugh. Russell was your Welsh male nanny. He used to drive you at high speed to go shopping. When your mother travelled to London by train it was always first class, with smart fur coats – your mother loved luxury, and was very impressed by grand people, whose political opinions she adopted eagerly, pro-hunting, anti-European etcetera.

Sometimes, in spite of her self-discipline, she seemed to lose her moral compass. One admirer and lover, used for his title and his letterhead cachet, helped garner support for the Rory Peck Awards for war journalists and cameramen – until he was chewed up and spat out. When this former admirer was packing up, he told me how he had accompanied your mother to befriend the Ogoni people, struggling to preserve their tribal lands in southern Nigeria from the encroaching pollution of oil exploitation by Shell, resulting in the murder of Ken Sarawiwa. Juliet had posed as their friend, while all the time being paid by Shell. Similarly, she befriended the 'Swampy' eco-activists living up trees to delay destruction of natural habitat for motorway-building, while actually working for the motorway lobby; so also her attempt to penetrate the operations of Cable and Wireless in the Caribbean, etc, etc. Her love of luxury, mixing with grand people and of devious manipulation came at a cost – people were hurt and they spilled truths with some bitterness.

She said more than once to me that if it were not for her children she would have given up the struggle to live. Your mother enriched our lives. She was a complex, often difficult character, but stylish, admirable, fun, courageous, generous and defiant. Her memory will live into the future, with her friends, and in you her children.

With love to you and Lettice,
Bruce Wannell

# A MODERN BATTUTA

# Taliban marching powder
## *Alamut, Iran, 2005*

**Kevin Rushby** *writes for the* Guardian *and is the author of a number of travel books.*

One sunny day in the spring of 1994 I was walking home through the Old City of San'a in Yemen. I lived at that time in a rambling old house in the labyrinth of alleyways that forms the old Jewish quarter. For anyone unfamiliar with the area the house was almost impossible to find, but that morning as I came into the long narrow lane where I lived, I spotted an unusual figure knocking at my door, a character dressed in a Chitrali cap and lemon-yellow shalwar kameez. We had heard reports of Yemenis who had gone to fight with the Afghan *mujahideen* and now returned preaching a new kind of hardline religion. I approached with caution.

He was talking to one of my neighbours, Muhammad the shopkeeper, and turned to greet me. 'You must be Kevin?' It was a voice that might have been heard on the BBC News, in about 1931, probably as the Royal Correspondent. 'I'm Bruce Wannell. Tim Mackintosh Smith gave me directions to your house and I thought I'd drop by.'

It was, I would come to understand, a classic Bruce moment. Having just arrived in Yemen from Pakistan, he had met Tim the previous day and was already mining his contacts, making connections, putting people together. Within a week he seemed to know everybody that was important to him: every musician of any ability, all the poets, the makers of obscure artisanal foodstuffs, the craftsmen, the chefs, the scholars and, of course, anyone with a house large enough to accommodate them all at a soirée. Over the next few weeks Bruce would be everywhere, often greeting you at someone else's door, the magician who had conjured a gathering. He would hand you a tray of tidbits: 'Try these "toot", dried sugared mulberries from Khorasan – they are delicious – would you mind handing them around?'

Within a month Bruce was a cultural fixture, the prime mover, an indispensable host, but sadly his tenure was cut short by war. As Yemen descended into chaos the expatriate community was scattered. With all the insouciance of a man boarding a Clapham omnibus, Bruce told me he intended to make for Somaliland by dhow. I fully expected never to see him again.

A year later, I had landed up in an obscure northern English backwater called York. The telephone rang. It was Bruce. 'Kevin, my dear, would you like to come over? I've got some Shirazi rose water tea and nettle soup. There's someone I'd love you to meet.' By sheer coincidence Bruce was living near York too with Juliet Peck, a friend from his time in Afghanistan and Peshawar. I went to meet him and within a few minutes was handing out sugared dried mulberries at a musical soirée.

Bruce moved into a housing association flat in York and carried on being Bruce, turning the wreck of a yard into a fine garden. One of the marvels of the man was how he managed to treat grey old England as if it had all the charm and interest of a fabled Persian citadel. His ability to befriend and connect people was irresistible; his kindness and compassion endless. During some dark days of the house he lived in, Bruce was robbed repeatedly by heroin addicts. When I went to visit one morning, he was putting food out in the kitchen for them: 'They do need some sustenance,' he said benevolently, 'so I put something out for them to pick at – just like for the birds.' When the junky thieves were sent to prison, Bruce visited, taking them beautiful Italian biscotti and rare herbal teas.

His house became a sanctuary of civilisation. For his fiftieth birthday Bruce somehow persuaded the ex-court musicians of the last king of Afghanistan to play. They came and sat on the floor in his kitchen and transported the rapt audience to the mountains of the Hindu Kush. Bruce loved such occasions, flitting from person to person, and from language to language. He was a gifted linguist. I asked him once how many languages he spoke and he looked at me in surprise. 'I've never actually counted them.'

I persisted. 'I know you speak Pashto, Dari and Arabic plus some Hindi, but what about European languages?'

Bruce was dismissive. 'Oh everyone has those, don't they?'

In fact he had learned French from his mother who was Belgian and gone on to study French and German at Oriel College, Oxford.

In 2005 it was those linguistic skills that I borrowed when I had an assignment to visit Iran. I travelled with Bruce as my translator. It was, I have to say, like travelling with Voltaire, or perhaps Dr Johnson in the Hebrides. In those days Bruce did seem like a character from the eighteenth century. In Tehran I was treated to a series of musical soirées and visits to old friends until I couldn't remember precisely if it was Bruce who was helping me on an assignment or the other way around. In the end I had to insist that there were no more soirées, but Bruce had already arranged a final treat: an all-night chanting session with some Sufi holy men at a famous shrine. As the hours rolled by and my knees became rigid, then died, Bruce and the others entered deep trances and ecstatic states. Unfortunately the ecstasy was interrupted when the chief savant's mobile phone went off. His ringtone was the theme to *Mission Impossible* and I got a severe bout of the giggles.

On the way home I had to explain to Bruce why this was funny. He had never heard of *Mission Impossible*. Neither did he comprehend how a theme tune could be co-opted into being a ringtone. In fact Bruce had often not heard of things relating to popular culture. As we travelled north towards the Caspian Sea, I remember a long bus journey when – for some long-forgotten reason – I had to explain *The Wombles*.

Our mission was to walk from the shores of the Caspian Sea over the Alburz mountains and on to the fort of Alamut, home to the Assassin cult. Bruce was dressed like an English cricketer from the age of W. G. Grace carrying a knapsack laden with artful culinary treats, plus a selection of scarves, each handmade by someone known to him. One night we stayed in a large hut with shepherds and – behind a rickety paling fence – their livestock. We ate bread baked under the fire and freshly made cheese. Bruce, of course, was in his element, discussing Persian poets and reciting verses from heart, much to the amazement of our hosts – and the cattle who spent the night enthusiastically urinating over the fence.

Next day we were chased up the mountain by snowstorms. At 4,000 metres Bruce fainted and when he came round, smiled beatifically at the shepherd guide and charmed him into carrying all his kit. When we reached the top, however, our guide dumped everything on the ground and pointing ahead shouted, 'You go that way.' Then he bolted back the way we had come. I looked ahead towards endless ranges of desert mountains without a single sign of human presence and said to Bruce: 'We are going to die.'

Bruce disagreed, pulling out a bag of sweet dried mulberries mixed with walnuts. 'Let's have some Taliban marching powder. I'm sure we'll find someone to help.'

He was right of course. An hour later we stumbled across a hut and in it a young man whom Bruce persuaded to carry his bag and guide us to his village, a mere six hours' walk away in total darkness. Bruce was certainly physically tough and for all his delight in the luxuries of life, he lived rather austerely most of the time. Sleeping on a wooden floor in a snowbound mountain village didn't seem to trouble him at all which was good because we were stuck there for three days. Bruce spent the time chatting to our handsome young saviour and persuading the mother to cook all his favourite Persian recipes – the way he liked them.

When we finally made it to Alamut, we were pretty ragged. We climbed up the fortress and bumped into an Iranian American visitor who was talking on a mobile phone. After our *Mission Impossible* experience Bruce was fascinated and had to have the gadget fully explained. It took almost as long as *The Wombles*, and then the man offered to let him try it. Bruce immediately rang a friend in Isfahan and fixed up another musical soirée. I think that might have been the first moment when Bruce realised the astonishing possibilities of new technology and how he might make use of it. A decade or so later he would take to WhatsApp with gusto.

Our journey continued west. We hired a car and driver to take us to Kurdistan, but as we set off I realised that the man barely knew how to operate the controls. We juddered and skidded and stalled all the way into the mountains, then started winding up very dangerous roads with huge precipices. As darkness fell, I had to point out the headlight switch. Then, after one particularly close shave that brought out an involuntary scream from me, I said to Bruce, 'I don't think Muhammad actually knows how to drive a car.'

This seemed to surprise Bruce who was sitting in the front passenger seat, totally unperturbed by every narrow miss and death-defying corner. Trying to reassure me, he questioned Muhammad on his driving experience then turned to me and said, 'He says he has never actually taken a test, but it's fine because his brother showed him how to drive yesterday.'

Soon after this fulsome reassurance, Muhammad stalled the engine on a rising hairpin bend and we began to roll backwards, apparently out of control, towards an unwalled precipice. I reached forward, pulled the handbrake on, and said, 'We are walking.'

Muhammad was inconsolable, but we walked away and went to the next village where we eventually found transport to take us to the ancient site of Takht-i-Suleiman. We arrived at dawn at what is an incredible natural and historical feature. Bruce loved that place and was the best kind of companion to be with. All his breadth of learning and zest for knowledge came alive. He was a polymath and autodidact, able to read inscriptions on ancient monuments and explain what lay behind them.

For Bruce that journey, like others, somehow never translated into storytelling. I remember many evenings sat around with the publisher,

Nick Robinson, who desperately wanted to do justice to our mutual friend in print. There was a vast manuscript of Bruce's travels, but neither of us could wrestle it into shape and in the end Nick had to admit, 'Nothing will ever do justice to Bruce.'

Just a few weeks ago, I met Bruce at his flat in York and we both knew we might not see each other again. As we said goodbye, he leaned on his gate in Holgate Road and said, 'Do you remember that time in Takht-i-Suleiman? Wasn't it wonderful?' We stood there, lost in memories for a few moments, then he smiled and said, 'Was Muhammad truly a bad driver? Did we do the right thing? I always felt bad for him.'

It was classic Bruce for a final time: wanting to see the best in another person, even after fifteen years.

In his later years I think Bruce just got better and better. His sense of humour, never much apparent in earlier times, came good. His learning, once a little ivory-towerish and sometimes overbearing, became more richly woven and textured by life experience. As I mentioned he mastered mobile phones and computers, taking to social media with aplomb. However his greatest gift, I believe, was for friendship – a gift that effortlessly bridged culture, class, financial status, language and background.

Bruce never stopped looking like, and sounding like, an Edwardian English gentleman setting out on a bicycle tour of Mesopotamia. He comfortably wore cravats, bicycle clips, and plus fours. I long to see him again at my front door, dressed in all those things, holding out a little package and saying, 'Kevin, my dear, here's a little sumac from Aziz – do you know him? He has a stall at the entrance to the souk in Aleppo.'

He was a musician, scholar, linguist, gardener, historian, but above all he was a generous friend whose memory we will treasure and none of us will ever forget.

# Bruce: back into the blue

**Tim Mackintosh-Smith** *is an Arabist, historian, traveller and occasional organist. At the time of writing he is in Kuala Lumpur, on sabbatical from the war in his adoptive land, Yemen.*

Writing about Bruce is like trying to catch and pin an exceedingly rare migrant butterfly – but a butterfly with a huge brain, and an even bigger heart.

The brain revealed itself from the start. 'Shouldn't there be a *maddah* on that *alif*, rather than a *hamzah*?' he said on our first meeting, in 1994, during a war in Yemen. Bruce had turned up out of the blue at my house in Sana'a, made for my library, and pulled a book of Arabic verse off a shelf.

'Oh . . . I gathered your subject was Persian,' I said, a little nonplussed. Bruce had explained that he was on his way from the Persian-speaking lands to England, via Arabia and East Africa. I looked at the text of the poem: he was right, of course.

'I have a little kitchen-Arabic,' he said, with a sideways smile.

For the next quarter-century, I went in awe of Bruce's intellectual *batterie de cuisine*, his inexhaustible larder of knowledge. When a book of mine on Arab history came out in the last year of Bruce's life, his copious notes and queries on it included, for example, the remark that 'When I was writing for my Kabul students a guide to the history of Islamic calligraphy, the Persian accounts of Nasta'liq I came across talked of a dream of rock-partridges in the mountains, not ducks on a pond.'

Avian anatomy, the story goes, had influenced Nasta'liq letter shapes. Bruce being Bruce – and therefore that almost extinct creature, an authority – his partridges probably have the edge over my ducks.

Even his questions managed somehow to display esoteric knowledge, as well as to seek it. His very last email to me asked: 'By the way, have you any idea where I could get hold of Sa'diya Gaon's Arabic translation of the psalms? I've heard they are masterly, if medieval.'

As well as joy in Arabic, we shared a love of keyboard music, and the message ended: 'This evening I was playing with a neighbour the wonderful transcription by F-X Gleichauf for piano duet of Bach's C minor Passacaglia & Fugue for organ: you probably play the original? Oceanic. Keep well.'

Oceanic; masterly; perhaps, at times, medieval: they are words that could describe Bruce's brain.

But the brain would have been no more than sounding brass without the heart. Bruce's heart revealed itself in snatches of kindness, in that constant and famous concern for friends, and in occasional gestures of the most Oriental generosity. Visiting an antique shop in Lincolnshire with him, I happened to admire a large and striking eighteenth-century etching of two girls with a youthful hunter. 'They must be Venetian,' Bruce said. 'Only Venetians have those pointed noses.' We read the inscription beneath the etching. He was right: the etching was after Piazzetta, a compatriot and contemporary of Canaletto.

I left the shop; Bruce lingered. When he finally caught up, he was carrying a big rectangle wrapped in brown paper. 'The Piazzetta,' he said. 'A present for you.'

I made some feeble, fish-gaping protestations; Bruce was, as often, down on his uppers. It made no difference.

Nothing ever did. Not even protestations, on another Lincolnshire visit, about the temperature of the North Sea. Bruce not only had us foraging in the salt marsh, but skinny-dipping in the freezing German Ocean itself; the latter was probably a first in the annals of our village. The afternoon ended with crabs and samphire on buttered toast.

Bruce, the rare – no, the unique – and gorgeous migrant, is perhaps uncatchable, unpinnable; but I sometimes wonder if he was trapped in this age of ours. His truer setting might have been the frame of some pre-modern miniature of gardens and princes and blue-domed skies; or, at the very latest, in a drawing room between the two world wars, with Harold Acton and Robert Byron and glass domes and quails' eggs. But maybe, just as he made himself at home everywhere, he would have been at home everywhen.

Now he has slipped the net of time.

I visited his room after he died. It was a chrysalis-case lined with books and bits and bobs, all precious and protective in his life, abandoned now for the next phase – into the blue beyond. *Antum al-sābiqūn wa-naḥnu al-lāḥiqūn*: you went before us, and we will follow on.

But we'll never catch you.

# Cairo transformed
*Cairo Iftar, February 1996 and Addis Ababa*

**Julian Reilly and Bojana Mojsov** *When they met Bruce in Cairo in 1996, Julian was studying Arabic ahead of his first diplomatic posting with the Foreign Office, and Bojana was Egyptologist in Residence at the American Research Center in Egypt. Sudan, Iran, Saudi Arabia and the Horn of Africa followed in various ways, and Bruce was always a part of the best bits of each.*

In conversation with two berobed monks, Bruce picked his way down the forest path and out into the hot sun by the sacred crater-lake of Zugwala, parasol and Ethiopian shawl setting off his linen shorts – and giving him the air of an Edwardian gentleman fakir. The climb (once the jeep gave out) to the volcano rim had taken in short lectures on horticulture at altitude and a break to pick juniper berries destined for a venison stew in York: growing at 10,000 feet apparently improves the intensity.

Having arranged for Bruce to join us at a conference in Addis Ababa, he had effortlessly turned the tables, instead giving us a whirlwind introduction to his Ethiopia: monastery pilgrimages and ox ploughing in Oromia, tea with the Pankhursts and coffee at the market. The colobus monkeys playing about us in the Zugwala crater were though equally an unexpected delight to Bruce.

Who had walked into our lives in the mid-nineties, sitting down crosslegged to break the Ramadan fast one sunset in the Cairo flat of an American Sufi academic and his young Sudanese wife? I was studying Arabic before my first posting to Sudan, and he transformed my Cairo. I had already fallen in love with the Islamic architecture, the souks, cafés and chaos, the endless layers to be peeled away. But Bruce always found the thread that led to the heart.

We had already spent the afternoon at a moulid in the Southern Cemetery, dervishes skewering their cheeks as they whirled down dusty alleys, children on old pirate boat swings, Bruce floating along in his galabia ('It's the only thing that doesn't itch after the required forty day ablutions'). But the best Quranic reciter was not on until midnight, as he had just learnt from an old Peshawar musicologist friend he had bumped into at the entrance to the saint's tomb. So after dinner downtown at a little French restaurant he was keen to try ('so-so'), we headed back down past the Citadel and into the cemetery, and the brightly lit mosque and overwhelming sound of tinny, massively amplified recitation, Sufi devotees mingling at the entrance with families in their saint's day best, the fair outside still at full throttle into the night.

Another afternoon it was tea on the lawn among the roses at a villa in Ma'adi, where he was already – although he had arrived in Cairo only a couple of months previously – an old friend of the family, and of the now much played grand piano in the drawing room. Friends, and oases of calmer pleasures, found and always shared.

When eventually I returned from Sudan some four years later, it was at the British Institute of Persian Studies summer lecture, in the stifling heat of Carlton Terrace, that I heard a familiar voice, turned, and, of course, found Bruce. Thereafter, twenty years of scurrilous gossip, scholarship, music and escapades; ringings of the doorbell when he spotted we were back in London after a year or two, notebooks full of names before we set forth, and even last summer an exploration of his sooty eaves in York for a report on political Islam that seems, inexplicably, to have slipped away.

Bruce and I had planned to meet for tea in Asmara this January. But his illness progressed too fast. News of his death the previous night reached us in Addis. That Sunday we went to the Trinity Cathedral, first visited with him four years earlier, to light a candle. That within half an hour, after much drama, a full mass was being sung by white-robed worshippers while his candle flickered in the Holy of Holies seemed entirely fitting.

# Bruce and Mahmoud
## Cairo, Egypt 1997

**Eric Stobbaerts** is a Belgian-Swiss born and brought up between Morocco and Portugal. He is a long-timer with MSF (Médecins Sans Frontières). His and **Adnan Ali**'s paths with Bruce have crossed on several occasions and in diverse geographies.

Often we associate Bruce Wannell with Pakistan and Afghanistan. But mention his name to me and flashes of Cairo surge. We had met in Peshawar much before at the Médecins Sans Frontières house and we kept meeting much later, at our place in London. Bruce has always been around ... always and he will not go that soon. Mashallah. I liked him.

Precisely seven years after musical evenings in the garden of University Town, Bruce reappears in Egypt. This is the summer of 1997. After decades spent in the East, Bruce has decided to return to Europe. This is a slow and gradual return, turning into an épopée. If my memory does not fail, the journey back took him about two years.

Was it procrastination? Was it fear? I don't think so, rather an enjoyable existence, wonderfully embedded in existentialism, alternative thinking, inspired from Descartes 'Cogito, ergo sum', 'les mises en situation' of Sartre and a shrewd oriental inspiration as a 'jouisseur de la vie'.

*Cairo-Flash* (*à la mode Ian Fleming*):
Anne Amzallag, my childhood friend from Casablanca, calls:
'I just met the most exciting character at a small mouled today in the City of the Dead. We went to Mokattam to hear Soufi Sheikh Yacine sing and we met this English gentleman in a gorgeous galabia wearing a pair of Church's. I was struck by the shoes. Yasser is convinced he is a spy.'
'Funny!'
'He comes from Peshawar and I inquired: he says he knows you.'

'It must be Bruce!'

'Yes, that is right. His name is Bruce.'

I smile and think of 007: 'Bruce, my name is Bruce Wannell.'

After only a few weeks in Cairo, Bruce was on everybody's lips. He had captured the spirit of the city, its people and their stories. Roland Huguenin, my friend at the ICRC invites us for dinner to finally meet Bruce.

Instants before the dinner, Bruce calls: 'Eric, I met someone in the Old City the other day. He seemed to be following me as I strolled. After a while, I turned back and faced him. We engaged in a sweet conversation and we have not left each other since then. Are you fine if Mahmoud joins us for dinner?'

'Of course, why not? *Ahlan wa sahlan.* The more the merrier.'

We spent a great evening the four of us. The diversity of pedigrees and of our whereabouts should have been a barrier. It was exactly the opposite and with a blend of colloquial Arabic, French and English, the conversation flew late into the night. As we were inquiring on Bruce's 'new trophy', to our dismay we understood that Mahmoud was a Mukhabarat and had very possibly been selected to follow Bruce. Only Bruce disagreed, or did he really? The information services under Mubarak would not miss a foreigner dressed up in a galabia and recently landed from Afghanistan. Undoubtedly one had fallen for the other but not exactly in the way the Mogamma had planned. Who had fooled who?

*Cairo-Flash* (adapted from D. H. Lawrence):

Bruce and Mahmoud could not find a decent and discreet place to stay over. As I headed to the Palestinian camp of Saloum on the border with Libya, I left the keys of my flat on Sharia El Montaza to Bruce. The views on the Nile are stunning from there and Bruce liked the place.

I thought: 'Bless them.'

After a few days, I am back at my flat. Bruce has kindly left the keys with large dates, a ration of *ichta* and a pot of wild honey.

I thought: 'So Bruce.'

A few minutes later, the bell rings at my door. It's Shireen, an Iranian journalist for Reuters. She lives opposite.

She says excitedly: 'Who is this friend of yours, who stayed here recently?'

'Bruce is a friend from my days in Peshawar.'

'Well I am totally fond of him.'

'What happened?'

'Well, I was just back from a long flight and came back home late.

As I went up and pushed the door of the elevator, the automatic light went on. I am staring at these two men in the most unsuitable positions. Silence, immobility, stupor. Brisk movements and within seconds, they are standing in front of me as if nothing. Your friend comes forward apologetically. With a few words, I played it down and Bruce smiles back with the most tender eyes.'

Bruce finally says: 'I sense an accent: are you Persian?' Shireen assents.

'And to my surprise, he answered back in Farsi and then the most amazing thing happens: we ended up the evening at home, talking about Iran and Bruce reciting classical poetry in the most refined ways.'

I miss him. This was only a flash, one among many. Colourful life. *Comme il portait bien sa vie!*

A few years later, Bruce was present when I got married with Adnan. On 21 December 2005, the first legal unions for same-sex couples were celebrated in London. Bruce cried with us in Chelsea Town Hall. He met my family and our friends. He has been in our hearts since then.

# Simon Everard Digby (1932–2010)

**Bruce Wannell**, *traveller and linguist, York, 12 June 2012.*

Simon Digby was a fellow of Wolfson College whom current fellows may not have encountered: those who did no doubt remember him well.

I was first introduced to Simon at Oxford, by a graduate student who had come to Simon at the Ashmolean Museum for supervision of his thesis on the Sufi shrine at Ajmer. My misty memory places that around 1974. Later in London, I was taken to visit Simon in his house in Kilburn, where he rented out the lower floors to Rastafarians and lived in a flat at the top, perched like a Buddha, or rather a Silenus, among treasures of Indian art and piled-up books, in an aura of squalor and magnificence.

I remember his booming voice, which could be heard in those sudden moments of hushed silence that affect auctions in the grander sales rooms – usually the booming voice was in full flow of some scandalous anecdote: Simon loved gossip. He was merciless towards fraud and humbuggery, especially that of the mystagogic Shâh brothers and their bamboozling of the Gurdjieffians of Combe Springs, Kingston, and of the credulous poet Robert Graves who, under their direction, retranslated the 'original twelfth-century manuscript' of Omar Khayyâm, with all the detailed misreadings of Heron-Allen's nineteenth-century prose translation! At the previews of these Islamic and Indian art auctions, I benefited from Simon's habitually generous sharing of his knowledge. He was obviously highly respected, regardless of his unkempt appearance – latterly a wispy beard, sandals, loose Indian shirt with the dye run, knitted sweater and knitted bonnet with holes, and invariably a cloth bag over one shoulder and a large Burmese pigeon's blood ruby mounted in gold on his finger. His avid collecting of Indian metalwork and Islamic manuscripts, his vast knowledge of textual sources in several languages, his wide-ranging travels, and his inherited sympathy for the subcontinent, made him a scholar of unusual calibre.

To the great 1976 'Arts of Islam' show at the Hayward Gallery in London, which was a turning point and opened many new perspectives for me, Simon had lent a beautiful Qur'ân from Gwalior in central India, dated 801 of the Hijra, equivalent to 1399 AD. It was written in *Bihâri* script and illuminated with finely drawn and brightly coloured flowers. Shortly after the exhibition, a disastrous emotional–financial entanglement forced Simon to sell it, and the Sultânate Qur'ân reappeared in 1979 at the Asian House gallery in America as the property of Sadruddin Âghâ Khân. Simon always proclaimed his belief in the necessity of goods circulating in the art market, of collectors following private passions and tastes to create new categories beyond stale orthodoxies. He never failed to point out the occasional failures of museums to carry out their basic duty of conserving the cultural heritage of the past. Whether due to theft or damage to objects under restoration or due to changes in fashion, shortage of funding or interdepartmental politics, objects had too often been removed from display, de-accessioned and sold off, or even destroyed, as was the case with the important eighteenth-century decorative woodwork from Gujarat at the V&A.

The 1399 Qur'ân is particularly interesting as its completion date coincides with the two months' residence in Gwalior of the greatest of the Delhi Sufis of that time, Sayyid Muhammad Gesu-derâz, who was travelling south with a large party of family, clerics and craftsmen, having escaped from the southern gate of Delhi just as the world-conqueror Timur the Lame defeated the Tughluq ruler and was entering the city from the other side to ravage and pillage it. When I was reading the great inscription band on the interior of the 1422 tomb of Feroz Shâh Bahmani (Gesu-derâz's host at Gulbarga in the Deccan for the last twenty years of his long life), I was struck by the similarity of the floral background of the inscription in what would have been brightly painted plaster, and the floral illumination of the 1399 Qur'ân that had briefly been one of Simon's treasured possessions. Sayyid Husain Husaini, now *sajjâda-neshin* (literally sitting on the prayer carpet) of his ancestor Gesu-derâz's shrine, showed me a Bahmani period *farmân*, a royal order granting possessions and concessions to the Chishti shrine. It is probable that craftsmen from the former imperial capital Delhi worked on the Gulbarga royal tomb inscription and used models of decoration which had been used earlier as the source of the Gwalior Qur'ân's illumination. Very possibly, this particular Qur'ân had accompanied the charismatic saint on his peregrination southwards.

When I returned from teaching in Isfahân during the Irânian Revolution of 1978–80, I met Sandy Morton, who proposed my joining the Royal Asiatic Society, where I again met Simon; there, as honorary librarian, he had taken the bold decision to have one of the greatest treasures of the society's collections sold. This was the c. 1310 manuscript of Rashiduddin's *Jâmi' al-Tawârikh* (collected histories), copied in the Rashidiyya quarter of Tabriz during the lifetime of the author-patron. The money raised was to secure the future financial stability of the old-established learned institution; the purchaser, Simon told me, was a Jewish dealer originally from Isfahân, who had benefited from his links with the Sultan of Brunei. Later a handsome facsimile of the manuscript was commissioned with a detailed critical essay from a leading American scholar, thus making the manuscript more widely available to the scholarly and general public than when it had been on loan to the British Museum.

Some years working in Peshawar with refugees from Afghanistan led to my being repatriated for medical treatment to the Hospital for Tropical Diseases in London, with a long convalescence that allowed me to meet Simon and Sandy frequently. They began then, and continued over the next several years, to give me offprints of their scholarly articles and books, Sandy's dealing mostly with Seljuqs and Safavids in Iran, Simon's primarily with India after the Muslim conquests of the twelfth century and before the Mughal conquests of the sixteenth century. The rediscovery of Sultanate art and literature, especially the collections of saints' lives (*tadhkira*) and their edifying talks (*malfuzât*), provided Simon with a rich seam to mine for the social and economic history of the Indian middle ages. His historian's salutary scepticism seized more on the underlying elements of social control enforced with spiteful vindictiveness, rather than on the Sufis' nebulous language of cloud metaphysics which overlay their specious claims to authority.

Early in the new millennium, I started collaborating with Willie Dalrymple in translating Persian materials from his books (*White Mughals* and *The Last Mughal*) and returned to India. This led to some happy chance meetings with Simon, once in Lodi – formerly Lady Willingdon – Gardens where we spent an afternoon reading the inscriptions on the fifteenth and early sixteenth-century domed tombs and ruined mosques, before going on to dinner at the International Club where he was one of the last remaining foreign members. Simon loved Delhi, which he had known when it was still a green and calm city over half a century before – deplored the dense urban sprawl and pollution of the mushrooming megalopolis, and the eclipsing of the city's traditions. He was a keen decipherer of difficult inscription and manuscripts, and would treat any problem case I brought to him as others might a *sudoku* or a crossword puzzle. My immersion in late eighteenth-century

Deccani material and mid-nineteenth-century British Imperial history also enlarged our field of common interests.

In 2004 he invited me to help him with an early sixteenth-century Persian text, the *Jawâhir-nâma*, treating of precious stones and rare substances, their origin, trade routes, prices, qualities, tests for recognising fakes, magical and medicinal properties. The invitation came rather suddenly, as he was due to leave imminently for Ladakh and had a spare air-ticket from London to Delhi. Of course I accepted, with the proviso that I would do some independent walking and visiting Buddhist monasteries, as well as help him translate.

Before we left Delhi, Simon asked me to deliver a message to a young man working in a restaurant in the west of the city... I later realised, when I found the young man installed in his bed in Manâli on the return journey, that this was an essential part of Simon's support system in the subcontinent. He would often say that, for him, differences of class and race were essential to any form of sexual interest. The young men were generously remembered, not only in the introductions to his books, but also in his will: but I was told that when the bequests were delivered to their families by Simon's chief heir and executor, they expressed dismay that the sums were not infinitely larger!

On the drive up to Ladakh, Simon was much preoccupied with death and made me promise to scatter his ashes in the river should his heart not survive the great heights of the Tang-lang-lâ Pass – some 18,000 feet. He repeated his admiration for his friend Penelope Chetwode and the loyalty of Bruce Chatwin, who scattered her ashes in Kulu according to her wishes. In the end it was Salmân Haidar, former foreign minister of India, who had the honour of scattering Simon's ashes. Once established in Leh, Simon reverted, in spite of doctors' warnings, to the regular and heavy consumption of the local rum: I kept him company for one glass in the evening, then left. But when I looked in the next morning, the empty bottles were piling up. Sometimes during the night, shouts and wails and roars would emerge from his room, waking the sleepers down the veranda corridor: was it night-blindness against which the *Jawâhir-nâma* proposed so many antidotes, or was it panic?

Work nevertheless proceeded during daylight hours, regularly but slowly, on the book of precious substances. I enjoyed our sessions: Simon's great historical erudition illuminated the text, and I called on all my Persian acquired in Iran and Afghanistan and also on what little knowledge of ceramic glazes I had been given by my friend Isabel Denyer the potter in Yorkshire, and of the traditional pigments by Joan Griffiths (who worked under her maiden name Seddon) the painting-restorer in Kew, and Don Baker the manuscript-restorer in Islington.

So, day by day, we teased out the knotty passages dealing with cobalt and lapis lazuli, and the grinding and washing out of a pure lapis paste after separating the residue of white calcite. Simon worked by accretion, and liked to add discursive footnotes to his long articles, reworking them with more and more parallels and explanatory passages in related literature. So we did not finish the project then...

Nor did we finish it on my subsequent visits, in 2005 and 2007, by ferry from Wareham, to Simon's house at Rozell in Jersey. It was an early nineteenth-century farmhouse with a large stone cider-press on the lawn, which he had inherited from an aunt, along with the support system of a delightful housekeeper and her gardener-husband. It was an escape from the low-life and poverty of Kilburn: here neighbours, such as Janey Malet de Carteret, Melissa Bon, Marcus Binney, would invite him for lunch or dinner or swimming, and a loyal young schoolteacher, Dominic Omissi, would swoop up on his motorcycle in a great flowing rain-cape, to put right any of those all-too-frequent computer hitches. Simon's London friends, Bob Alderman, George Michell, would receive phone calls, beginning with his characteristic wail of irritation and anguish, as when his passport was lost just before he was due to leave for a conference on medieval Kashmir: as soon as he'd acquired a new passport, the old one was found under a heap of correspondence on the hall table.

The habit of accumulating – papers, books, projects each in a series of cardboard boxes climbing the stairs, encumbering the dining table and invading the guest bedrooms – had lasted from Kilburn days. The guest bathroom was overflowing with medieval Indian bronze pots, jugs, spouted ewers. One of his great treasures was in the cabinet in the drawing room, a sixteenth-century Gujarat inlaid mother-of-pearl pen-box, which had belonged to a previous Dalâi Lama and had been smuggled out of Tibet. The chest of drawers in the dining room was full of manuscripts in one of which I found a fine early sixteenth-century Timurid copy of Dawalatshâh's *Tadhkiray al-Shu'arâ*, containing a mythic Sufi poem by Âzari of Tus, who had migrated from Khurâsân to the Deccan to become court poet of the Bahmanids. The kitchen wing was filled with porcelain from East and West – alas, Simon's failure to maintain the property led, just after his death, to the collapse of that entire side of the house, and the reduction of the porcelain collection to fragments and dust.

Simon commissioned a series of wooden blocks on which he mounted his finer small bronzes, which he did with the greatest delicacy, precision and tenderness. Everywhere hung his mother's watercolours – she had taken him, after his father's death, on a painting trip to

Pachmarhi and Kashmir in the early 1950s; later she committed suicide, leaving him a note telling him not to take it personally, she'd just had enough. The more recent suicide of his colleague and friend, Aditya Behl, left Simon saddened and, after a drink of whiskey, lachrymose. He brightened when telling of his father, the judge in Jabalpur, and his overnight train journeys in France before the Second World War, where he would emerge at a destination, dishevelled and wearing the ticket-collector's trousers.

Simon told me that he intended to leave his collection, at least the entire, coherent ensemble of early Indian metalwork, to some institute of higher learning, as a study collection for the students to handle. One of his recurring criticisms of contemporary oriental *academe* was that the study of texts is divorced from the study of material culture. The recent visit of an art dealer, keen to make offers on items of the collection, was memorable chiefly for the armoured racing car in which he arrived, after purchasing it from the King of Jordan. Other art dealers – personable, charming, rapacious – followed, and the decision was taken by the executors of Simon's will to disperse the collection piecemeal in a series of sales, in order to raise money for bursaries for younger students. Will another Simon be found to build up, over years, with painstaking and detailed love of objects and their literary and social background, another such collection?

In the last two years of his life, I saw Simon when he came over from Jersey and I down from York: usually we met with Sandy Morton at a Greek *taverna* on Camberwell Grove, before cancer also claimed the life of that other great scholar.

On the last evening of 2009, I was ferried in a coracle down the Tungabadhra River between the large granite boulders that slow its flow from Hampi to Anegondi. A large moon was rising, and night had fallen by the time we reached the mango grove where the New Year's Eve and birthday party was being given. Naked village boys, painted red like the monkey-god Hanuman, jumped out of the trees to greet the guests with flaming torches and drumming, leading us along the paths to the fireworks display on the lawns and the Indian classical dances on the veranda of the estate bungalow. 'Simon should be here, there are so many of his Indian and Indianist friends here' was a comment I heard more than once that night.

A few days later, while I was working in Bijâpur on a revised reading of the Persian and Arabic inscriptions of that exquisite early seventeenth-century garden tomb, the *Rauza* of Ibrâhim Âdilshâh, I heard the news that Simon had just died in hospital in Delhi; pancreatic cancer had ended his life in its seventy-eighth year.

'They are all gone into a world of light.'

As an older generation of scholars dies, I am keenly aware that time will not wait: unfinished projects are all too often jettisoned. The social and economic circumstances that allowed serious, amateur private scholarship and an intimate, grainy and lived knowledge of the land, society and material culture of former colonial territories have all but disappeared. Sandy's last words of advice to me, when I visited him in the hospice where he was dying were: 'Finish what you have started – no one else will do that for you.'

I hope, as a tribute to my scholarly, erudite, sceptical and generous mentors, Simon Digby and Sandy Morton, to finish the work we started on the *Jawâhir-nâma* and to bring it to publication very soon.

*wa lâ taufiq illâ billâh* and success lies with God
*innâ lillâhi wa innâ ilaihi râji'un* we belong to God, return to God

# Shaykh Abdu Rahim al-Bura'i, the Sufi
*Sudan*

*This essay by Bruce was edited from his travel book, written for Nick Robinson but never finished, and published in* Meetings with Remarkable Muslims (*Eland, 2005*).

I arrived at Zariba as the moon was rising. In a large courtyard, Shaykh Abdu Rahim al-Bura'i's lanky teenage son, Jayli, presided on a mat in the sand. There was no electricity, so I enjoyed the rare luxury of natural darkness and moonlight. Jayli told me that he had twenty-two brothers and fifteen sisters, as the seventy-two-year-old Shaykh had married nine wives in the fifty years he had been running the masid. The nine wives, even when marriage ties were dissolved (there were never more than the allowable four wives concurrently) were left with their own houses around the *masid*, and they and their children were fed and clothed out of common funds.

When Jayli's grandfather established the mosque and school at Zariba, the area had been a notorious badland of robber-nomads: this Sufi centre had spearheaded a more settled and lawful life among local tribesmen. Initially, it was not easy to gain their confidence, but the first shaykh visited their families and invited all to meals of honey and roast meats till they began to treat the *masid* as their own centre and spontaneously came to the shaykh to resolve their disputes and difficulties. A market had grown up outside the walls, allowing not only students but also locals to dabble in commerce, so that the spread of Islam was accompanied by the growth of commerce. Religion brought with love had been a major factor in the evolution of society.

After the night prayer, a rumbling sound started up and continued all night – it was the oil mill, which pressed oil from cottonseed, sesame and groundnuts for sale to Omdurman and El Obeid – the *masid* was now underpinned by agro-industry as well as by commerce.

A sudden whooping of joy from the students and a stampede towards the inner courtyard heralded the arrival of Shaykh Abdu Rahim al-Bura'i. I finished my bowl of sweetened yoghurt with Jayli and walked slowly to see the arrival – I found the old Shaykh stretched on a string-bed with three students massaging his limbs.

'Such an effort,' I thought uncharitably, 'to step from the plane into his air-conditioned Pajero which stands gleaming there beside him in the moonlight!' But then I remembered all the massages I had enjoyed, a civilised pleasure I had never disdained. No doubt massage of his aching muscles was welcome to the septuagenarian, as the bumpy ride along desert tracks must be tiring, even in a Pajero.

Here was, I feared, a phenomenon comparable to other cult-gurus. The posters and photographs of the Shaykh that were sold, along with his volumes of poetry, in the market outside indicated a cult of personality that seemed far from ascetic. But this personality cult is modest compared to the monstrous self-promotion of American television evangelists. It was only after several meetings with the Shaykh, and close observation of the crowd of visitors that my mind and my heart began to accept a different concept of sanctity, one based not on repression and denial, but on endless and boundless generosity.

The old man certainly had a remarkable reproductive success (enviable even to monarchs and alpha-male apes) with his thirty-eight children – and all of them educated, at least in the Islamic sciences. His students and devotees spread all over the country. I was accosted later in the streets of Khartoum by a worker recently expelled from Libya who had seen me at the *masid*, so I gave him lunch at an Iranian restaurant. In Port Sudan, months later as I was leaving the country, a petty trader who had heard my speech at the Zariba *masid* after Friday prayers gave me a long article published in the papers about the Shaykh shortly after I'd left – the journalist had quizzed me about my education and my purpose in coming there. The Shaykh's poetry in praise of the Prophet was known and sung not only in Sudan, but in Egypt and even in Syria – a year later, I met a *munshid* religious singer in Aleppo who regularly sang the Shaykh's religious poetry, and that of his fourteenth-century ancestor and namesake from the Jabal Bura' in Yemen.

The Shaykh had also taken over one of the traditions of African kingship, that of mass marriages. At the last occasion in June, some two and a half thousand people were married in the *masid*: divorcees, the poor and unemployed, all those who could not afford the expense of marriage or were debarred from the lengthy and complex negotiations to secure a partner, would come here to find a mate and be married and blessed and even receive a little money from the Shaykh to set up their new ménage.

I began to think differently of the oil-mill chuntering and grinding through the night: it was a good investment of pilgrims' donations to allow the *masid* not only some financial security, but also a continuous redistribution of wealth. The lorries carrying the oil daily to sell in Khartoum kept open the *masid*'s contact with the outside world, as well as offering free transport to pilgrims on the way. The profits went back into the school and guest accommodation, as well as financing a string of new mosques in most towns of the Sudan, giving focus, and employment, to the Shaykh's progeny and devotees.

The multiplicity of the social functions of the *masid* seemed inexhaustible.

One of the visitors was a Saudi who'd just flown in from Riyadh to be cured after being touched by Satan – *lams-u-Shaytan* – the Satanic stroke commonly supposed to be the cause of impotence.

Another was Zubayda, an upper-class woman from Khartoum, who had lived for seventeen years in Saudi Arabia and Abu Dhabi keeping house for her husband, bringing up her children and working in an office. On a visit to her aged father in Khartoum, she had received a phone call from her husband announcing that he had divorced her, was keeping the children and had installed his new wife in the house! Thanks to his connections with the current government, he blocked her appeals for justice and had even had himself appointed head of an Islamic Relief Charity! Her ex-husband was now in his late forties, the restless age, sick, on his own. Zubayda almost felt sorry for him. She was back at college to get a Masters in nutrition so that she could eventually work and help her children. Meanwhile, she had come to ask for the Shayhk's prayers for a solution to her problems. I asked if she did not think it was time to organise an Islamic Women's Movement to protect the rights of women in Sudan, as professional women had started successfully in Pakistan. She looked at me uncomprehendingly.

Next to veiled Zubayda was a local Arab tribeswoman, dishevelled and completely naked above the waist, suckling an infant on her pendulous breasts, come to beg a charm for the health of her child. Other peasants pushed and shoved to present their petitions.

The Shaykh was imperturbably kind and attentive to each one, reading the scraps of paper, answering the questions, offering a prayer, blowing on a sick child, patting a bowed head, occasionally making a joke, receiving the shower of bank notes and putting them away in his capacious pockets, always with patience and good humour; and when he'd had enough, he arose majestically and walked off in a slow procession.

Jadidi Mahmud at-Taba'i was the visitor I spent most of my time with. He was Tunisian and spoke French – it turned out that, like me, he was born at the end of August 1952, and like mine his mother was from

Brussels. Beatrice van der Kerkhoove had married a cardiologist, my mother's sister had also married a cardiologist. His father, a Tunisian *sharif*, eventually returned to his estates near Tunis and started his own private, and very profitable, hospital in the capital. Jadidi had, according to his own account, the only one I had to go on, spent an extremely luxurious, dissolute adolescence and early manhood in Tunis. Aged forty, he dreamed a dream, the same dream every night for a month – Shaykh Abdu Rahim al-Bura'i would appear, summoning him to Zariba. Jadidi consulted a Sudanese neighbour, obtained his father's blessing, packed his bags and set off by lorry through Libya, Chad and Darfur. He arrived at Zariba after two months' exhausting journey. He was now living in a small room with two large porous clay water jars whose dripping water cooled the air. He was learning the Quran by heart, the basic step in any traditional Islamic education, and progressing on the spiritual path. After two years, he had been made a shaykh of the Sammaniya 'tariqa', I hoped with better justification than my elevation to that rank a few months earlier in Ethiopia.

We sat on the sand and talked at length as the moon rose about our lives: I told him of my hopes to go on the Umra and then by sea to Egypt and to see my aged parents in England before they, or I, died; of the careless, solitary life I'd led 'au jour le jour', never thinking of tomorrow nor of the need for financial security, accumulating experiences but no material wealth, giving and sharing what I could but now, in my mid-forties, with neither family nor home nor established profession.

'What of it?' countered Jadidi robustly. 'If it is your fate, live it, live it to the full and enjoy it! Some of our greatest saints never had families. That didn't stop them from giving to those around them. Do likewise. Keep faith, keep trusting!'

I lay coughing on the sand till I fell asleep. Jadidi's friend, a thoughtful student who had travelled to Egypt and kept a stall in the market, woke me with a hot bitter infusion of sage leaves and ginger root to clear my chest.

In the library of the Shaykh's eldest son Fatih, I came across that wonderful book of spiritual aphorisms, the 'Kitab ul-Hikam' of Ibn Atallah al-Iskandari. One saying seemed to echo Jadidi's encouragement:

'Let it be no cause for despair, if, in spite of your insistent prayers, there is delay in granting gifts: for He has guaranteed to answer your prayers as He chooses best for you, not in what you choose for yourself, and in the time He wishes, not in the time that you may wish!'

Jadidi later told me that he'd asked the Shaykh to do one of his special *fatiha* prayers to intercede for the successful outcome of my

119

journey, including the pilgimage to the Hijaz, the return by sea to Egypt, the reunion with my parents and brothers. I was haunted by Ibn Batuta's return to Tangier after his long absence, to find his mother already dead. Certainly in that distant stretch of central Sudan's savannah, home seemed a long way away, and the Shaykh's assurances were comforting.

I spent a week at Zariba, sitting on the dry red sand in front of the Shaykh's reception room during the day when he was performing his *dhikr* litanies of commemoration in a closed room. I studied in the shade of a big baobab, leaning against its trunk and at night slept on a string bed on the back terrace; when I stood after midnight to recite the supererogatory *tahajjud* prayers under the full moon, I would see tame gazelles come out from their pen and step delicately around the sleeping guests.

The organisation of the *masid* was quite an undertaking. Students, disciples and visitors were given early morning milk tea, mid-morning *futur* of *asida* for the general public – eggs, red beans and tomato salad for guests – mid-afternoon *ghada* of roast meat, honey, stews, *kisra* and *weka*, salad and fruit which the Shaykh would heroically share with rank upon rank of guests who came to eat from the same dish with him. Late at night, *asha* of bread and sweetened yoghurt was served, a feat of organisation, mostly cooked by the Shaykh's nine current and ex-wives.

There were several hundred students and disciples, mostly adolescents, willing but untidy, fifty or more visitors daily and a rush at weekends. Pilgrims arrived on Thursday evening, entered the brick and concrete compound, marching with flags and chants, drumming and dancing, till they had covered the prescribed itinerary around the tall, domed tomb of the Shaykh's father where strip-lighting blazed just this one night, around various concrete excrescences, a pseudo-hillock where the older shaykh had died, some false wells occasionally filled by bucket for pilgrims. These were all significant features of the landscape of piety. Had veneration of the founder, dead barely fifty years, replaced some pre-Islamic ancestor worship?

But the *masid* was also a centre of traditional Islamic learning, strengthening and renewing the inherited but fragile cultural identity of these mostly rural Muslims. At different levels, there was the basic memorisation of the Quran for elementary students, then the study of *hadith* traditions, of *fiqh* canon law for the more mature, and, for the more advanced, even commentaries on the Quran and books of Sufism. In Shaykh Fatih's library, I found not only that classic of Shadhili mystic psychology, the *Hikam* of Ibn Atallah, but also a book of the ten variant readings of the Quran by Ibn al-Jazari *Kitab u-Nashr fi Qira'at'Ashr*, the *Ihya Ulumi-d-Din* of Ghazali, the supreme legal textbook *Muwatta* of Malik, the poetic *Diwan* of Umar Haddad, the great dictionary *Taj ul-'Arus* of Zabidi and other treasures. Reading was as much part of my Islamic journey as physical travel and meetings with Muslims.

I find the essential message of the Quran text convincing, the themes of preaching recur as leitmotifs in various combinations, with the personal polemic tone often supporting the traditional idea of the divine revelation fitting in to the purported biography of the human recipient. The genre of prophetic utterance was perilously close to, and therefore had to be emphatically distinguished from, that of the Kahin sorcerers and the Sha'ir poets. But the Quran's cosmology of seven heavens, seven gates of hell, three paradises, shooting stars to punish eavesdropping Jinn, are all difficult to square with modern concepts of the universe. Our astronomers do not have seven or three of anything, their quantities are altogether vaster.

For me, and for many non-Arab Muslims, one of the most essential problems remains the relationship between innate natural religion and its culturally specific seventh-century Arabic revelation as defined by the limited geographical and historical scope of references in the Quran.

How Arabic should Islam be, if it is to be a universal religion?

Also, I do find the increasing identification of Ego, the Prophet, and superego, God, rather disturbing. There has already been enough of that in Christianity, hero-worship taken to the point of deification!

And yet, and yet, if there is not a perfect concordance of will and consciousness between God and Prophet, what does the Semitic tradition of prophecy amount to?

All this was grist to the mill of my critical mind, which worked overtime and refused to give up its addiction to examining, questioning and doubting. However much my heart wants faith, would even be satisfied with superstition, my reason refuses to believe.

When I finally met the Shaykh to talk with him, after a long wait outside his door when I almost lost my temper and banged on the door while he was performing his extended devotions, I tried to explain my predicament to him: 'My heart believes, if God wills, but my reason refuses to believe.'

He referred to verse 46 of the Chapter of Pilgrimage: 'It is not so much eyes which go blind, but rather the heart in the breast which goes blind.'

'Did you not see me in your dreams last night?'

'No.'

'You are still clouded. This intellectualism could drive you mad.

121

Look at life and at faith from the point of view of *rahma* – mercy, not *ikhtilaf* – dissension.'

He also quoted verse 118–19 from the Chapter of Hud: 'and they do not cease to differ, except those on whom your Lord has had mercy; and to that end He created them.'

'Were men created for mercy and unity or for dissension? A Muslim must love the Prophet and therefore stick to his exemplary *sunna* habitual practice – so don't emphasise differences; just believe in the unseen *ghayb* – the all-powerful God. You cannot know all, so use allegory as well as literal commentary to approach the truth, which is all one Truth.'

'As for Arabism,' the Shaykh continued, 'Arabic is the privileged language of this revelation, but never forget the saying "*khatib u-nas 'ala qadri 'uquli-him*" – speak to people according to the level of their understanding. You don't have to become Arab to become Muslim. So keep your vernacular language, keep your local name Bruce, providing its significance in your language is neither idolatrous nor insulting.'

The Shaykh did not want me to leave until after the Friday prayers, so I took the chance for more talks with him, about dreams, idle thoughts that obstruct concentration and prayer, about asceticism. The more I saw him the more his kindness and wisdom impressed me.

'Did you hear or see me in your dreams last night?' he asked again one morning.

I was not aware of having had any dreams since coming here.

He described *zuhd* asceticism: 'renounce what is your own, God will love you for that; renounce what is other people's, they will love you for that.' The ascetic is one who envies not what is in others' hands and gives freely of what is in his own. This seemed to describe the Shaykh's own practice.

To a student he repeated one of his father's favourite sayings:

*alay-kum bi-t-taqwa: wa hiya*
*al-khawfu min al-Jalil*
*wa-l-'amalu bi-t-Tanzil*
*wa-rida'u bi-l-qalil*
*wa-l-isti'dadu bi-yawmi-r-rahil*

Your duty is Piety, that is: fear God,
act according to the Revelation,
be content with little,
be prepared for the day of departure, death.

Turning to me he warned: 'Contemplating God's attributes must not go to the point of questioning His essence; the human attributes are those of *ubudiya* – being a servant of the Lord – therefore concentrate on those human attributes, humility, spiritual poverty, a sense of your own nothingness in the face of God's majesty.'

'Work cleanses; service to human beings is the real expression of religion; heaven is outside time and place, outside our experience and our comprehension, and therefore described in elusive, allusive, allegorical language. The heavenly spirit breathed into each human being by God at his creation "*wa nafakhtu fi-hi min Ruh-I*" in the Chapter of Hijr verse 29, this is what lasts and, if God wills, this is what returns to Him, the light returning to the Light.'

I was late for the Friday sermon and prayers and was hurrying over the sand to the mosque after all the others had already entered, when the Shaykh came in my direction. He took my hand as we both approached the mosque, and asked me, almost apologetically, explaining that some people were worried by the presence of a Westerner, to repeat the *shahada*, the profession of faith.

I was shocked, but repeated the formula while holding his hand. '*Ashhadu an la ilaha illa Allah, wahda-hu la sharika la-hu, wa ashhadu anna Muhammadan abdu-hu wa rasuluhu*'; I bear witness that there is no God other than the One God, and that Muhammad is His servant and His messenger.

The Shaykh then led me into the mosque by a back stair up to the preachers gallery in full view of the assembled two or three thousand. I was confused and abashed, and did not know what to do.

The Shaykh gave a powerful sermon on the text of the Chapter of the Afternoon:

> I swear by the afternoon,
> that man is indeed at a loss,
> unless it be those who believe
> and do good works,
> and encourage one another to hold on to truth and patience.

After the prayers, he turned to me and said: 'Now you talk to the people.'

Pushing me forward, he gave me a glowing introduction that seemed to confirm my undeserved status as honoured visiting scholar. So I talked very simply in my basic Arabic about my trip through different Muslim countries to see how my Muslim brothers were living, and to see the strength and solidarity of Islam lived in the lives of ordinary people.

I felt at first as if I were being thrown to the lions, perceived as an outsider from a hostile culture. People seemed to appreciate what I said which was as positive and tactful as I could make it. It was obviously not the place to air text-critical quibbles. In fact the shock of repeating the *shahada* had quite driven such things from my mind. My intellectual pride and nihilistic undermining of faith suddenly seemed irrelevant, unworthy.

On Saturday, I looked for the Shaykh early and found him in the furthest part of the *masid*, in the radio-room where he was giving orders by radio to his various centres at el-Obeid, Umm Ruwaba, Wad Madani, Port Sudan, Omdurman. He had just received news of the previous night's car crash where his son had escaped unhurt but the driver had broken his wrist. Despite his suspicion of much modern mass culture – football, cinema – there was no unwillingness to make use of useful modern technology.

The Shaykh's youngest son, an infant, at-Tum, was climbing all over the place with a runny nose. I wiped his face clean with a tissue and the Shaykh, noticing my gesture, immediately gave me a pack of tissues.

The whereabouts of the Shaykh did not long remain secret and soon more visitors crowded in and were served with trays of bread and bowls of red beans with raw onion and peanut oil and fresh tomatoes, followed by basins of wild honey and ghee, then fruit and tea, a never-ending profusion.

Finally, I plucked up courage and asked for permission to leave, to travel onwards with his blessing. He looked at me and asked: 'Do you really want to go?'

'Yes.'

He embraced me, kissed me on the neck, then dug into his capacious pockets and emptied all the money accumulated there: 'Take this for your journey!'

Shaykh Abdu Rahim al-Bura'i used to talk about his recent trip to Fez in Morocco when he was the guest of the Tijani order. The descendants of the founder, also Maliki in legal observance, quoted some fifty hadith in favour of praying with hands-open, hanging by the side – just as I remember the Shaykh standing, leading the long lines of worshippers in prayer on the sand. This, as opposed to the arms crossed over the chest of Hanafi and Wahhabi. In some parts, these minutiae are taken in deadly earnest: a traveller joined the prayers in northern Nigeria, folded his hands across his chest and was promptly stoned to death.

Is that akin to a musician outraged at a favourite melody played too fast, with botched phrasing, or a cook enraged by a classic dish over-peppered or disfigured with tomato ketchup? Etiquette and aesthetics and fashion can command our obedience in the smallest details of taste and ritual, but not religion, not anymore, not in the rationalised West.

So are the Muslims who worry passionately about the ritual efficacy of a particular gesture or length of beard or woman's veil wrong to do so? A ritual or a custom can encapsulate values and beliefs, but should remain transparent; otherwise there is the risk of idolising outer forms, the risk of attempting – an intolerant and futile attempt – to limit the free-flowing inner Spirit.

One of the most concise definition of Sufism, that it is 'entirely about good manners', stresses precisely this attention to details of hierarchy and etiquette, not in a dry, but in a loving way. It is also a realistic way, recognising and giving to each person or thing its proper place and value. What greater respect and courtesy than that is needed in the presence of the Divine?

I keep the memory of a great and saintly man, one who had no false modesty nor false austerity, a giver, who gave back manifold everything that he was given, a fount of generosity – in that sense at least, the ideal of Muslim sanctity which reflects the unending generosity of God who perpetually sustains and renews His creation.

The echoes of this meeting have continued with me throughout my travels in Egypt and Syria, and even now in cold, damp Yorkshire.

# The book that never was by the most interesting man in the world

**Nova Robinson** *was Nick Robinson's second wife. The letter about Bruce that she refers to at the beginning of this piece was written by Nick Robinson and addressed to his two children, Mathew and Tilly, to be opened after his death (August 2013). You can read it on page 342.*

I stumbled upon the letter [published at the end of this book] written by Nick Robinson about his lifelong friend Bruce Wannell. Barnaby had asked me to dig around in Nick's papers to pin down a few facts. So I donned my detective hat in an attempt to discover the truth behind the rumours that Nick paid Bruce a £10,000 advance to write his travel memoir. I giggled at the amount when I read Bruce's obituary in *The Times*. We (Robinson Publishing) didn't pay those sorts of advances in those days. And so began much rummaging on Nick's old laptop and through his random correspondence (a decade's worth in each plastic carrier bag).

My first memory of Bruce was when he came to stay with us at Fox Farm. I forget exactly when, I feel I have always known him. Like others, I too have many entertaining stories and memories of Bruce. As I drove Bruce back to London that damp spring Sunday evening, I pointed out the wonderful old tithe barn as we left Tisbury, the longest in the country, almost derelict, rarely used except by the local drama group. Of course Bruce made me stop so we could take a look. We walked around it, completely locked up. 'We must go in,' insisted Bruce as he took off his rather smart overcoat and laid it on the floor below the barn door and we rolled in below the door to take a look.

Nick first met Bruce in 1974, in Paris aged nineteen, long-haired and wearing an old Afghan coat, on his gap year before heading to study History of Art at Cambridge. A like-minded soul, Matthew Harragin offered Nick his floor to sleep on in Rue Saint André des Arts in the sixième. Matthew knew Bruce from Oxford, Bruce also in Paris would often pop round. Matthew shared a tiny flat with a French couple, Alain and Martine. Alain took photos of tourists outside the Louvre and made a non-stop succession of joints from one of those pop-up metal boxes. Martine was half North African, with an impressive embonpoint, exaggerated by a regular diet of baklavas, which satisfied their 'munchies'. Perhaps a bit of an eye-opener for Bruce (and Nick), but a setting Bruce would have been quite used to later in life.

Drifting in and out of each other's lives for almost forty years, Nick and Bruce knew each other so well, and were often seen bickering like an old married couple.

Nick became a publisher, setting up Robinson Publishing at his flat in Shepherds Market in the late '80s. Talk of a book with Bruce began in the early '90s, mentioned often in letters in '90 and '91. In one written in red ink dated 26 Feb 1991, Bruce outlines his travels and writes: 'If we did something I would have to come back to England and I'd have to have an advance of at least £10,000...' In another letter dated June 1991 replying to two of Nick's, 'It'll take a year to write – can I pay rent, running costs, word processor and still eat for £5,000? YES!!' (he also writes: 'I actually took the plunge and became M [Muslim] because I fell in love – details unprintable!').

Over the following years Nick tried many ways to extract some form of manuscript from Bruce. Eventually I found an old journal of Nick's. An entry in March 1997 reveals this is the period Bruce is living at Nick's flat 'writing his book'. Filled with many tales of musical soirées and extravagant breakfasts, eventually Bruce moved on, soon after Nick was heard to say 'so darling, are we living together now?'

NR writes:

Wednesday, 13 August 1997
*Outline arrives from Bruce. Too much detail as ever and my heart sinks as I read through it. And then, at the end, is a passage about coming back and how he feels he has fallen between two cultures, how his family have not helped him at all (and they haven't), how materialistic everyone is and how the spiritual world seems over in the West. This is the theme for the book – the spiritual world is ending all over the world and has ended in the West. Bruce has seen the last of it in the East, whose traditions are being corrupted by the cars and the concrete of the West. In the outline, Bruce tells a story of travelling with a Sufi master in a car and driving into a gun battle between two bands of robbers. Both sides lay down their weapons and come out from behind their rocks to meet the Master.*

Friday, 1 May 1998

*Lunch with Bruce. Bruce is living in a housing association bedsit in York, because as he says, he can live there on no money, save up and then every 2 or 3 months come to London and see friends, have fun and spend what little he has, whereas if he were living in London the whole time he'd never save and never be able to afford to do anything. Shiningly intelligent, then he tells me he wants Volume 1 of his travels to cover leaving Pakistan through to the Sudan. Not so bright.*

Thursday, 20 August 1998

*Bruce comes to breakfast. We talk for two hours without stopping: about his book, about his watching two troops of monkeys in Tanzania and how he thought they were just like the Yorkists and Lancastrians; how the family is so important in the Islamic world because there is no other form of protection for the individual. B. gets more camp and more affected but he should have the title The Most Interesting Man in the World.*

A letter to Bruce dated March 1999

*We've reached a point where friendship is running into business. I can't reasonably tell my colleagues that there is a private Wannell advances account without telling them something about the book.*

*So far the advance paid comes to £4,299.95. This wouldn't be a problem if we were making progress towards the book you and I had agreed you would write. Unfortunately, we're not. Instead of a book about your conversion to Islam, we are getting a book about your disillusion with Islam, and acting as a mortgage house.*

*If you look at this from our point of view, we are going to end up with a book of your African travels which may not have a very wide appeal, for which we will have paid, by the time we're finished, an advance of £5,000. We'll then have to wait another four or five years for the book on Islam for which you'll obviously need another advance.*

*The time has come to ask straightforwardly when you plan to start writing the book on Islam and when you plan to finish it.*

*I may be wrong, but I believe there is an enormous difference between the levels of interest there will be in the two books. In Iran, Afghanistan and Pakistan you are caught up in world events and underwent a conversion. This is the seedbed for inspiring stuff. In the second book you travelled through a number of poor countries in Africa and underwent a process of disillusion. Forgive me, but this is different.*

*Come and have lunch on the 18th and let's talk about it.*

2001, an unsent letter... Nick thought better in person.

*I fear you think we are no longer friends because of the book, whether on Africa or Afghanistan, or rather the book that never was or could have been. This seems to me to be a pity and I hope you think so too. Whenever you're next in London would you like to come and have lunch? I talk to Kevin Rushby from time to time who gives me news of your wanderings.*

In late 2002 Nick made another attempt, an extended invitation to Bruce to stay at Fox Farm, while Liz (Nick's PA) would sit and transcribe the tales of his journey and of his thoughts. After around ten days of sitting in the huge armchair in the sun at Fox Farm, regaling Liz with his stories, Nick finally admitted defeat, returning instead to the great friendship he had missed.

# Recollections: returning to Afghanistan
## June 2006, Kabul

*This piece was written by* **Bruce** *for an intended new (2007 edition) of* Afghanistan: A Companion and Guide *published by Odyssey. Bijan Omrani told us, 'I remember when he actually handed over the original manuscript copy – Magnus and I went to meet up with him in a theatre in east London, where he was rehearsing a group of Persians for a performance of Persian poetry, in aid of Amnesty or another charity. When we walked in, a Persian girl was on stage, reciting Hafez. Bruce waited patiently for her to finish, then jumped up, gave a patient, pained and very forensic explanation of how the metre actually was meant to work, and then recited it himself, stunning the Persians with his pitch perfection and leaving them rather shamefaced at their own inadequate grasp of Persian prosody. His recitation was extraordinarily beautiful.'*

I transferred to Dubai's second airport for the connecting flight to Kabul; the waiting area filled with overweight, muscle-bound Americans, crew-cut or pony-tailed, looking like military sub-contractors or mercenary bounty-hunters. The Afghans seemed to be making an effort not to notice them: the teenagers too busy, in their uncertain approximations of Western fashion, trying to put a brave face on the inglorious condition of being refugees in west London or Cologne or Lille – they told me they were returning for some death or wedding in the family; the taut-faced woman I'd shared the taxi with boasted of her husband's profits from American building contracts and petrol-pump concessions and renting out luxurious villas; two older men, traditionally dressed in loose trousers and long shirt turned out to be Hazara menial workers returning from the Gulf oil states to their impoverished valleys north of the capital – the Qandahari white-on-white khamak-duzi embroidery as much a statement of social advancement for them as jeans for the urban teenagers! All invited me to visit them in their villas or villages.

On the creaking Aryana flight, middle-aged, badly shaven stewards showed the tenderest care for a hysterical little girl resisting her exhausted mother's efforts to calm her. Once we arrived, an elegant young couple headed straight for the German embassy. In the passport queue, an older American, of the lean and starched type I associate with pioneers and missionaries, told me at length how he was committing ten years of his retirement to working in Afghanistan: 'Four years down and six to go! Of course I make money, but I also employ Afghans. Look, we're helping this country – we've just built the biggest warehouse in Asia.' 'Who uses it?' 'Our American military, of course!'

The carpark inside the airport compound was a frenzy of vociferous taxi-drivers, so I turned my back on the freemarketeers, and walked out to hail a cheaper local taxi on the main road by a stall selling mangoes imported from Pakistan. We drove through the wealthier suburbs now occupied by Western troops, embassies and aid bureaucracies, whose presence was signalled by festoons of razor-wire over each wall and gateway, and by triple rows of concrete gabions which squeezed the traffic into a frustrated single-file trickle.

The old-fashioned guest house and courtyard garden I'd been recommended near the Passport Office was closed for redevelopment into a high-rise block of flats. Imported flush lavatories and washbasins spilled out in profusion onto the pavements from rows of shops; past the Silo grain depot, we passed stacks of sheet marble also imported from Pakistan – all part of the privately financed building boom affecting the city. A luridly decorated guest house down a sidestreet proclaimed the new money and the bad taste that had oozed in from the Gulf and Pakistan. The *chowkidar* guard was stacking metal grilles at the gate ready for making more concrete gabions to service the paranoia of the Western-alliance bureaucracy. He pointed down an unsurfaced dirt road, with open gutters clogged on either side, to a Muslim language school. 'Ask there!'

This quarter of the city consists in modest middle-class courtyard houses being rebuilt after the ravages of the *mujahideen* civil war which all but destroyed the capital after the Russian withdrawal. Before dusk, boys played cricket on the road, men gathered at the water pump, others wandered to the little mosque set into the perimeter wall of the university. I heard as much Pushtu as Dari Persian on the streets and in the local bakery and grocery. People were friendly but not intrusive.

My host, an experienced agronomist, lived in a low-walled compound belonging to the extended family of his Afghan business partner. Once through the green gates, I found myself in a garden full of hollyhocks and sunflowers, overlooked by small terraces. The family was sitting around the TV watching an Ismai'ili private news channel (the same business which controls most of the current cell-phone boom) showing more footage of more foreigners killing more Afghans in remote rural areas – 'Just like twenty years ago when the Russians were here!'

The electricity failed, interrupting the self-congratulatory televised carnage. Half-wild dogs paraded, scampering along the roofline under swaying, sighing trees in the fading light. A baby cried next door, sounds and smells of dinner being prepared also wafted over. Talk turned to the recent riots which had spread from the northern suburbs below the Khair Khana pass to the city centre. I later saw the damage done to accessible Western targets – the closed shops on the ground floor of the Agha Khan's Serena Hotel, the glass smashed and windows boarded up; the burned-out offices of the American aid agency Care International, roof buckled by fire. I was told that the riot had been sparked by an American military driver who had knocked down civilians with aggressive insolence and utter impunity (much the same grievances had fed discontent with the Shah's regime in pre-Revolutionary Iran, and similar incidents have been reported from Romania). Local outrage found a ready response among the poor Persian-speaking community who resented the waning influence of their representatives in the police and the army, and eagerly decried the foreign military occupation of their city, the corrupt and predatory puppet government. As a result, security measures for the foreign resident bureaucrats have tightened, and those responsible for rebuilding the country have retreated even further into their bubbles of unreality behind razor-wire and concrete gabions and high walls; meanwhile their Afghan counterparts vote with their feet and send their families to live in Dubai or Pakistan, and commute from there to work in the Kabul offices.

When I walked through the crowded street markets to the Pol-e Kheshti mosque, where I stopped to buy translucent greenish stone prayer beads from the mine near the Shah Maqsud shrine, the vendor commented: 'We don't see many of you foreigners walking about town anymore.'

The next day we drove out east of the city, past 'godam' warehouses and building-supply depots, then north following the sweep of mountains confining the Shomali plain, with a few nomads still herding their flocks towards the higher summer pastures. Outside the American Bagram airbase – notorious for the extra-judicial torture of uncounted Afghans – is the smugglers' market where, the day before, a car bomb had exploded. Today trade was as normal – mounds of military boots, shoes, trainers, army surplus clothes, knives, canned food, powders to expand your muscles, anything that had 'fallen off the back of a lorry'.

I stood at the door of one shop, absentmindedly fingering my prayer-beads, when an old Afghan asked for his son 'How much for the boots?' 'I'm sorry, I'm not the shopkeeper.'

Towards Istalif, tall plane trees rose above the orchards wherever the torrent was channelled into square boulder-lined pools. A large mound below a mosque was covered with rams' horns – the grave, we were told, of a saint who had tunnelled all the way to Ghazni and still gave relief to sufferers from toothache. Higher up, we came to a spring flowing beneath vast ancient plane trees in a narrow side valley: it is sacred to the 'green man' of fertility, Khwaja Khizr, who can be recognised, by the aspirants who come here at night, by his thumb which has no bones! So the young man told us, who had elected to be our guide for the morning and get away from the boredom of sewing endless leather jackets for some aid project. I had with me photographs taken fourteen years previously of a religious leader, a much-respected *mowlawi* who had invited me to feast on sweet white mulberries in his garden. The face was immediately recognised, but the *mowlawi* had recently died, so we found his son, who took me to offer prayers at his father's grave on the dry slopes above the village. He then invited our party into the same garden to sit on mats by the same water channel, while his children shook the trees to make the ripe mulberries fall onto sheets spread out below; they put them on wicker platters and lowered them into the cool flowing water to wash off the dust before serving. Another photograph found its model, a successful potter, now older, greyer, fatter, in a shop down on the lower outskirts of the potters' village: 'It's good that you've come back, that you've not forgotten us!'

Composting is a passion of my agronomist host; so, since handing over his fruit tree nurseries to the new government, he has started a trial composting project in Ghazni. Even the Emperor Babur mentions in his sixteenth-century memoirs that the thin, wind-eroded soil of Ghazni needs top-dressing every year. That laudable habit had fallen into abeyance, and meanwhile the town was choking with uncollected rubbish. It is reckoned that up to 30% of household waste in this area is biodegradable, so an efficient project to collect, sort and recycle the rubbish would leave not only cleaner and healthier urban areas, but also help stabilise and fertilise fragile agricultural soils.

The project sounded attractively low key, likely to benefit Afghan farmers, even if not corresponding to the high-profile, high-spending projects beloved of the big agencies who prefer accountable bricks and mortar to dot the landscape. I asked if we could go and have a look at the project. 'Of course we can go, but can we come back? Security is not good.' The ambassador who had agreed the initial modest funding of the project had announced his intention of formally inaugurating the project; the governor had prepared to receive him royally; hours before the visit he, perhaps sensibly, cancelled; the governor was put out, lost face, calling his failed guest a 'poltroon' or the Afghan equivalent!

In Ghazni we were received by the governor's young assistant, who confessed that the administration barely controlled the area five kilometres outside the town, and that the composting project would be exposed in case of attack. A large open hangar shaded a dozen young men and women, sifting and sorting the household waste of the town, their faces wrapped up against the dust they were raising with their spades. Having observed that a good part of the 30% biodegradable waste was not actually being separated for composting, I left my host to settle a labour dispute with his quarrelsome Hazaras, and went to pay my respects to Sultan Mahmud, the conqueror of India: the entrance to the tomb precinct was blocked by three American armoured personnel carriers, with soldiers peeping out covered in full body armour, padded carapaces, helmets, goggles – like space-age tortoises, not an inch of humanity, eyes or even skin, to be seen. 'How can hearts and minds ever work with such people in charge?' I wondered.

We went to a sidestreet in the market to buy vats of the local honey, and on to the shrine of the preeminent Sufi and Persian poet of the Ghaznavid period, Hakim Sana'i. As I finished the *fatiha* prayer over the grave, I notice a young man looking at me rather sharply. He came towards me: '*Shoma Bruce astid?*' Are you Bruce? 'I am.' He embraced me and explained that he used to come to my house in Peshawar fifteen years ago with his father, a *robab* player. He had now come to the shrine to seek help for his sick children.

So perhaps, I felt, in spite of an often brutal foreign military occupation, an unrealistic, top-heavy aid-bureaucracy, an embattled and ageing local administration, a precarious, inefficient and predatory government, a countryside resistant to centralised control, there is room for cautious hope. Perhaps, these fragile networks of friendship and recognition and personal trust can form a path for progress in difficult times. Certainly those foreigners I met who are still working with the Afghans after one or several decades, have networks of personal contacts which might allow them to be seen in their own right as friends of the Afghan people, not as mere pawns of current power politics.

# FREE-SCHOLAR, TRANSLATOR
# AND TEACHER

# Bruce in Kabul

**Thomas Wide** *is a curator, historian and translator. He lived in Afghanistan for several years where he worked as the Managing Director of the cultural heritage organisation Turquoise Mountain. He holds a D.Phil in Afghan history from Oxford University. He currently works at the V&A.*

> *Since brass, nor stone, nor earth, nor boundless sea*
> *But sad mortality o'er-sways their power,*
> *How with this rage shall beauty hold a plea,*
> *Whose action is no stronger than a flower?*

It was in the garden of the French Archaeological Mission (DAFA) in Kabul that I first heard Shakespeare's Sonnet 65. Bruce was in full swing, wandering through the small rose garden crisscrossed with concrete pathways, wrapped up in an oversized jacket with hood, something of the Derek-Jacobi-as-Cadfael about him, chattering away. It was my favourite kind of Kabul day: bright winter's sunshine, shockingly sharp light, a 'windless cold, that is the heart's heat' in T. S. Eliot's words.

Bruce recited the sonnet (or the first four lines at least, he couldn't remember the rest and we looked it up on my iPhone) as we looked up to the city walls visible from our spot in Shashdarak, our compound dwarfed by the ISAF military base behind us. The poem was a particular favourite he said, and that made sense to me. The Bruce I knew had such a strong sense of beauty and its fragility in the face of worldly force. The sonnet felt particularly apt for post-2001 Kabul, a place where civil war and a trillion-dollar foreign intervention had left an ancient capital disfigured by brain-grey concrete slabs, blank beige blast-walls, and red-and-white checkpoint signs.

Bruce was back in Kabul for just a few weeks, tidying up a 'little book' on the tombstones found scattered across several sites in Kabul's

Old City: Babur's Garden, Asheqan-o-Arefan, and the Mausoleum of Timur Shah. That little book, *Kabul: Elite Burials* and its sister work *Herat: Elite Burials* were the only books he ever published. Printed in Kabul in a run of only a few hundred copies, and distributed for free primarily within Afghanistan, they are now almost impossible to get hold of outside a few specialist libraries.

Despite their modesty of scale and distribution, these two books comprise an important body of work. Indeed, they have a claim to be the most valuable pieces of scholarship ever written on epigraphy in Afghanistan. They serve as essential documents of an element of Afghan cultural heritage almost completely unstudied and in serious danger of being lost. The books owe their genesis to the far-sightedness of an old friend of Bruce's, Jolyon Leslie, the heroic (though he would detest the term) former director of the Aga Khan Trust for Culture (AKTC). Bruce was invited in 2006 to visit an AKTC project, the magnificent restoration of Babur's Gardens in the west of the city. In typically Bruce-ish fashion, he had spent his time walking around the garden pointing out errors in the information panels and the mistaken orientation of certain relocated headstones and footstones. Jolyon called Bruce's bluff, asking him to come back to do a proper project of researching, documenting and analysing such graves. Over the following six years Bruce made several trips to Afghanistan, focusing first on the gravestones around the Gozargah shrine in Herat and then turning his attention to key sites in Kabul.

The books took a long time to write, and Bruce was his usual infuriating self: disappearing for long stretches of the day on trips to have beautiful clothes made by his favourite Kabuli tailor; not responding to emails for weeks as he disappeared on his travels. But it was worth the wait. The books are miniature masterpieces of meticulous scholarship, deep learning, and insight about life, art, memory, human love and human vanity. In cataloguing, describing, and transcribing the texts of dozens of gravestones of elite Afghans, stretching from the fifteenth to nineteenth centuries, Bruce offered the most comprehensive survey of the subject ever created, building on and far surpassing in detail and insight the only other significant work on the subject, Muhammad Ibrahim Khalil's *Resala-ye mazarat-e shahr-e-Kabul* (Kabul: 1339 HQ / 1960 AD).

The works offer so many insights in their brief pages. From an art history perspective, they illustrate how tombstones were a key medium for presenting the visual vocabulary of various Central and South Asian dynasties, most gloriously that of the Timurids and Mughals. Bruce also brilliantly traced the changing nature of this vocabulary, from the early Timurid designs to the new style of stela introduced by Mughal Emperor Jehangir (1569–1627) in the headstone he created for his great-grandfather Babur (1483–1530) and whose influence can be followed over the following two hundred years. From a cultural heritage perspective, Bruce's beautiful descriptions of these memorials – a headstone, for example, is topped with a flourish 'like a peacock's tail rustling open' – make us see anew the value of these endangered sites and should inspire us to seek their longterm preservation. From a socio-political and religious history perspective, these tombstones also have much to tell us about emotional attitudes to loss and death amongst elite Afghans of the period, the public practice of mourning and memorialisation, and the religious beliefs that underpinned it all. Of particular interest here is the frequent presence of verses from the Quran inscribed on headstones, something which today is shunned as 'un-Islamic' by many literalist Afghan clerics. By illustrating what Bruce called in his introduction to the Kabul volume the 'diversity of historical fact' as it relates to the use of Quranic verses on tombstones, Bruce was challenging the literalism of the present, and providing pathways to a more tolerant, inclusive form of Islam than that frequently practised today in Afghanistan. Bruce also noted in his introduction that the cataloguing and presentation of these beautiful and moving artefacts might also 'provoke a wider sense of responsibility for preserving the cultural heritage of a whole society.' His two books certainly do that and will be essential catalogues for future generations. While it is a common lament amongst Bruce's friends that he did not write more, let us pause for a moment and celebrate properly the superb work of published scholarship that he *did* complete.

The books are also testament to Bruce's modesty and generosity. The Herat book is described as being co-authored by Wahid Amiri and the Kabul book by Khadim Hussein, both young Afghan employees at AKTC. When I spoke to Wahid recently, however, he was at pains to point out that despite the co-author status it was Bruce who was very much the *ustad* [teacher] and Wahid the *shagerd* [student]. The whole project was – for Bruce – a teaching opportunity and he used his time in Herat and Kabul to train young Afghans in the technical skills of surveying, analysing calligraphic styles, reading faded stone-carved Arabic and Persian quotations, and the highly complex system of *abjad* dating used for the headstones. In Kabul, he ran workshops for Kabul University students, bringing them out to the graveyards and shrines on fieldtrips. Wahid was astonished not just by Bruce's learning but by his firsthand knowledge of so much of the country: 'it was fascinating to see an Englishman who knew all the places in Herat – and its surrounding rural areas too; of course, he knew it because he had been there in the times of the *mujahideen* [in the 1980s].' Wahid also felt deeply supported by Bruce: 'He so wanted me to learn this work so that in the future I could keep going on my own; he was my *ustad* [teacher] and *rahnama* [guide]'. The work was hard, with long hours as Wahid and Bruce moved slowly from gravestone to gravestone at the Gozargah Shrine in Herat. But Wahid recalls the time as *khaterat-e shirini* (sweet memories), with Bruce combining a seriousness of purpose with a delight in scandalous jokes, rude stories and plenty of silliness. Wahid remembers that, one day in Herat, a local government official named Agha Moftizadah came to try and stop their work, saying that they didn't have permission: 'Oh Brother, why don't you come and work with us rather than trying to stop us?' Bruce responded. 'You say your name is Moftizadah [son of a Mofti], but you're really more of a *moftkhor* [freeloader]!' This punning insult from Bruce somehow managed to defuse the situation, and they all ended up collapsing into laughter.

Bruce's support to Wahid, and to so many other young Afghans, stemmed from a firmly held belief that it was up to Afghans themselves to take charge of their own history and heritage. He was deeply sceptical of international 'expertise' and was highly critical of foreign interventions in Afghanistan, as elsewhere. He was not, however, an isolationist. For Bruce, human relations and friendship across difference were central to all meaningful activity, and this applied to international development and cultural heritage as much as his personal life. He was deeply sceptical of abstractions – he scorned the abstract processes of institutional frameworks and agreements that were peddled by governments, the universalizing language of 'core competencies' and 'transferable skillsets' used by institutions, the patronising development jargon of 'capacity building' or 'upskilling' so prevalent in Afghanistan at that time. For Bruce, everything was personal, everything was context-specific, everything was mutable and fragile and precious. One of Bruce's favourite books was Tolstoy's posthumous masterpiece *Hadji Murat*, the story of a charismatic Caucasian Muslim leader who ends up being betrayed and killed during the wars with Russia in the mid-nineteenth century. On Bruce's interpretation, Hadji Murat represented a world of honour, courage, courtesy and care which was swept away by a new colder, more corrupt, more cynical order, represented by imperial Russia. Bruce was always and for ever on the side of Hadji Murat.

Bruce came to stay with me in east London for a couple of days in September 2019. Idly wending our way, in a familiar pattern, up Brick Lane towards Leila's Café for lunch, we stopped off at the Brick Lane

Bookshop for a browse. Bruce was shortly off to the Caucasus for a tour, and we discussed suitable travel reading. He mentioned his love of *Hadji Murat*, and that made me think of my own favourite Tolstoy short story, *The Death of Ivan Ilyich,* which Bruce said he had not read. I bought him a copy. On 1 November I received a WhatsApp message: 'Your gift of Tolstoy's *Ivan Ilyich* was prophetic/diagnostic; ever since I'd fallen & broken 3 ribs, I had a dull pain: I heard yesterday that it's pancreatic cancer, far advanced, leaving me only a few months to live.' The parallels were uncanny. But where Ivan Ilyich was beset with rage and fear at his impending death, Bruce faced his death as he faced his life: with courage, honesty and love. A true *musafir* (traveller), I treasure the memory of my *ustad, bruce-e aziz.*

# Timurid epitaphs, harpsichord and saffron

**Andy Miller** *is an archaeologist and heritage specialist, having spent the last two decades engaged on cultural and conservation programmes throughout Afghanistan, Iraq, Kurdistan and south-east Turkey for UNESCO, the Aga Khan Trust for Culture and the British Museum.*

L ike many of his friends no doubt, my first encounter with Bruce was not a conventional one. Tasked with supporting a new consultant whilst working for the Aga Khan in Herat, we were introduced. Bruce, dashing and windswept (unusually sporting khaki and an old Hermès scarf rather than his usual more local attire), had been commissioned to produce a corpus on the 'political poetry on fifteenth–sixteenth-century carved gravestones', a somewhat niche but entirely fitting subject. Working together at the early fifteenth-century shrine within the  Abdullah Ansari Shrine Complex, the national staff were both fascinated and intrigued by this latter day Sufi mystic polymath from York… Completely engaged in the beauty of the carved tombstones and their complex  text, many hours were spent in the searing heat transcribing and recording, punctuated at weekends by the occasional jaunt to a remote shrine, holy hermit or monument hidden away in the countryside. Having the opportunity to spend time with Bruce in Afghanistan over many years offered the occasion for all sorts of sanctioned (and not so) encounters. Too many (and perhaps also too risqué) to recount here, whether it was sourcing honey from Nuristan in the bazaar, attending a clandestine poetry recital, or the endless search for a patient tailor, Bruce was engaging, stimulating and a constant surprise. Of course, the main reason I believe Bruce came to Kabul every year was to acquire a whole new wardrobe. The scourge of the tailors of the Old City, and with an eye for perfection and nouveau-orientalist chic, trips to choose cloth, fitting and alterations were numerous, rarely short, never straightforward, but always an adventure!

## *Post-conflict piano*

An accomplished pianist, Bruce was always on the look-out for the opportunity to play the piano in Kabul, not an easy task with the only two we knew of at the time (2010) being at the Serena Hotel and the German Embassy. One day in early summer, not many hours after a semi-botched grenade attack earlier that day, we found ourselves in the Serena, Bruce trying to make the best of the 'woefully out of tune' lobby piano. I am still not quite sure how we were able to visit so soon after the incident, not quite dust settling on the floor post-incident, but very close to that. A memorable afternoon listening to some beautifully performed Chopin, much to the surprise of many of the usual Serena clientele (stocky gentlemen in checked shirts sporting interesting body art). Some weeks later, again through Wannell guile and persuasion, I find myself acting as impromptu page-turner in the German Embassy. In the ambassador's absence we (Bruce) had been granted access to play the piano in his private quarters, in the bizarre setting of a beautifully decorated apartment within the heavily fortified embassy, itself nestled inside Kabul's 'Green Zone'. I think this was particularly pleasurable for Bruce. I believe he had performed here previously to a somewhat larger audience in the heady, formative 1980s.

## *Gatecrashing a Baroque flute masterclass*

Encounters with Bruce also extended to Europe in many unconventional guises. Invited to a mutual friend's wedding in the hill-top town of Cordes-sur-Ciel in the Occitanie, Bruce was charged with mastering the impressive, yet temperamental, early nineteenth-century organ as a central part of the wedding ceremony. It was originally from Notre-Dame (the organ, not Bruce) and hidden away in the loft high above the transept, requiring multiple mirrors to enable observation of the priest and ceremony below. My suggestion of using a mobile phone to text instructions (rather than mirrors and half-visible hand signals) was greeted with a look of incredulity and quickly dismissed. The performance was accomplished with the flair and aplomb one had come to expect and with only a modicum of heat- and fear-induced profanity, all contributing to a wonderful occasion.

Lunching with Bruce two days later I knew we were in for an unusual afternoon. We left the first venue after the owner refused to accommodate Bruce's specific lunchtime music requests. Setting off for a walk as the clouds opened, we found ourselves on the riverbank approaching a water mill, where Bruce had heard a rumour there was a musical recital taking place. Climbing a barbed-wire fence, ignoring the obvious *propriété privée* signs, traversing the riverbank, now both completely drenched by torrential rain, I expected to be shot by an angry shotgun-toting resident as we crept across formal lawns and knocked on the kitchen door. I would have given up on this course of action before the barbed-wire fence. To my astonishment, we were met by a delightful English woman, very surprised but enduringly polite in the way only perhaps the English could be in the circumstances, who explained that yes, there was an international historical flute masterclass being held at the mill, participants from around the world receiving instruction next door. Whether by chance or design the internationally renowned historic flautist, Georgia Browne, was running the course, Bruce adamantly claiming to have met her previously at the Romanian(?) Embassy in London some years earlier. Whether she remembered this encounter or not (and I think perhaps not), Georgia was extremely accommodating. Bruce was as charming (and musically knowledgeable) as ever, and we were welcomed in to dry off in front of the blazing medieval fireplace, at the back of the last session on baroque flute techniques, behind the now completely mystified participants, doubtless wondering who on earth we were.

### *Harpsichord and saffron*

Languishing in Richmond one late summer morning, assuming Bruce was leading a tour party in Baltistan, attending a poetry recital in Samarkand or gardening in York, I received a phone call out of the blue. 'Andy, I'm in Kew, come for Persian lamb'… Apparently a 'short-term' house guest (I assume the owners knew although I never met them), I find myself with Bruce in a stranger's kitchen, amidst the aromas of the Orient, Bruce producing saffron from a little pouch in his wallet, as one does of course. An enthusiastic and very accomplished cook, Bruce revelled in preparing such a delightful dish, only once interrupted by the teenage son of the hosts, apparently oblivious to the fact that Bruce was staying but seemingly undaunted that two strangers were cooking lunch in his parents' kitchen. An engaging and entertaining catch-up as ever, followed by an unexpected musical interlude. Bruce, having noticed his hosts possessed an antique harpsichord, promptly summoned his brother from the other side of London with cello, treating us all to a wonderful post-Persian lamb.

I quickly learnt that you should never, if at all possible, turn down an invitation from Bruce.

# A Sufi returns
## Oxford, 2015

**Fitzroy Morrissey**

A sign of success at the end,
Is the return to God at the beginning;
He who is illumined at the beginning;
Will be illumined at the end.

Ibn 'Atā' Allāh of Alexandria (d. 1309), *Kitāb al-hikam*

By temperament, learning, and experience, Bruce Wannell was a Sufi. (Indeed, it is perhaps more accurate to say that he was an āref – a purveyor of that heady and distinctively Persian blend of 'high' Sufism, Aristotelianism, and Twelver Shi'ism known as 'irfān.) As chair of the shortlived Oxford Society for Sufi Studies, therefore, I was delighted to invite Bruce to come and share some of his hikmat with us.

A date was set for June 2015. The idea was that Bruce and Robert Maxwell, with whom he'd recently published a volume of Persian poems, would come to Wadham, the centre of Persian studies in Oxford, to read and discuss some of the highlights of that collection. The meeting of the society was scheduled for the evening, but Bruce, as was his custom whenever he returned to Oxford, wished to take tea at the Randolph beforehand. Over Earl Grey with lemon, and cucumber and smoked salmon sandwiches, he held forth on the Sufi doctrine of *insān-e kāmel* (the 'perfect man'), the difference between *fanā' fī'l-shaykh*, *fanā' fī'l-rasūl*, and *fanā' fi'llāh* (respectively, mystical 'annihilation' in the Sufi guide, in the Prophet, and in God), the deeply held Sufi proclivities of Ahmed el-Tayeb, Grand Imam of al-Azhar, and the sayings of 'Hazrat 'Ali'. As Bruce glided seamlessly from one topic to another (as if trying to prove the Sufi principle that all things are connected) one sensed that his insight, as traditional Islamic education required, was derived less from books than from direct 'audition' of living Sufi masters.

Finally we moved on to Wadham. On arrival, Bruce decided that both the subject matter and the balmy summer's evening demanded that we decamp from the sterile seminar room that I'd booked to the Fellows' Garden. Once there, he suggested we arrange ourselves into a circle – again emulating Islamic educational practice.

'One may call the master of a gathering the 'pole' (*qotb*) of that gathering,' writes the great Sufi Ibn 'Arabi, and Bruce was certainly the *qotb* of our gathering that evening. He chose two poems from the collection to recite in his perfectly polished Persian. The first, by the fourteenth century Aleppan poet Shah Ne'matollah Vali, eponym of the popular Ne'matollahi order (today headquartered in Notting Hill and Banbury), contained a classic statement of the Sufi doctrine of *wahdat-ul-wojūd* (the unity of existence) – 'O seeker, is any creature devoid of truth? No! / As a true mystic, in all things, seek out the truth' – as well as a bombastic claim on the poet's part to be the 'pole' of the universe, the 'perfect man' embodying all of the divine attributes. The second was by the early modern poet Bidel, the chief exponent of the so-called *sabk-e hindi* ('Indian style') of Persian poetry, reflecting Bruce's particular fondness for the Persianate culture of India and Afghanistan. (In his last lecture in Oxford, he encouraged students to delve into the relatively unexplored world of Indo-Persian literature.) Reading them back now, the Indian poet's verses take on an added poignancy:

You have not studied the world:
Take a step out of yourself
If you transcend yourself.
You will reach everywhere.

As your body wearies and fades, Bidel,
Let this be sufficient grace,
That you reach a discerning ear
Like a distant echo's trace.

Before he left, Bruce signed my copy of his book – 'with thanks and admiration', he kindly wrote. The feeling was certainly mutual.

# … and then from his cape pulled out a box of fresh Yorkshire butter, French cheese and some homemade apricot jam
## *Notting Hill, 2017*

**Moin Mir** *is a writer born and raised in India but based in London. He is the author of* The Prince Who Beat the Empire *and co-author of* Mirza Ghalib and the Mirs of Gujarat. *He is currently writing a book set against the backdrop of Sufism.*

### 1817, The Red Fort, Delhi

The weak and penultimate Mughal Emperor of Hindustan Akbar Shah II lounging on his throne issued a *Sanad* in Persian with the sanction of the all-powerful East India Company and the Jam (Maharaja) of Nawanagar in Gujarat. Standing before the Emperor was the nobleman who was being decorated – Sayyid Mir Sarfaraz Ali Khan, a descendant of the Prophet whose ancestors had been at the Imperial court for centuries. On him were bestowed the lands that ran along the river Badar in Kathiawar, Gujarat and the small town of Kamadhia as an Imperial Grant. Subsequently, the East India Company recognised Kamadhia as a princely state and since then that *Sanad* has been in my family for seven generations.

### 2017, 110 Palace Gardens Terrace, Notting Hill, London

Exactly 200 years later as I was researching my book *The Prince Who Beat the Empire* I looked closely at a copy of the *Sanad* my father had emailed me, desperately trying to study it and understand each detail. The last to speak Persian in my family was my grandfather's brother. After him all of us spoke Urdu and English. Persian, which had been our language for generations, was lost to us. Every line I tried to read only took me to the doors of frustration and up went my hands in utter despair. It was then that I thought of Bruce Wannell and our first meeting a few years ago. It was summer and I had been introduced to him by James

Mallinson, a scholar and friend, at a book launch. My first impressions of this rather fragile looking, high-cheekboned man with piercing blue eyes were of immediate curiosity and fantasy. That evening he was dressed in a green Afghan cape similar to the one Hamid Karzai wore and what we would call in Urdu *deewar topi* or the high-walled woollen cap. 'How fascinating,' I had thought to myself, 'here in the heart of London to encounter such a man.' Bruce and I spoke about everything that dazzled us about the Orient amid the chattering and clamouring crowd. We seemed lost in the world of Herat, then Isfahan and Delhi. Like birds we flew from one city to another oblivious to the peak and the end of the evening. Before he left Bruce had mentioned he did translation work as a profession and had scribbled his details and thrust them in my hand. Now, sitting at my desk, I looked for his details in the drawers and card holders. When I eventually found them, I wasted no time in calling him. Almost immediately he recognised me. 'Moin *Jaan*,' he said ('*Jaan*' being an address of endearment in Persian and Urdu). 'Bruce, I need your help in translating a Persian *Sanad*. Can you please help me?'

'Well, I'm in London today and off to York tomorrow… might not be back for a while.' Then, almost as if he thought I'd lose interest, 'But I can come today and see you wherever you are!'

'Today?' I almost thought it to be an imposition.

'Yes.'

'Uh…Alright…I'm in Notting Hill do you think…'

'That's fine. I'll see you in two hours.'

'…well alright see you then.'

Bruce entered my apartment at 6 p.m. sharp dressed in a flowing white cape and a light grey *deewaar topi*. Leonie, who was my fiancée then, couldn't take her eyes off this extraordinary man as he played with his rings, looked around the living room and then from his cape pulled out a box of fresh Yorkshire butter, French cheese and some homemade apricot jam. Almost instantly he had charmed Leonie. We spread out the copy of the *Sanad* on the dining table and like a bee attracted to a flower Bruce moved towards it. I could see his eyes light up when they fell on the beautiful Persian script. Each letter felt the love of Bruce Wannell's meticulous studying gaze. His fingers flowed under each line and then like a magician from the Orient he swished his cape, reached deep within and pulled out a magnifying glass. His love for the language was so evident as he refused drink or food till he had got the translation right. He muttered to himself, then shook his head, scribbled away, looked closer, gasped in frustration, yelped in joy and finally rose from the desk and embraced me. The translation had been done. It was midnight by now and Bruce had worked non-stop for six hours.

I insisted we break for dinner and at 12:15 a.m. we had supper. Kebabs from a nearby Persian restaurant and saffron rice followed by the delicious French cheese he had brought. At that moment of sharing a meal both Bruce and I knew we would become good friends. Before he left he looked at me, at the *Sanad* and then gently caressing a finger over the seal of Emperor Akbar Shah II he said, 'Moin *Jaan,* keep this safe with you. It will in time be a guarantor for your lands, for it clearly says they must be in your family for generation and generation'. As I waved him goodbye, Bruce in his white cape resembled a pearl disappearing into the dark night.

We met regularly after that. We recited Hafez together. We got drunk on the verses of the Sufis. We recited Saadi together. We got lost in discussion on the tilework of Samarkand. We recited Sanaai and we realised we had a special friendship. Like most people, the last time I saw Bruce was at the opening of Willy Dalrymple's fabulously curated show 'The Forgotten Masters'. Bruce came up to me, took off his *deewar topi* and placed it on my head. 'It suits you better Moin *Jaan*,' he said with premonition in his voice. Those were his last words to me. I thought he might leave me with the cap. But he didn't. And rightly so. Towards the end of the evening he came and took it off me and left with a wink. *Shab-ba-Khair Dost*. Good night my friend.

# Whenever our paths crossed

**Tahir Shah** *is the author of forty books, many of which seek to lift the veil on the hidden layers of societies through which he travels. Spanning fiction and non-fiction, and bridging East with West, his work is regarded as especially original. He is currently working on the fourth novel in his* Jinn Hunter *series.*

Everyone knew Bruce Wannell, but at the same time I feel as though none of us really knew him at all.

On my travels he popped up in the most unlikely places. From the tribal wildlands of northern Pakistan, to the baked red deserts outside Marrakech; and from the sweltering jungle of the Yucatan, to the serene crescents of Georgian Bath. Each time we met, I glimpsed a little more of his life, viewed through whom he knew and how he knew them.

Someone once wrote of the other great Bruce (Chatwin) that 'he was always leaving or about to arrive.' The line described both Bruces perfectly.

Whenever our paths crossed, Bruce would ask what I was up to.

As I spewed a tidal wave of ideas, encounters, and adventures, he would listen in a way that no one ever listened to anything I say. When he listened it was as though the world around us was paused freeze-frame.

Listening was only one of Bruce's many talents.

An even greater one was giving advice at the exact moment it was needed.

The best example I can remember was when Bruce turned up by chance on a Sunday morning in London's East End. His appearances were always by chance. Twenty years ago I was living in a little Georgian house in Whitechapel, under the Air Ambulance helicopter. Bruce seemed intrigued that anyone could withstand such a deafeningly loud background to life.

He suggested we go for a walk.

During the promenade through streets piled high with ripped black sacks of rubbish, I spewed the latest instalment in my encounters and adventures.

As usual, Bruce listened.

I told him how I'd recently studied magic with the godmen of India, searched for King Solomon's gold mines in Ethiopia, and taken Ayahuasca with a former head-shrinking tribe.

Suddenly, Bruce grabbed my arm.

I stopped walking, and talking, and peered into his eyes.

That moment is burned into my memory. For the first time in our friendship it was *my* turn to listen.

Looking at me hard, Bruce said: 'Never be afraid to embrace the ordinary.'

Washing over me like a bucket of ice water, the advice was what I'd waited to hear my entire adult life.

I've never allowed it to leave my mind.

Like a key that can open the most impossibly secure lock, it's enabled me to glimpse something more extraordinary and precious than anything else...

The ordinary.

# Bruce at Galle
*Sri Lanka, 2018*

**Razeen Sally** *is half Sri Lankan and half British. He is a professor at the National University of Singapore, having previously taught at the LSE. His book* Return to Sri Lanka: Travels in a Paradoxical Island, *is published by Juggernaut.*

On a hot afternoon in late January 2018, I made my way down Galle Fort's narrow lanes to Southlands College, hard by the western ramparts. In the large school hall a panel on translation had just begun. A Sri Lankan professor at a US liberal arts college talked about translating Homer's Odyssey for his philosophy class. Then a German who had written a novel about Kafka spoke. And then a Swiss-French translator from Geneva. But the panel's moderator talked most, a silver-haired, trim-bearded sixtysomething with a pukka English accent, precise diction and a rich verbal repertoire.

He mentioned a stone slab Admiral Zheng He brought to Sri Lanka in 1417 on one of his voyages from China. It had lettering in three scripts – Chinese, Tamil and Farsi – and was presented to the Vishnu temple in Dondra, farther down the coast from Galle. He said something about the Farsi script, and emphasised Farsi's far-flung influence over centuries as a trade language. That fixed my attention, for I had seen this object in the National Museum in Colombo. Here, if you like, was a choice specimen of premodern Chinese 'soft power': a Ming dynasty, Chinese Muslim naval superstar gifted a stele in three trade languages to a Buddhist temple honouring a Hindu god.

The Zheng He stele gave me a pretext to engage Bruce in conversation after the panel discussion ended. Half an hour later he was still talking, non-stop, on the steps of Amangalla. I always thought of this huge pile as the dear old NOH (short for New Oriental Hotel), Sri Lanka's oldest hostelry dating back to Dutch times, where I had stayed often as a child. I told Bruce I was desperately keen to attend his travel-writing workshop at Amangalla the next morning, but it was fully subscribed. 'Oh I think we can fix that, dear boy,' he said, tapping me lightly on my arm. 'Just come along at nine in the morning.'

Just before 9 a.m., in Amangalla's lounge full of Dutch period furniture, there was Bruce playing something complex on the grand piano. He was wearing his glasses and totally absorbed; sweat streamed down his face and soaked his white linen shirt. Ten minutes later he appeared in the little library at the back of the hotel, joining the ten or so participants in his travel-writing workshop.

An hour-and-a-half passed in a flash. It was a masterclass, delivered in Bruce's flawless slowmotion English. He introduced three of his favourite travel books – Nicolas Bouvier's *L'Usage du Monde* (*The Way of the World* in the English translation), Norman Lewis's *Naples '44* and Peregrine Hodson's *Under a Sickle Moon* – extracting lessons from each for the aspiring travel writer. He engaged each of us, gently and patiently, to talk about our travel-writing interests, and encouraged us to overcome our inhibitions and write our stories. He fed off our remarks to make his larger points. He mentioned his own travels occasionally. And gave us his key tips. Think of your experiences that might be significant to readers. Read your writing out loud: *hear* what you write. Read old travel writing; some of it is still alive. Don't talk down to the reader. Don't dumb down. Expect the highest of your readers. Turn the abstract into the concrete, liveable and accessible. Use the techniques of fiction – character, plot, pace – to sharpen your material. Think of your model writers as a start to finding your voice. Use your travel writing to refine your sense of identity. Read widely.

It was a mesmerising performance, rich and subtle, and seemingly effortless. I felt as if my more than quarter-century reading of travel literature had been distilled into this ninety-minute essence.

Later that day, Bruce gave a lecture to a full house on his travel experiences in Iran, Afghanistan and Pakistan. It was in a marquee, just outside the Old Gate of the fort, with the British coat of arms and 'Anno 1659' inscribed above the arch of the outer wall, and the Dutch East India Company's coat of arms on the inner wall.

He spoke for forty-five electrifying minutes. About Isfahan when the revolution broke out in '79. How his students refused to denounce him – an example of the decency, friendliness and grace of ordinary Iranians. Mountain trekking and drinking Russian vodka to wash down Iranian flatbread. Driving his best friend's putrefying corpse from Tehran. The death threat issued by Gulbuddin Hekmatyar's *mujahideen* when he was in Peshawar. His treks on foot and horseback through wartime Afghanistan. How his guide was killed a few feet in front of him. Treating badly wounded Afghan villagers with his kit of painkillers. The unbounded hospitality of Afghan villagers, despite their deprivation and brutalization.

He ended in the best tradition of English travel: soaking himself in a hot bath in Herat after a fortnight without washing, with shells flying all around, saying his mental thankyous to those who had been good to him in case this was to be his last bath. His final words rang as clear as a bell in a forest hermitage: 'Be open to travel, for minor miracles will happen to you.'

On Christmas Day 2019, I texted him excitedly from Bogowantalawa, the 'golden valley' of Ceylon tea. I had just been to the grave of Julia Margaret Cameron, a mid-nineteenth-century pioneer of photography, and his friend William Dalrymple's ancestor, who lived out her days in Ceylon. She and her husband lie side-by-side next to a simple little Anglican church surrounded by tea bushes. He texted back, saying he looked forward to our meeting in York in June, 'unless my pancreatic cancer carries me off before... Keep well, dear friend. LB.'

# Someone I needed in my life
## *Wigmore Hall, 2010*

**Richard McClary** *left behind his life in the mountains of British Columbia in 2010 to study Islamic art and architecture in the UK. After an MA at SOAS and a PhD in Edinburgh, he is now a lecturer at the University of York. Throughout this whole process Bruce was an endless source of advice, support, and, most importantly, friendship.*

Having spent many years living in a very rural community in the foothills of the Rocky Mountains in western Canada, and travelling in the winter months to a wide range of countries across the Islamic world to document surviving examples of medieval Islamic architecture, in the spring of 2010 I finally decided to leave my old life behind and move to London in order to embark on a Masters degree in Islamic Art and Archaeology at the School of Oriental and African Studies. After spending so long in a part of the world that was, while incredibly beautiful, somewhat devoid of culture and intellectual stimulation, the opportunity to live in Pimlico for a year meant that I was able to spend many evenings attending concerts across the city, especially at the Barbican and the Wigmore Hall. One evening, while settling in to listen to what turned out to be a rather pedestrian Monteverdi concert, I turned to the pair of well-turned-out gentlemen to my left and struck up a conversation. They asked if I was a music student, to which I replied no, I am studying Islamic art. Both of their faces lit up, and immediately with a flourish of his left hand, one of them pulled a packet out his jacket pocket and announced: would you like some nougat, I just bought it in the market in Isfahan this morning. I knew immediately that this was someone I needed in my life, and after the concert Bruce, George Michell, and myself went to a nearby Carluccio's and spent the rest of the evening discussing our shared passions for the Islamic world. We exchanged numbers, and as a result of this chance encounter I met someone who was to become a very close friend, a most kind, generous, and exacting mentor, and the person who was responsible

155

for a huge amount of translations of the Persian inscriptions in not only my doctoral thesis, but several subsequent books and articles. We went on to meet regularly, be it in London, Ullapool, Fife, Edinburgh or, most memorably, chatting late into the night in his attic room in York, discussing everything from Iranian politics to the finer points of tree felling. We never had the chance to explore Afghanistan together, which is a country close to both our hearts, but Bruce inspired me to travel further into Central Asia and Iran, and we spent a great deal, but not nearly enough, time together over the last ten years. After his diagnosis I was so touched and felt it a great honour when he asked me to be his executor and to help plan his memorial. While there are many of his friends who knew him for far longer, and travelled with him in far more exotic locales, he asked me to contribute this specific anecdote to this volume a few hours before he died, as he lay in pain, but beatific and at peace. I kissed him on the head and told him I would do my best to honour his wishes. We shall not see his like again.

# Editing Bruce
*York*

**Bijan Omrani** *edits* Asian Affairs *and is the author of various books on Asian and classical Roman history. He is a trustee of the Royal Society for Asian Affairs, the co-director of the Shute Literary Festival, and writes for the* Literary Review.

I first met Bruce many years ago at his house in York. As a young editor, I had been commissioned to work with him on a guidebook to Iran. All I had been told of Bruce beforehand was that he was a formidable scholar, and a convert to Islam. I was therefore slightly puzzled when his opening gambit was to offer me a Kir Royale cocktail, during Ramadan, at lunchtime.

This sort of greeting was typical of Bruce: unexpected, and generous; ebullient, and yet refined. He was soon in his garden, harvesting salad for lunch, his discourse jumping all the while between Sufism, the Quran, the cultivation of herbs, a concert of Persian music he had recently held in the garden, and a harpsichord recital he had recently led in York. Within a few minutes, I understood that it was going to be a privilege to know Bruce. Seeing him then as I was, a young person just out of university, he was for me the paradigm of the renaissance man: the scholar and traveller, untrammelled by convention, an aesthete and *bon-viveur*, who knew how to reconcile good living with a deep and transcendent spirituality.

It was never possible to keep up with Bruce's perfectionism, or his talent to generate the unexpected. As a houseguest whilst working on the Iran guide, although offered a bed he insisted on sleeping on a Persian carpet, 'like a dervish'. His irrepressible flow of knowledge – architecture, food, film, calligraphy, ethnography, religious history – was only put on hold when he went off to play Bach partitas on my moth-eaten piano. The only thing to wind him to a standstill like a cat chasing a feather was the challenge of creating an infallible scheme for the transliteration of Farsi. This led to the first manifestation that I saw

157

of a very Bruce-ish habit: downing tools to email or telephone a world expert for their opinion, which he would then relentlessly critique: Professor X's advice on transliteration, was 'good, but some of his policies (Tehrananizing an already turkicized Arabic) lead to monstrous hybrids like *torbe*, *hekme*, *monkez men al-zalal*, etc, which elicit at best a "double-take".'

Indeed, it was rarely possible to keep up with Bruce *per se*. His scattered communications, received from him on the road whilst on the way to or from absolutely wherever – Yerevan, Chanderagore, the Carinthian Alps, Al-Ahwaz, Susa, Choqa Zanbil, were always a source of joy. 'I'm enjoying perfect weather in Islamabad, aka Islam-les-Bains.' An email postcard from Afghanistan: 'We landed at Kabul on fire, the firemen covered us in foam, and we got out by the back exit down a slide – none of the other 5 was working – and now another bomb has just gone off next to Ministry Interior / Indian embassy, windows rattled and huge dust cloud from beyond the Asma'i mountain. Meanwhile I'm getting on with calligraphy and epigraphy... I'm also tutoring some callligraphers from the university and giving a public lecture in the restored domed tomb of Timur Shah before flying to Herat for more Timurid tombstones.' These emails from the road were often accompanied by gloriously recondite invitations or requests for scholarly information: to join him at a 'Mongol handbag exhibition... not as frivolous as it sounds'; a lecture he was giving at SOAS on the *Jawaher Nama*; questions about references from Pausanias and Diodorus of Sicily; 'I'd be grateful if you could find out if there's anything left of Sayyid Ali Hamadani's tomb-shrine in Kulab – he died on the way back from Kashmir to Samarkand in the C14th – after spreading Iranian arts in those parts, as well as Sufism, of course...'

Later ending up for a time as a schoolmaster, I was able to introduce Bruce to a number of schools as a lecturer. His visits have never been forgotten. At Eton, the Persian phrase *chiz nist* (it's nothing) is still a catchphrase amongst various beaks and old boys, thanks to a poetry reading he gave there. Also invited to judge and present an essay prize there – a ceremony which conventionally is conducted in dark academic gowns – Bruce turned up in a particoloured Bukharan silk *khalat*; jumping in his speech from Persian, to Turkish, to Arabic, no-one regretted granting him that licence. At dinner afterwards, for variety, he fell into conversation with a modern-languages beak, and sat reciting large chunks of St John of the Cross to him, in Spanish. At Wellington College, by contrast (his old school, which he esteemed greatly) he set off the fire alarm at breakfast after an absent-minded encounter with a toaster; whilst the entire school scattered in confusion from the dining halls, Bruce sat magisterial and unmoved at the scene in the gathering cloud of smoke, savouring his coffee.

We shall miss his house visits – his perfectly judged presents of Indian circus lanterns for the children and tea 'from my favourite tea merchant in Delhi'; his endless food-related quests: 'my dear, do you have some fresh sage? My absolutely favourite new breakfast is to fry some sage leaves in butter, and then an egg on top – it's divine' (cue a hopeless 7 a.m. hunt through our garden, and then our neighbours' gardens, for a sage bush which was never to be found); or through the grocers' of several towns in a hunt for broad beans at the end of the season to make *baghali pilao* – when some elusive beans were eventually tracked down, the extended family were sat around a garden table laboriously to shell them, in imitation, he explained, of Persian social custom when making such a dish; it was, when finally produced, a most excellent dinner.

We shall miss his friendship, his conversation, his learning, his talent for the unexpected, his tailoring, and his rare spirit. If he possessed erudition in abundance, he also possessed humility. After the Iran guide was published, he emailed a short request about his author biography, which had not been run by him before printing: 'I'm a little embarrassed to be trumpeted as an EXPERT on anything at all, let alone on anything as elusive and complex as Islamic mysticism/Sufism, where it would count as the height of bad manners to claim to "know it all" – which I certainly don't.' Perhaps this was so, but if there was anyone who could know it all, and feel it all, Bruce was certainly the closest.

# Meet at Rustem Pasha

**Janet and Paul Starkey** *live in the Scottish Borders. They have known Bruce since 1980; travelled and lived in the Middle East for many years; and have published extensively on travellers to and from the Middle East. Janet was a lecturer on the Anthropology of the Middle East at Durham University. Paul is Emeritus Professor at Durham University, Chair of ASTENE and of the Banipal Trust for Arab Literature, and until 2018 was Vice-President of the British Society for Middle Eastern Studies (BRISMES).*

In Islington in the spring of 1980, Janet's cousin, Ian Blois, who had just returned from a year in Australia and New Zealand, introduced us to Bruce as they had been at Wellington College together. Bruce was recently back in London after leaving his teaching jobs in the University of Isfahan and later the British Council following the Iranian Islamic Revolution which broke out in January 1978.

We had much in common with Bruce: Janet had led a somewhat nomadic existence around the Middle East for several years, but by 1980 was running the first computer project on the ethnographic collections at the British Museum and Museum of Mankind. Paul had studied Arabic and Persian at Oxford, had recently completed a D.Phil on Tawfiq al-Hakim for which he had lived and researched in Egypt, and by then was a Principal with the Treasury. Both of us had travelled widely in the Middle East, including (in Paul's case) Iran and Afghanistan. With so much in common we became lifelong friends, meeting in unusual places, exchanging postcards, and comparing experiences of places and people. Bruce was a regular visitor at our home in Islington as we lived near him; and he would attend parties with friends from the British Museum and enjoy dinners with us too. We heard many times of his unhappiness about working for the Inland Revenue. Like us, he had taken the civil service exams in the hope of getting into the Foreign Office: Janet too had been offered a post in the Inland Revenue which she almost instantly declined, while Paul was anxious to move back into the academic world — a move he achieved when we moved to the University of Durham in late 1983.

We also met Bruce in the Middle East itself. In the summer of 1983, we had driven to Istanbul and then along the Black Sea before turning inland to go on to Konya. We had arranged to meet Bruce at the Rüstem Paşa Mosque near the Mısır Çarşısı (spice bazaar) in Istanbul at 3 p.m. to celebrate his birthday on 25 August with, as we eventually remembered, his instructions for Paul to climb its twisty stairs from the Hasırcılar Çarsisi (straw mat weaver's market). We had bought a *rabab* as a birthday present for him and a couple of instruments for Paul's collection too. Mid-August in Anatolia can be punishing: rapidly running behind schedule, with hail, rain and thunderstorms that were so violent that we had to pull off the road several times until the worst had subsided, it was a stressful journey and the ferry crossing to Europe (there was no bridge then) was rough. We eventually arrived at the mosque several hours late — but Paul was relieved by the sight of Bruce sitting chatting to the imam and other worthies about aspects of Muslim tradition — as he had presumably been doing for several hours. Once reunited, we inevitably all had to dine in a certain fish restaurant under the Galata Bridge nearby that he particularly favoured. Bruce was staying in a flat just north-west of the Pera Palace Hotel and lent it to us after he left on his own adventures. It had an impossibly inadequate water supply, but he explained that when necessary he simply dropped into the Pera Palace for the odd shower, tea and coffee, in true Bruce freeloading style.

We would go for long cycle rides across the fens from our cottage in Swaffham Prior to Ely in the 1980s and strenuous walks in the hills around Weardale once we moved to Durham. It was just after his return from eight months in Peshawar and Afghanistan that Bruce undertook a major three-year tour around the Mediterranean to learn Arabic, visiting Egypt, Sudan, Ethiopia and Yemen as well as other parts of North Africa. We were always sent postcards from places he visited where he would inevitably encounter our old friends and acquaintances along the way. Our daughter, Katie, then about fourteen years old, remembers with horror an occasion when Bruce had just returned from one of his expeditions and took her to the Guide and Scout shop in Durham to buy hiking socks — for which, to the immense confusion of the elderly lady assistant, he tried to barter. On another occasion, Bruce with Katie and Anderson Bakewell were striding across farmland at a rapid pace, in complete disregard of any trespass laws. The expedition came to an abrupt conclusion when they were confronted by an irate farmer brandishing a loaded gun and threatening to shoot them if they did not get off his land that instant. Bruce inevitably calmly talked their way out of the episode.

Bruce stayed with us during the eighth Royal Anthropological Institute Film Festival that we organised for Durham University in 2003 and enjoyed viewing many of the films, not least *The Kabul Music Diary* made by John Baily, now Emeritus Professor of Ethnomusicology at Goldsmiths College, London. With Bruce's help, Baily collected, preserved and performed Afghan music in its diaspora whilst music was banned in Afghanistan by the Taliban. Sometimes, Bruce would entertain visiting musicians and invite us to concerts, though we could not always attend. With his profound understanding of classical Persian poetry and Islamic mysticism, Bruce translated poems by Rumi and his beloved Hafiz for John and on his return would discuss their finer literary points with Paul.

Occasionally, after he settled in York, we would visit him there for meals in his house, and we particularly recall the haunting music performed at his fiftieth birthday party there. We were part of Bruce's northern or Scottish circuit any year he was in the UK, and he would usually try to make a visit coincide with the Paxton Music Festival. Schedules were at first arranged with his little black book: 'Do you mind if I use your phone to arrange my next visit with x or y?' or more recently with his mobile phone and its extensive lists of contacts. Our son also likes to remember him at Ednam House Hotel in Kelso, when Bruce was attending Neil and Jane Stratton's wedding and came down for breakfast in this rather grand hotel attired in a splendid robe and slippers to the amazement of other guests.

For several years, Bruce would time his visits so that he could give a lecture on Afghanistan on Janet's Anthropology of the Middle East course at Durham University and enthral another generation of enthusiasts with details of life with its peoples, music and places. He attended several lectures and conferences we gave around the UK and in 2001 gave a paper on 'Ventur de Paradis: Reports from Tunis' at the ASTENE conference in Edinburgh. Inevitably, someone in the audience had benefited from his kindness or had been helped with Persian translation by Bruce. Whenever they met, Paul and Bruce would discuss the finer points of Persian and Arabic literature, cultures and translations and ponder on matters of Islamic mysticism. He was particularly proud of his collection of translations of *Persian Poems* he produced with Robert Maxwell in 2012. Whenever he came to stay, he would produce whatever text he was reading or translating, to discuss it at length before settling down to play piano duets and enjoy good food. Always, as so many others recall, bearing some exquisite gift: homemade jams, walnut bread, honey.

We have always enjoyed travelling long distances to remote places, but wherever we went around the Middle East we would inevitably return to discover that Bruce had been to the same places before us, or else was about to visit and needed some tips to help him enjoy the place more. He often had an extra snippet about a location we had only partly explored or with amazing recall could provide details of relevant places, people, histories and travel lore. Thus, it was no surprise to receive a WhatsApp message from Bruce after we had arrived in Bishkek in September 2019 to begin a marathon drive through Kyrgyzstan, Kazakhstan, Uzbekistan and Tajikistan: 'Good morning, dear Janet and greetings from Daghestan. Don't miss the wonderful early Scythian petroglyphs just north of Issyk Kul. Happy travels LB' and attaching two images. We were then by chance sitting on the shores of Issyk Kul.

He was just then near the end of a tour of the Northern Caucasus, Sochi to Makhachkala, when he wrote:

… some magnificent landscapes & wonderful hospitality. Hope to see the Sasanian walls of Darband tomorrow LB

PS a lot has been rebuilt/over-restored/sanitised/securitised, but some parts are still worth seeing: I like the drive over the Takhta Qaracha pass to Shahr-i Sabz, don't miss the original turquoise glazed tile flooring described by Clavijo.

Also the open-air shrine of the Naqshbandi Khwaja Ahrar, the giant Qur'an stand for the Umar Aqta/Baisunqur copy which now stands in the courtyard of the Bibi Khanum Mosque, the blue raisins mayviz from the farmer's market next door, & the magnificent Soghdian wallpaintings @ Afrasiyab: the reconstructed paper mill nearby on the Kan-i Gil meadow is also quite interesting LB

The 3 states south of the Caucasus are bigger & rather more independent, though still precarious. I wonder whether a loose federation within an overarching system with a common language is not slightly better than fragmentation into unviably small units – providing the centre is benign rather than brutal…

A message in early January leaves nothing more to be said:

Thank you, dear Janet

Yes, life does occasionally ambush us, & death too… at least I've been given a few months to prepare, & the new painkillers seem to be working. It also gives me the chance to thank you & Paul for the friendship & many interests we've shared since first meeting in Islington over 40 years ago Iraq fascinating but ravaged.

Let's meet soon

LB

# Lothians to Lahore
## *2011*

**Isabel Buchanan** *is a barrister. She is the author of* Trials: On Death Row in Pakistan *(2016) and a contributing author to* Protecting Children in Armed Conflict *(2018).*

Directions to find a teacher of Indian classical dance and her liberal lawyer husband, to the 'best qawwali singing of the sub-continent', to the home of a recently unwell writer and a recently deceased musician, and to Basant parties on the roof of a haveli in the Kashmiri Mahalla; with love from Tehran and an apology that whilst travelling he didn't have his address book to hand. So Bruce Wannell sent me from the Lothians to Lahore. The journey – taken aged twenty-three as a recent law school graduate, moving to Pakistan to apprentice myself to death penalty defence lawyers at the Lahore High Court, and my first time away from lowland Scotland – was peppered with further instructions. Received while waiting for my connecting flight in Doha: 'Don't miss the Wazir Khan mosque, the Gulabi Bagh gateway, the interior of Ali Mardan Khan's tomb (and all the waterworks he designed after defecting from the Safavids) … the angel paintings in the Musamman Burj of the Fort … the tile mosaic animals on the exterior wall above the ditch, and the Austrian oil painting of Bahadur Shah Zafar'; not to mention the more elusive 'pool where Biruni measured the curve of the earth while accompanying Mahmud of Ghazni and researching his book on India' and Babur's stone throne 'overlooking an orchard and a lake'.

On docile Saturdays after a week of prisons, petitions and perspiring in Court, I set out for places on this list. Looking over old-city rooftops from a mosaiced minaret or lost in a rickshaw in search of a last remaining twelfth-century Hindu temple, I got to know and began to love this man I had then not yet met. As we became friends over the next nine years, Bruce opened up more of the world. From the story behind a small ceramic bowl or a recipe for cheese biscuits at a Holgate

Road lunch, to days in Delhi scaling the ruins of the Firuz Shah Kotla in search of dervishes and the truth of murders rumoured in eighteenth-century texts, to Schubert *lieders* in Scotland and late London dinners glinting with delicacies and good, ever erudite, company – I adored what he brought to life. And I hope that as it began with instructions in his absence, my friendship with Bruce will live on through acts of adventure, generosity, loving, learning and, one day, finally finding where Biruni measured the curve of the earth.

# Speak to that gentleman over there
## RGS, London, 2012

**Gianni Dubbini Venier** *is an independent scholar and writer. Before concluding a PhD in Indian art at the University of Venice Ca'Foscari, he graduated in History at the University of Milan and in Art History at SOAS, University of London. He lives and works between his hometown Venice and the countryside of Friuli.*

In the summer of 2012 I was twenty-five and I met Bruce for the first time at the Royal Geographical Society. William Dalrymple was about to give a talk on his book *Return of a King* and since I had met him previously in Venice and read the final draft of the book, I wanted to attend. At some point an old lady who saw me wandering alone with a lost look on my face in the foyer of the RGS said to me: 'Go to speak to that gentleman over there, his name is Bruce Wannell and he is a very nice man.' A minute later I gathered up my courage and approached him. He initially looked puzzled but once he understood that I was an Italian student, to my surprise he immediately switched the conversation into my own language and offered me my first experience of his extraordinary generosity. He invited me to participate as auditor at a unique seminar on eighteenth-century India, organised by the University of Swansea in the historic house of Gregynog, Wales. I believe Bruce brought me luck, because a few months later I became a postgraduate fellow at the RGS and was accepted as a graduate student in Art History and Archaeology at SOAS, University of London.

That day initiated one of the most important friendships of my life. This was fuelled by long discussions on Persia, India and Venetian travel accounts (he encouraged me to collect them), particularly those of Nicolò Manucci between the Safavid empire and Mughal India. Bruce came to visit me in Venice many times. He supervised all my PhD work on Manucci and my academic publications, giving severe but fundamental advice. He was a sort of 'jedi master' on how to live, how to travel and stay curious, and how to conduct myself as a scholar. An independent scholar and an independent man.

It is therefore with strongly felt emotion that I present here recent memories of Bruce in Friuli, Italy.

'*Caro mio*, you must have attention deficit disorder...'

'What?'

'Yes, you know, with those social networks you all always use: attention deficit is what you get!'

I stared at him through the silence that followed and slowly put my iPhone down. He ignored my questioning gaze and continued his imperturbable examination of the document, with his back ramrod straight at the table where we worked. He then emitted his verdict.

'The transcription you have made is a partial one...you chose the easier path! *Ragazzo mio*, you must show more endurance: this is an incomplete job!'

I muttered: 'Bruce, please give me a break. I just finished my PhD, I'm a bit sensitive right now...' Pointing at the sheets of paper: 'You know... this took me months: *per favore, non essere crudele!*' (Please don't be cruel!)

He was not listening. I could hear his clockwork brain ticking, entirely focused on the object of our dispute: the early nineteenth-century will of an Italian in the Indian Subcontinent that I had recently discovered.

I looked into the sympathetic eyes of my Belgian Sheperd Artù, tied by a rope nearby, the only witness to the scene. This is how my master–disciple ordeal began.

That morning Bruce had taken a solitary promenade around the park. I could see him from my bathroom window, through the branches of the high trees. He spent a long time contemplating the oak tree. Then, he went into the house, gathered up books and my laptop, and brought them outside to the shaded colonnade of the church. He created a beautiful *ritiro*, an open-air study, where we could work while listening to the birds and the leaves in the breeze.

Bruce liked to move from my bachelor's apartment near San Giovanni in Bragora in Venice, where he had a small room with a bed, to my family's villa in Friuli. Avoiding tourists and the chance to discover a lesser-known region of Italy, while helping me with literary projects were attractive prospects for him.

Over the years he became a frequent visitor to Sterpo, where our country house sits, and some signs of his presence are still visible there today. One particularly hot July day, he led a team to collect plums near the pond, and managed to drop an incandescent pan full of the jam he had made from them onto the precious *tatami* table my grandfather had imported from Japan. This left an indelible mark. He made this mistake in front of my mother's very eyes. Her shout echoed across the kitchen and could be heard across the other side of the ample park.

Bruce enjoyed cycling the country roads around the villa, spotting the ponds where the 'white witches' of Celtic Friuli practised, as described by the historian Carlo Ginzburg, or walking along the river Stella, ancient *Anaxum* of Pliny the Elder, or visiting with my parents the architect Sanmicheli's Renaissance fortifications in the walled town of Palmanova, on which he was an expert.

His favourite Italian phrase for proposing a plan was '*si potrebbe…*' (we could do this, we could do that…). It was '*si potrebbe*' if we were in Venice, for a private visit to the eighteenth-century *filatoi* of Fondazione Tessuti Bevilacqua or to see Carpaccio at San Giorgio degli Schiavoni, or just to chill out at *osteria* Arco. He loved Arco's *cicchetti* (he particularly liked '*folpetti*' – small boiled octopus served with bread and olive oil) as much as a *sandólo* (rowing boat) tour of the Arsenale on which I rowed. Or in Friuli when he had the idea of cycling to the villa of the Last Doge, near Sterpo, or of a stroll through the vineyards, oblivious to the risk of ticks in the high grass. '*Si potrebbe*' meant he really would have loved to do something, and it was impossible to refuse a guest with such a sense of initiative and fun.

The coloured Murano glasses he chose reflected the spring sun, creating pleasant light effects across the surfaces of the piles of books. We sipped apple juice from them as we 'relaxed' during the breaks in our transcription of the will.

'*Sicca* rupees!' he burst out, 'It's not rupees, Gianni! It's *sicca* (issued in British Bengal before 1836), it's very different, it's double or triple the amount…I don't remember. You must check this in the Hobson-Jobson dictionary. Have you got it here?!'

He looked at me with those austere grey-blue eyes, that had seen Afghanistan's tribal areas torn apart during the civil war. I could not contain my fear and muttered confused words in bad English. I knew what the Hobson-Jobson dictionary was but in my nervousness I could hardly remember.

'Hobs….-Job….s… yes, I know…I don't!'

The punishment arrived like an arrow (he must have been suffering from the heat).

'Of course you don't fucking know!!!'

The dog emitted a cry.

After a couple of days like this we had transcribed the whole inventory of the will: it was an outstanding exercise and I was exhausted. But we also made time to savour good food and each other's company. Bruce's digestion was ailing. So we chose a diet based on fresh salads and our locally farmed smoked trout. We also indulged ourselves with the lovely Ribolla Gialla wine of the Collio.

Our longstanding and trusted groundsman at the villa had retired. The new temporary keeper was a short, swollen man with small eyes who dressed in *camouflage* uniforms like a member of a Russian militia in the Donbass and didn't hide his love for the Italian far-right leader Salvini. While Bruce and I fought to ignore his presence, we were lucky enough to still have with us Luigina, our housekeeper since the time of my grandfather. She was more than seventy and would retire forever the following year. Bruce had complete trust in Luigina and gave her his finest clothes and silk shirts to iron. He spoke to her very kindly in Italian and often tipped her generously for her services. But unexpected problems were facing the villa.

That year the northern Italian countryside faced an almost unbeatable enemy from far away: the Asiatic stinkbug (replacing the native population of the common green stinkbug). It was proving to be a total disaster for the crops and the farmers were suffering. The fields around the villa became infested and like an invading army the bugs soon managed to hide and reproduce in small nooks and crannies inside the villa. The Asiatic stinkbug doesn't bite, or do anything bad to you, apart from dirtying surfaces and stinking when killed or burned: hence the name.

One morning Bruce stormed into my room, waking me and complaining: 'They've even got inside my bedcovers and I've got them in my beard!' I offered to change rooms with him many times but he constantly refused, because he liked the nineteenth-century painting of Saint Catherine over his bed too much.

Determined to outrun the stinkbugs, or at least to stop thinking about them, we wound my Mini round the upper hills of the Collio, near the Italian border with Slovenia, a vast hilly region of beautiful countryside. We went to the local wineries and as we turned the bends in the road we found ourselves sometimes in Slovenia, sometimes back on Italian soil. We often had to ask a local which country we were in. The hilltop views of valleys below covered in cherry-tree-dotted vineyards, stretching up to the horizon under the bright light of the afternoon sun, became photographs on Bruce's phone.

On one of his last evenings in Sterpo, Bruce remonstrated with me for the hundredth time that I was spoiling my dog. It upset him when

I gave the Belgian Shepherd scraps of food from the table while we ate dinner. But once he understood that Artù was able to sit politely if told to do so, Bruce's Edwardian strictness fell away. Particularly when I demonstrated how the dog performed his most elegant move – the sphinx pose – in reward for culinary favours. Bruce wanted to try it himself – no matter anymore that we were eating – and ended up by granting full slices of *prosciutto crudo* to the big black dog beside him.

The expression on Bruce's face became most tender.

# Persian grammar

**Charlie Gammell** *is the author of* The Pearl of Khorasan, *a history of the city of Herat, and worked as a Pashto and Dari interpreter in Afghanistan for the International Committee of the Red Cross, as a cultural consultant for UNESCO and spent time in Afghanistan researching the history of Herat. He currently works for the FCO, and is writing a novel about antiquities' smuggling in Afghanistan in the chaotic days after the fall of the Taliban.*

B ruce and I were catching up over tea and toast in Gwendolyn's house in Scalter Street, east London. It was bitterly cold. In between heaping praise on Gwendolyn's rare quince jam and freshly baked artisanal loaf, Bruce was helping me translate some rather complicated medieval Persian poetry and chronicles. Bruce breezed through the texts, ever so slightly admonishing me for getting my grammar all in a twist, but doing so with the good grace and generosity that we all came to love and admire in him. We covered in half an hour what it would have taken me hours; there was no need for a dictionary, and as he plucked allegory and obscure Islamic references from the texts, I felt in the presence of a true master, generous with his time and learning, and kind too. I was off to Kabul the next day, Bruce in a few weeks' time, and so we talked about our forthcoming trips. Bruce asked me if I had packed yet. I replied that I'd not done so and Bruce asked me if I wanted advice on packing for Afghanistan. I said I would love some, anticipating a life-changing nugget of traveller gold, hewn from decades of experience. Bruce said that one's Afghan packing should always, always be done as if one were heading to a country house weekend, or making up a shooting party. I still don't know if he was teasing me or not.

# Sour maids and other career advice

**Ben Cuddon** *grew up in London and studied at Edinburgh (History) and Harvard (Middle East Studies). He then worked as a history teacher, before setting up a charity called Climate Ed, which teaches children about climate change.*

B ruce very kindly took an interest in my career and gave me advice on the matter whenever he was passing through London. I had studied Middle Eastern languages at university and, because I had a particular interest in Iran, he was keen to help a fellow Persianist.

Bruce warned me against academia as he felt Middle East Studies in the UK was dominated by a group of 'sour maids'. He applied his scholarship through tour-guiding, and on one occasion invited me to cover a tour around Iran which he couldn't manage himself. He could be scathing about the 'blue-rinse brigade', but he cared about helping them. 'Teach them to see,' he said, 'to really use their eyes and see for themselves.'

Bruce certainly taught me to see. The last time I saw him we were walking through St James's Park. Looking up at the trees, and the delicate spread of interwoven branches, he taught me the French term 'en filigrane'.

That day Bruce was mournful. He wasn't ill, but expressed a weariness with life. 'Sometimes I wonder how to keep going,' he said. 'But then I think of music, and the opportunity to create music with my friends, and that keeps me alive.'

Bruce was immensely generous and cared about people. Whenever we parted he would follow up our meeting with an email 'in Polonius mode'. He said you didn't have to find the *one* thing you wanted to do in life. But whatever you did, you should do it with passion, energy and commitment. And, because he was an aesthete and a man of incredibly sophisticated taste, he always issued a warning about stooping low in life. 'Don't end up in the slurry,' he would often say. Popular culture appalled him.

I suppose I remember Bruce most of all for his kindness, and also his incredibly sharp tongue. He didn't suffer fools gladly. I remember once he formed a low impression of a scholar whom he deemed an imposter. He seemed to relish dismantling his scholarly facade and exposing his pretensions, which he did so utterly ruthlessly, mercilessly, and comprehensively, but somehow also with great humour and humanity. He had no ego as in a way he had so little to protect; no academic career, no 'reputation', a limited livelihood. His own career was precarious, and he often expressed concern about 'staring into the financial abyss'. But that meant he could do and say whatever he wanted, and was always on the 'right' side, batting for the right team, for what was good; for knowledge and sharing it, for understanding, for enlightenment and spreading it as widely as possible.

Humanity. Bruce was thoroughly humanitarian. I recall meeting him at SOAS once and he was in a rage. 'I've just got back from the Middle East. The way the FCO treats visa applicants disgusts me', he said. 'It *disgusts* me.'

And of course, he was a mystery. A mutual friend was convinced he was a spy. But for whom? He could quite plausibly have been a quintuple agent. And when you thought he might be off to brief some bureaucrats at MI6 he would throw you off guard. 'I must catch a train,' he said. 'I have an appointment to sing for the King of Belgium.'

# 'over the Kachikani glacier into Swat, lots of gentians and edelweiss'

**Nick Buchan** *is a writer. He has worked and studied in Central Asia and travelled in Iran, India, Pakistan and China. He studied Russian and Persian at Wadham College, Oxford, and has a long-standing interest in the study of comparative religion. Among his Bruce-inspired pursuits are nastaliq calligraphy, Persian translation and travel.*

I was sifting through old emails following Bruce's death when I came across some correspondence with him from my time in Tajikistan which drew my attention. I'd emailed him asking for travel advice, to which he responded:

> I would thoroughly recommend a walk through Tajik Badakhshan, perhaps over the Pamirs and Wakhan [...], even over into Chitral, where the erstwhile royal family were friends [...] Perhaps you could go for the polo on the Shandur Pass, always a good event; I walked over the Kachikani glacier into Swat, lots of gentians and edelweiss, and rode through the forests of Kalam to Tal Lamutai and Dir and over the Lowari Pass to Chitral and left the horses for the summer on upper pastures on the slopes of Tirich Mir.

I only received this email on returning to London from Tajikistan and I read it, as I recall, with amusement and regret. Amusement, because it was so quintessentially Bruce and regret, because it appeared I'd missed every place on his list! Reading it again after his death, I was filled with the deeper regret that this great traveller and adventurer was no longer with us.

Bruce had an appreciation and knowledge of Persian art and literature that was at times overwhelming. During conversations with him I was amazed how he could move between Sa'di, Mughal miniatures and architecture almost in one breath, without compromising on detail

174

or authenticity. Working under him on a translation project I noted how he could understand archaic vocabulary and forms and also the cultural practices (since lost) that underpinned various obsolete idioms that, but for his explanation, were completely incomprehensible.

He also had little patience with half-hearted 'dabbling' and I remember being loudly upbraided by him in a packed (and silent) reading room in the British Library for querying the point in reading certain obscure Persian texts. The flip side to this seriousness was his well-known mischief, which could turn our translation sessions into fits of hysterical laughter and result in our expulsion from various reading rooms.

It was Bruce's appreciation of beauty and his sense of adventure that, along with an ability to converse with and amuse people of any society, made his company so enlivening. I'm sure that during times abroad in the future I will have cause, as I have before now, to invoke Bruce's memory — whether before producing an inappropriate couplet of 'Ubayd-i Zakani, or labouring to identify the hidden date of an old and long-forgotten structure, or staring into a sublime landscape far from the humdrum of daily life. I know others will do the same, and will share in the solace of his memory.

# Breakfast with Bruce
## York

**Lydia Wilson** *lives in York, but spends much of the time travelling, researching and writing on conflict and terrorism, mostly in the Middle East. Recent essay topics include Syrians in Jordan (*New York Review of Books*) aboriginal life in Australia (*Cambridge Literary Review*), the Christchurch attack (*Times Literary Supplement*), and Belgian filmmakers the Dardenne brothers (*Times Literary Supplement*). In the autumn, a series on the history of writing, presented by Lydia, will be broadcast on BBC Four.*

Whatever the start of the conversation – 'I work on terrorism', 'I'm going to Uzbekistan', 'Do you know so-and-so?' 'Have you read such and such?' – what was sure to come at some point was: 'Well, why don't you come to breakfast? Sage eggs and coffee, 9 o'clock?'

You were greeted with a phenomenal array of both artefacts ('Oh yes, I picked that one up in Nepal' or 'Don't you know Isabel? That's one of hers') and delicacies from around the world (cardamom sweets, Turkish delight, tea from Russia) or from his garden or foraging or cooking (the sage for the eggs, blackberries from Scarcroft allotments, homemade marmalade). At some point I started bringing contributions from my own travels, tastes he missed from different parts of the world – za'atar from Jordan, sweets from Turkey, Chinese tea, cardamom coffee, spices.

Whatever it was that we were supposed to be talking about, there were books for me to borrow (some subjects required a visit to the attic room for plundering those incomprehensibly densely packed shelves), and contacts to be generously shared. Many conversations would meander and spread far from their starting point, resulting in follow-up WhatsApp messages and phone calls – and often another breakfast. We had so much in common, though you didn't even need much in common to talk to Bruce. You just had to be interested in the world.

His travellers' tales were, of course, extraordinary, though for me these were all secondhand, around the breakfast table; I didn't have the good fortune to have travelled with the intrepid orientalist.

I'm writing this in Abu Dhabi, where I've met Bruce's friend William Dalrymple, been to talks about Shakespeare in the Arab world and how printing shaped the development of Arab thought, and seen some of the top musicians alive in the Arab world today, including the Lebanese band Mashrou' Leila, banned in most of the region for their notorious defence of gay rights. The first thing I would normally have done when I got home was to ring or text Bruce to say what a fascinating time I'd had, and the response would of course have been, 'Well, why don't you come for breakfast? Are you free tomorrow?'

Sharing and analysing experiences, from gossip to geopolitics via the history and culture which shapes both people and countries, was the meat of those breakfasts – Bruce could talk about all these things (and often produce a book to illustrate his point) for every country I've ever been to, and far more besides. Going through his library now, cataloguing and book plating the shelves and piles and boxes of books, sifting through bags and baskets of papers, I am continuously amazed at the breadth and depth of his reading; a single tour involved immense amounts of academic papers, carefully annotated, maps, brochures, guides, photos, and exquisitely kept notebooks. There is a wealth of material to shed light on his thinking and knowledge, but how much more fun it was to hear his expertise over sage eggs and coffee, as I'm sure he'd agree.

'All this reading, languages, people – where does it go now?' Bruce asked me as we were washing up together after one breakfast soon after his diagnosis. We spoke of the nature of consciousness, his Sufi training making an appearance, and how I wish now I had pushed him further on this mystical side that keeps popping up in all corners of his room. But I hope it was the Hindu–Buddhist tradition which dominated by the end, so that I can believe Bruce has been reincarnated, to wander the world again, and come back for breakfast.

# A garden close to the tomb of Sa'di
## *Iran, 2006*

**Robert Maxwell**'*s working career began in international mining and finished in health policy and management. For seventeen years (from 1980 to 1997) he was Chief Executive of the King's Fund, a royal foundation based in London. He read English at Oxford, where he won the Newdigate Prize for Poetry. With Bruce Wannell, he published* Persian Poems *in 2012.*

I first met Bruce when, in 2006, he was the scholar guide for a journey along the western part of the Silk Road, organised by Warwick Ball of Eastern Approaches. It was a group of about eighteen, including my wife Jane and me. We travelled by bus from Tashkent to Tehran, crossing Uzbekistan, Turkmenistan and Iran in the process.

Bruce was the perfect guide for this. He had the languages needed (whoever we met, he could find some common tongue and something to talk about), he knew and loved the places we were visiting, and he combined charm with common sense. Despite the long drives, there were few dull moments. Even crossing the borders was not without its interest. He had allowed plenty of time and warned us to avoid any word or action that might rouse the attention of a guard: 'These people have an extremely dull job. They long for some excitement. Whatever you do, don't give them any.' Our crossings were entirely without incident.

Cities like Samarkand, Shiraz and Isfahan, and sites like Persepolis, are so full of interest and beauty that visiting them is a joy, particularly in Bruce's company. There's so much to learn and reflect on in the history and cultures of the region, the role of the Silk Road and the trading along it. Each evening Bruce would choose somewhere to gather us and talk to us about something we had just seen or were about to see. One of these was in a garden close to Sa'di's tomb, where he read a number of Sa'di's poems, translating them into English once we'd listened to the Farsi. Many Iranians (mostly young) were camping nearby and reciting them to one another from memory.

Bruce said that his aim as a guide was to give each individual experience as close as possible to that of someone travelling alone. He often succeeded. For example, rather than take us to a café for lunch, he'd organise a picnic: one day that resulted in watching the red and turquoise of rollers as they flashed around us. On our last evening in Tehran he took us to his favourite café in a garden, where an elderly man was singing Farsi songs to his family and grandchildren. We sat nearby to listen and were in due course made very welcome by the singer. Along the route he would take us to anywhere where he remembered a craftsman or a good eating place. In Iran in particular, we got a feeling for the people, who are much more sophisticated and independent-minded than I had realised. Young women would wear smart clothes under their regulation dress. They were testing the limits. Occasionally, while we were there, that would call down the wrath of the police.

After our return to England, I wrote to Bruce to say how much we had enjoyed the trip. I also said that I was keen, as a poet, to try to translate a Persian poem into English verse. Could we work on one together? To my delight, he agreed and we set a date. That started a joint project that lasted five years and produced a book, *Persian Poems* (Libanus Press 2012). It contains thirty poems by twenty poets spanning a thousand years.

Our first meeting was at Bruce's house in York. It was convenient that at the time I had frequent meetings in York and Bruce's house was in walking distance of the hotel where I usually stayed. Bruce had chosen a poem from the manuscript collection he had built up over the years, often from oral sources. He settled me with a cup of green tea and a delicious cake or biscuit and read the poem several times in Farsi. He translated it as the mood took him and I wrote down his words verbatim. Then we had some discussion about it. I asked about anything I did not understand. He talked about the poet, any allusions (e.g. to the Quran, to myths or to other poems) and about rhythm and metrics, before reading it again several times in Persian.

I took my notes away and worked at a first draft. That usually took me two or three weeks. As soon as I was ready we'd fix a date and place at which to meet next. I would bring the draft with me. We'd start by his reading the original aloud and then I'd read my draft, probably several times. He'd give me his reactions and we'd critique the draft, line by line and word by word, before I took it away to revise it.

Once we'd agreed to continue the process, he would also pick a new poem and we would follow the same process, so that next time we had one first draft to consider and one second (or third) draft of a different poem. We would set them on one side only when we were both satisfied.

Bruce was excellent to work with: wholly reliable and focused, while also making the occasion a real pleasure, whether as host or guest. He was a perfectionist in that he would not accept anything until he was satisfied we had it 'right'. His choice of words was different from mine. He tended to use more words and phrases with a Latin or Greek derivation, whereas for poetry I prefer the more earthy and visual Anglo-Saxon. The fact that we came from different directions in our choices was helpful in clarifying meanings and in building poems. We were both pleased with the final result, which is, among other things, a beautiful book, thanks to Libanus, Hampton Printing and Celia Ward's cover, based on the birds that occur in the poems. It's now out of print but can still be downloaded from Amazon at modest cost.

Bruce and I became comfortable in each other's homes. 46 Holgate Street surprised me in several ways when I went there first. It's a neat York house where Bruce is a longstanding tenant, with several others, who are much younger and have been there less long. They all share the ground floor kitchen and the garden. The garden is very much Bruce's creation: long and narrow and divided into a series of 'rooms', with lovely plants, places to sit and tables to share. It was ideal for working on our shared task. Bruce's private space was his bedroom on the top floor, which was also his scholarly place for reading and thinking and talking.

He was a most welcome guest. Jane knew him from the Silk Road and my children came to know him well too. He always brought gifts of some kind with him – not expensive gifts, but thoughtfully chosen, sometimes for Jane, sometimes for one of my children. All of us are missing him. A star is no longer here.

In early January 2019 Bruce rang to ask me to join him at the Galle Literary Festival in Sri Lanka later that month. He had good contacts in Sri Lanka and had been invited to participate or lead in several sessions, including one about our book of Persian poems. He wanted me to present this session with him. He also invited me to join him for the week before the festival at a house lent to him free by friends, with a garden and pool and a majordomo to look after us. We could do our preparation there, explore the coast a bit and visit a site or two. I would have to pay my own fare – his was being paid – but there would be few other expenses as I could share his hotel room during the festival for which I would have free entry. When I sounded hesitant about coming at short notice and about the airfare, he suggested I bring copies of the book with me and sell them at our session. He thought there would be a demand at a price higher than we could charge in the UK.

I accepted the invitation and it was all a great success. Galle is an attractive old city and the festival is a major English language event, which attracted some interesting speakers, including Maggie Smith, Sebastian Faulks, Alexander McCall Smith and David Puttnam. After the festival Bruce went up to the north of Sri Lanka with friends to visit an island where there are wild horses of uncertain origin. (I think the party relied on the Sri Lankan navy to get them to and fro.) I contacted my daughter who joined me at short notice to explore the middle of the island.

# Persian cooking

**Bruce Wannell**, *from the* Odyssey Guide to Iran, *reproduced here by kind permission of Magnus Bartlett.*

Iran has one of the world's great culinary traditions, based on a once-vigorous nomad pastoralism in the semi-arid steppes and a rich agriculture in the few well-watered areas of oases, rivers and the mountain valleys of the Alborz and Zagros ranges and the coastal areas along the Caspian Sea and the Persian Gulf. Iranians remain hospitable and courteous, and good food, though harder to find, is still there when the doors of hospitality open to travellers: the traditions of Iranian javanmardi (generous and chivalric) and of Islamic hospitality survive in spite of social and economic pressures. The discriminating and persevering traveller will find his/her way beyond impoverished modernity to a still-living tradition of fine eating and generous entertaining.

However these traditions have been severely endangered, if not quite destroyed, by the galloping industrialisation, pollution, destruction of the natural and social environment as well as the population explosion of the last thirty years – leading to uncontrolled growth of towns and cities, engulfing limited agricultural land, contaminating water, decaying traditional extended family structures and increasing reliance on imported food and standardised supermarkets and restaurant culture.

The Esfahan oasis has lost the life-giving water of the Zayandeh Rud to a hare-brained project in the deserts of Yazd, with a resulting death of upwards of fifty kilometres of orchards and rice-paddies upstream; the Caspian coast has been parcelled up into tiny plots for holiday villas, where once productive agricultural land is sold off for building, whilst the valleys and forests of the Alborz slopes no longer offer a livelihood to shepherds, instead the trees are felled to make lavatory paper in Sari; the semi-deserts have been turned into motorways and factories, and nomads no longer drive their flocks across the landscape; tax-concessions encourage most villages to house small and inefficient factories which pollute the atmosphere, while the last twenty-five years have seen the traditional mud-brick vernacular architecture of even the remotest areas swept away almost without a trace, to be replaced with ugly concrete-and-steel-girder boxes.

The death of the single-storey courtyard house, open to the sky and housing the extended family around its courtyard and its central pool, means not only a loss of traditional identity and of a varied local architecture suited to the climate, but also, importantly for food in Iran, the loss of the mutually supportive workforce that traditionally ensured the regular, labour-intensive preparation of delicious Iranian cuisine. Now as often as not the harassed lone woman of the nuclear family has to take a paid job outside the home and returns to the bleakness of a small flat with strip lighting and synthetic moquette and blaring television, too exhausted to go through alone the once-communal rituals of traditional cooking and eating.

American-style convenience food, with its attendant evils of flatulent obesity, is all the rage. In Tehran, there are some reasonable restaurants serving an approximation of the varied traditional domestic cuisine, but even there the fashion is for greasy hamburgers or dimly lit preparations that aspire to pass as Mexican. The situation is little short of a catastrophe.

The lone traveller may be fortunate enough to be invited to Iranian homes where traditional food is still prepared, as Iranians continue to be gracious and hospitable. The tourist in a group will have to rely on his/her guide negotiating with the hotel chef to produce something a little better than the usual carelessly repetitive one-night-stand fodder. Group tourism alas, like factory farming, seldom if ever encourages gastronomic excellence!

One of the problems is that non-elite public eating in Iran derives from the bazaar cookshop tradition, which never was intended to give a complete diet, only to provide essential protein and carbohydrates to the workforce: hence the endless kebabs and flat-bread or rice, with barely a sprinkling of sour red sumac seed or strained yoghurt with mountain garlic *mast o musir* to enliven them, let alone a relish of pickled vegetable *torshi* (homemade they can be superb, especially matured garlic pickle often twenty years old: the quality of the vinegar is crucial – much factory-made pickle, as in England, is inedible because of the cheap chemical vinegar used). Kebab is still regarded as the main form of public eating, so vegetarians will have a hard time of it! Even carnivores will tire of the overuse of chemical tenderiser on low-grade over-refrigerated meat smothered in passe-partout saffron – at home or for picnics, the freshly slaughtered local lamb or mutton is marinaded overnight in onion and lime juice or in yoghurt and garlic before being roasted on skewers (*sikh*) over a charcoal fire – and the result is delicious. In Ramazan, a meat and wheat porridge called *halim* is served in the market at dusk; a thick broth (*ash*) is traditionally served on Thursday evenings, based on grain and pulses, with herbs and dried whey (*kashk*) and fried onions with dried mint; a traditional workman's breakfast is boiled sheep's head and feet (*kalleh-pacheh*), too strong for the uninitiated, and a delicious lunch (*ab gusht*) cooked and served in stone pots (*dizi*) a liquid stew of mutton, onions, chick peas and dried limes, eaten with bread, accompanied by a raw onion, and a fresh yoghurt drink (*dugh*) – the pre-bottled variety almost always tastes of preservative, so is best avoided, as also the sickeningly sweet fizzy drinks that are routinely offered; bottled water is fairly safe and at least doesn't interfere with the taste of the meal.

Iranian fruits and fresh herbs can be superb, with intense flavours that shame the watery productions offered for sale in English supermarkets. A favourite ending to a meal is a dish of fresh herbs, including tarragon, lemon basil, chives, mint, etc, served with white sheep's cheese and thin flat bread to wrap the selection in small rolls or triangles, very cleansing to the palate. There are a variety of flat breads baked in the *tanur* (the communal clay oven) – whose origins go back to ancient Mesopotamia – thin *lavash* and the standard *nan*, with sesame or black-onion seeds, slapped onto the clay walls; *sangak* oven-baked on a bed of pebbles; *barbari*, crisp and ridged; very fine breads baked on convex metal plates by nomads like the Qashqai, while shepherds in the mountains make a thick crusty bread under the ashes of the big log fires that keep them warm and the wolves at bay. Snacks of white feta-like cheese and flat bread are served with watermelon or with fresh grapes and walnuts in the autumn. Another snack sometimes served at lunch is a stiff herb and spinach omelette (*sabzi kuku*) fried on both sides, served with bread and plain yoghurt; another end product of milk is *kashk*, a slightly acrid residue of boiled-down and dried whey and yoghurt, added as a souring agent to soups and stews, and notably to fried aubergine (*kashk badenjan*); grated cucumber and chopped fresh mint is used in *mast o khiar*, and lightly boiled strained spinach with a little chopped garlic for the other yoghurt classics *burani esfinaj*; yoghurt side dishes are also made with steamed, peeled and fried courgettes, or even with a large de-thorned thistle (*kangar*). Fresh dates in their own syrup, *rotab*, pale golden-yellow from Shahdad or Jahrom, darker from Bam, are served with plain yoghurt as a breakfast snack or dessert, as is sesame-halva. Dried and salted melon seeds and the excellent pistacchios form an ever ready snack, or appetizer during the long wait before the dinner, when conversation meanders and the host/ess peels little cucumbers and other fruits for the guests before the meal is served at the end of the evening.

Sweet and sour is a recurring feature of Iranian cooking – the refreshing taste helps cut the heaviness of the favourite fat lamb or mutton, and quenches the thirst in a very dry climate. Pomegranates are one of the marvels of Iran – translucent seeds varying from pale to darkest ruby, they are delicious simply as they are, providing you don't mind the woody inner seed, or as a fresh juice, or as a concentrated *robb* used as a souring agent in cooking *khoresh fesenjan*, a stew of wild duck or pheasant or even chicken: the restaurant version is too often totally inadequate – the battery chicken separately boiled in water with just a dribble of the pomegranate and walnut sauce splashed over it, eked out with lemon juice and sugar – whereas it should all be stewed long and slow together to form a rich sauce that is not cloyingly sweet; served with a plain *chelo* of the finest white rice, it is at its best unbeatable. Another pomegranate and walnut preparation, also originating from the Caspian coast, is the preserved olive, *zeitun parvardeh*, which has recently gained currency throughout Iran. Another souring agent for stews is the aromatic dried lime *limu 'ammani* cooked with herbs, red beans and fried mutton in the classic *qormeh sabzi*. Other lamb stews soured with rhubarb, *khoresh rivas*, or with quinces, *khoresh beh*, are typical of the north-east. Small sour grapes are sometimes added to the aubergine stew, *khoresh badenjan*, and sour grape verjuice (*ghureh*) is also used as a souring agent. All these stews are served with *chelo*, plain long-grained white rice which is rinsed and soaked before boiling, then drained, sealed and steamed for up to an hour, so that each grain is separate and light: an additional refinement is to line the pot with thinly sliced potatoes and oil before steaming, which results in a crisp crust *tah-dig*. This complex preparation indicates the prestige status of rice in Iran: this style of cooking rice became prevalent under the Safavid Shah Abbas (d.1629) as recorded by his chef Ustad Nurullah: since the oil-boom of the 1960s rice-consumption has become generalised throughout Iranian society, even in the poorest classes.

The other main form of rice preparation is *polo* also known as *pilav*, similar to the first stages of *chelo* until the steaming stage, when various enrichments are added: sour cherries (*albalu*) or barberries (*zereshk*) – both of these are also used to make delicious refreshing sherbets. The greatest of the *polo* rice dishes is *baqali polo* where peeled fresh broad beans and quantities of fresh chopped dill and chunks of lamb marinated in turmeric and cumin and fried in its own fat are added for the final steaming, with a scattering of rice grains perfumed with saffron added on serving. A plain yoghurt is the only relish needed. A Shirazi speciality is *kalam polo* with cabbage and herbs shredded in rice, which is served with meatballs. The most famous meatballs, giant in size and built around apricots or plum with a forcemeat of chopped lamb and crushed chickpeas is the *kufteh tabrizi*. The other great festive *polo* is made with slivers of blanched bitter-orange peel, pistachios and saffron – *shirin polo* also known as *narenj polo* – with chicken stewed separately and incorporated at the last stage. Bitter oranges are also used to squeeze on to fried fish or grilled kebabs, when they are in season.

Iranian sweets are also varied and delicious, if properly made with good ingredients: among the best known are the butterscotch-like *sohan* from Qom made with the sweet flour of germinated wheat, clarified butter, saffron, pistachios etc; the fine layered pastry stuffed with almond and cardamom paste drenched in rosewater syrup *baqlava*; the lozenges of saffron almond paste, *lozineh*, from Jolfa Esfahan; an Armenian speciality is *shirovharz*, a lokoum of grape-juice and walnuts and spices sun-dried to the consistency of a stiff jelly; and the rosewater and saffron rice-pudding, *sholeh zard,* is offered in the street on feast days.

The repertoire of Iranian food is greater than what has been sketched here, and its influence reaches in the Caucasus, Mesopotamia, Central Asian and even India, areas with which Iran shares much history and many traditions – even the Spanish and South American dish *escabeche* has a distant Iranian origin via Abbasid Baghdad and the Arab advance across North Africa to Andalusia. All food is not only a necessity but also a luxury, its study is a prism for studying the health and history of a nation, its cultural and agricultural imports and exports through time. The Iranian tradition of food is a great tradition, but now beleaguered and endangered, threatened by a tragic loss of quality and authenticity, which in turn threatens the health and even the identity of the nation.

# Sufi poetry for Amnesty

**Graham Henderson**

B ruce Wannell came into my life, as he did into the lives of so many of his friends, with a cavalier flourish. I was running the arts organisation Poet in the City and Bruce approached me with the idea of doing a Sufi event in the auditorium at Amnesty UK's headquarters in Shoreditch, where the charity held regular events. It quickly became clear to me that Bruce was a great expert on the history of Sufism and of Islamic culture in general. He was a one-man whirlwind of sparkling wit and erudition. Together we created and published a booklet of Sufi poetry to accompany the event, a beautiful little publication which blows away many prejudices and misconceptions about the Middle East and its heritage.

Little did we know that the event at Amnesty in September 2007 would take place only a few weeks after the bombing atrocities of 7/7 in London, and at a moment of palpable Islamophobia. With music by the Afghan tabla player Yusuf Mahmoud, and songs performed by Veronica Doubleday, the event told a very different story about the Muslim world. As an event it felt both special and important, and it was a reflection of Bruce's deep knowledge and passionate commitment to the subject, and to his admirable perfectionism. It was a magical evening of poetry, percussion and song.

With Bruce came many friends and connections, and new ideas. A string of other events followed over the next few years which were either influenced by Bruce or which directly involved him, including events celebrating the poetry of Rumi and Hafez. In the process I got to know him as a friend, and marvelled at this modest man who seemed to me a spiritual heir of Hugh Leach, Wilfred Thesiger and T. E. Lawrence, an Englishman who (as the saying went) 'had got sand between his toes'. In Bruce's case his travels had taken him all over the Middle East, Far East and Central Asia, including much time spent in Afghanistan, and in and out of danger. Sitting on a lovely day in his garden in York, sharing a meal of humus, peppers, flat bread and tea, it felt as though I was in the company of a kind of English Bedouin, someone who had absorbed the simplicity, spirituality and generosity of some of the remote regions where he had travelled.

His knowledge was not limited to the Islamic world. He was a polymath and polyglot, a gifted musician, and a champion of all the arts. In later years he would appear from time to time in London and sweep my wife Judith and me off to a recital at the Wigmore Hall or (on one memorable occasion) to a small-scale performance of *The Marriage of Figaro* in an obscure Victorian theatre in Teddington. Sometimes he would stay overnight with us in Twickenham and we would converse easily over the dining room table about all manner of subjects: the arts, literature, history, music. It seemed that Bruce was knowledgeable about everything. He was also a gifted raconteur, and our evenings were always characterised by gales of laughter. On the last occasion when Bruce stayed with us, Judith and I said our farewells to him on the edge of the River Thames in Twickenham. We watched him clamber aboard Hammerton's Ferry, the small foot ferry which still runs daily on summer days across the river to the Surrey shore at Petersham. Bruce was the only passenger and we were amused to see that, by the time the boat was in midstream, he was already in animated conversation with the ferryman.

Bruce's death leaves a great gap in my life and represents an inestimable loss to all those who knew and loved him. I shall always remember his rakish charm, humour, intelligence and irrepressible lust for life. I know that he will be sorely missed. When a person like Bruce dies a great storehouse of knowledge, memories and experience passes out of the world, leaving all of us poorer. Only last year Bruce and I were making plans for him to perform piano pieces by Chopin at a fund-raising event for my current charity, the *Rimbaud and Verlaine Foundation*, and a magical evening I am sure that it would have been...

# Rumi

**Alan Williams** read this in the original at Bruce's funeral. *After studying Classics, then Persian and Arabic at Oxford he took a doctorate in Iranian Studies at SOAS, University of London on Zoroastrianism. While teaching at the universities of Sussex, SOAS and, for thirty-four years, Manchester, he has published on ancient, medieval and modern Iranian literature, and most recently a new parallel text edition and translation of the* Masnavi *of Rumi, of which two volumes are now in print (IB Tauris 2020).*

For years a man is living in a city,
    as soon as his eyes drift off into sleep,
He sees another city good and bad,
    and nothing of his own place is remembered,
Recalling "*I was there, this city's new
    – this is not mine, here I am just a guest!*".
But no! He thinks that he has always been
    here in this dreamland city, born and bred!
What wonder if the spirit's own abodes,
    which were its dwellings and its former births,
Are now forgotten? For this world, like sleep,
    enfolds her as the clouds obscure the stars.
More so, from all the cities she has trodden
    the layers of dust are unswept from her sight.
She has not striven ardently in order
    to purify her heart and see what's happened,
To raise her heart out of the pit of mystery
    and see with open eyes both first and last.

At first we came to inorganic realms,
    then from the inorganic to organic.
For years we lived in the organic state,
    and now forgot the inorganic world.
And when we passed from plant to animal

سالها مردی که در شهری بود
شهر دیگر بیند او پُر نیک و بد
که: من آنجا بوده‌ام، این شهرِ نو
بل چنان داند که خود پیوسته او
چه عجب گر روحِ موطن‌هایِ خویش
می نیارد یاد؟ کین دنیا چو خواب
خاصه چندین شهرها را کوفته
اجتهادِ گرم ناکرده، که تا
سر برون آرد دلش از بُخشِ راز

یک زمان که چشم در خوابی رود
هیچ در یادش نیاید شهرِ خود
نیست آنِ من، در اینجا ام گرو
هم در این شهرش بُدهست اِبداع و خو
که بُدهستش مسکن و میلادِ پیش،
می‌فروپوشد، چو اختر را سحاب
گردها از درکِ او ناروفته
دل شود صاف، و ببیند ماجرا
اوّل و آخِر ببیند چشمِ باز

## أطوار و منازلِ خلقتِ آدمی از ابتدا

آمده اوّل به اقلیمِ جماد
سالها اندر نباتی عمر کرد
وز نباتی چون به حیوانی فتاد
جز همین میلی که دارد سوی آن
همچو میلِ کودکان با مادران
همچو میلِ مفرط هر نومُرید
جزوِ عقلِ این از آن عقلِ کُل است
سایه‌اش فانی شود آخِر در او
سایهٔ شاخِ دگر ای نیکبخت!
باز از حیوان، سوی انسانی‌اش
همچنین اقلیم تا اقلیم رفت
عقلهایِ اوّلینش یاد نیست
تا رَهَد زین عقلِ پُرحرص و طلب
گر چو خفته گشت و شد ناسی ز پیش
باز از آن خوابش به بیداری کشند
که:چه غم بود آن که می‌خوردمبه خواب؟
چون ندانستم؟ که آن غم و اعتلال
همچنان دنیا که حُلم نایم است
تا برآید ناگهان صبحِ اجل
خنده‌اش گیرد از آن غمهای خویش

وز جمادی در نباتی اوفتاد
وز جمادی یاد ناورد، از نَبَرد
نامدش حالِ نباتی هیچ یاد
خاصه در وقتِ بهار و ضَیْمران
سِرِّ میلِ خود نداند در لبان
سویِ آن پیرِ جوانبختِ مجید
جنبش این سایه زآن شاخ گل است
پس بداند سِرِّ میل و جست و جو
کی بجنبد، گر نجنبد این درخت؟
می‌کشید، آن خالِقی که دانی‌اش
تا شد اکنون عاقل و دانا و زَفت
هم از این عقلش تحوّل کردنی است
صدهزاران عقل بیند بُوالعَجَب
کی گذارندش در آن نِسیانِ خویش
که کند بر حالت خود ریش‌خند
چون فراموشم شد احوالِ صواب؟
فعلِ خواب است و فریب است و خیال
خفته، پندارد که این خود دایم است
وارَهَد از ظلمتِ ظنّ و دغل
چون ببیند مُستَقَرّ و جای خویش

there was no memory of the state of plants,
Except a feeling which we have for them,
    so strong in springtime with its fragrant flowers.
And we, like babies feeling for our mother,
    know *not* the secret of the urge to suckle,
Like every novice's obsessiveness
    towards his noble Pir of generous fortune.
This finite mind is from that Perfect Mind,
    this shadow's trembling's from that Perfect Bough.
Our shadow passes into Him at last,
    and then we know the secret of the quest.
How can the shadow of another bough be stirred,
    O blessed man, if *this* tree does not tremble?
Again the Lord Creator whom you know
    takes us from animal to human nature.
And so we've passed from state to state like this,
    till we become enlightened, wise and great.
There's no recalling prior states of mind –
    from *this* one too there is advancing onward.
So we escape this mind of greed and gain,
    to see a hundred thousand minds of wonder.
If we should fall asleep and lose the past,
    how could we be abandoned in oblivion?
They bring us back to wakefulness from sleep
    that we may laugh at our own sleepy state:
Saying "*What was that sorrow suffered in my sleep*
    *and how could I forget the truthful states,*
*Not knowing that those sorrows and those ills*
    *result from sleep, deceit and fantasy?*"
Such is this world, which is the sleeper's dream!
    The sleeper thinks it truly is eternal,
Till suddenly the dawn of Death shall break,
    and we escape thought's darkness and deception,
And laughter at your sorrows overcomes you
    to see your true abode and dwelling place.

*Masnavi* of Rumi Book 4, vv. 3629–57, ed. M. Este'lami,
tr. Alan Williams

# Designing books with Bruce

**Celia Ward** *is a painter and textile designer, Holgate Road garden admirer, swapped china and ceramics with Bruce, fellow expert in falling asleep at the dinner table.*

I can't remember how I became embroiled in designing for Bruce. I think our first partnership started with my being asked for advice. Robert Maxwell and he had translated a selection of Persian poems, which they wanted to have printed. For Bruce it was a two-year determined quest to get it done as well as possible. A young Iranian had started laying out the pages in Word.doc but it became difficult making contact with him, and Bruce was anxious for his safety. Meanwhile, out blackberrying in York, Bruce met Stephen Bentley and persuaded him to help, I think by working through a succession of delectable lunches and teas. He wondered if I also could be involved, but I said I was no book designer. We looked at getting the printing done by the friendly and highly professional commercial printer at Prontaprint in Barking, near where I lived and with whom I had often worked. We drove there from East Ham, over the North Circular where London seemed to end and East Anglia begin, Bruce intrigued by the east London cityscape. He spent two hours talking to the man at Prontaprint about printing and esoteric matters, after which we both decided that to meet Bruce's great expectations for the book we would have to look further. I was very embarrassed about the length of time we had taken up.

There followed a period of sitting in heavenly gardens, looking through fine books over dainty morsels of food, until it was clear a small press was what was needed. Happily Robert had an idea for how this could be paid for, and the Libanus Press agreed to take on the job. Bruce asked if I would do the cover, suggesting it should feature the various birds that appear in the poems. Unfortunately, as in the case of the nightingale, beautiful song is not always matched by beautiful plumage. I did two versions of birds amid a design of roses, and Bruce liked both, so one went on the front cover, the other on the back. Meanwhile all was going fine with Libanus until the first proofs arrived. Bruce hated the layout of the Persian text. Not only was he finickety to an extreme, he also, despite having no clue about the nuts and bolts of design, started telling Libanus how to do their job. I became very embarrassed again by the extended email and phone row. Many times Bruce asked me to intercede, to turn his furious feelings into polite and acceptable emails that might succeed in getting the changes he craved. It transpired, however, that Bruce's eye was as deft as his manner of expressing himself was infuriating, and everyone was delighted with the end result.

Our second partnership was for a community textile project which I ran in Newham. The project was doing a series of embroidered hangings, each one featuring the alphabet of one or other of the major languages spoken in our area of east London. We had already produced an Arabic alphabet, and the embroidered letters had been digitally photographed and incorporated into a little booklet.

Bruce had kindly checked that the decorative cover pages made up of random letters did not inadvertently spell any outrageous words in Arabic. Our next booklet was Hindi, and I needed a brief history of that alphabet as an introduction. However, I could find no-one to write this until I mentioned it to Bruce, telling him we had £175 in our budget. He proceeded to work on it for about sixteen hours a day non-stop for two weeks. The final text was scholarly and not at all the kind of thing one would normally expect to find in a community production. Then, I discovered, he wanted to design the booklet. He began by giving advice, but this quickly turned into total control, while I became reduced to computer technician. We both loved the result and he gave many copies to friends and families. I am glad that before he died he saw the copy grandly bound by The Wyvern Bindery and exhibited, alongside other work by our textile project, at The Watts Gallery and The Art Workers Guild.

By way of a thank you for my help on *Persian Poems*, Bruce insisted on taking me out to lunch. We had a delicious meal at a fashionable restaurant (Ralph Fiennes at the next table), and after paying the bill Bruce announced he now had a grand total of £53 in the bank. He was adamant I should not contribute. 'I can always sell a carpet,' he said.

I have worked since with both printers, and neither said a word against Bruce.

# A formidable but modest scholar

**Warwick Ball** *is a Near Eastern archaeologist and author who spent over twenty-five years carrying out excavations, architectural studies and monumental restoration throughout the Middle East and adjacent regions.*

On a visit to us in 2016 I showed Bruce a recent publication that I had just purchased, a book on the Friday Mosque of Herat, one of the more important monuments in the eastern Islamic world. Mainly Timurid from the fifteenth century and later, a part of the original twelfth-century mosque is preserved in the form of a magnificent portal decorated with an elaborate turquoise glazed Kufic inscription dated 597 AH/1200 AD, one of the very few surviving monuments of the Ghurid dynasty centred on western Afghanistan that ruled an empire stretching to Delhi in the twelfth and thirteenth century. On a casual browse through the book, Bruce glanced at the translation of the inscription and immediately spotted an error, which he pointed out to me and corrected. It was only a minor error that did not alter the overall interpretation of the monument, but it demonstrated Bruce's extraordinary skill at reading Arabic and Persian monumental inscriptions, a highly specialised skill that even few art historians master, a skill furthermore in which Bruce was entirely self-taught.

His mastery in written Persian and Arabic made Bruce a sort of unofficial consultant to more established scholars, but sadly led to only one publication of his own, *Kabul Elite Burials: a wounded heritage* with Khadem Hussain, published in Kabul in 2013 by the Aga Khan Trust for Culture. However, being a complete novice in this area myself, it is to an entirely separate branch of scholarship that I would like to draw attention where Bruce excelled: Roman mosaics. In particular, two mosaics that Bruce brought to my attention.

The first concerns one of the best-known mosaics of the ancient world, the 'Alexander Mosaic' in the National Museum of Naples, originally from the 'House of the Faun' in Pompeii. It depicts one of the most important battles of the ancient world, the Battle of Gaugamela in 331 BC between the forces of Alexander of Macedon and those of Artaxerxes III of Persia, both of whom are shown leading their forces. The mosaic dates from the end of the second century BC but it is believed to be a faithful copy of an earlier Hellenistic painting, probably made soon after the event it depicts. Following a visit to Naples in 2011 when he was able to examine the mosaic closely, Bruce came to us in considerable excitement having concluded that the artist who painted the original picture on which the mosaic was based had to have visited Persepolis. In support of this, Bruce pointed out details of the Persian weaponry and costume that were identical to those depicted on the Persepolis reliefs and nowhere else, so could only have been observed at first hand. A huge amount has been written about this mosaic but as far as I was aware, nobody had picked up on this. I urged Bruce to write this up as an article and submit it to a scholarly journal, but he was reluctant – indeed, Bruce was always frustratingly reluctant to put pen to paper.

Soon after, a forthcoming conference was brought to my attention, *Persepolis: 40 Years On. An International Conference on the Archaeology, History, and Reception of Persepolis* at the University of Edinburgh later that year. I immediately wrote to Bruce that this would be an ideal venue to present his discoveries and urged him to attend. He accordingly came, we gave him a crash course in Powerpoint the evening before, and he presented a very well thought out and persuasive paper at the conference the following day (I attended, but merely as a member of the audience, not a participant). The paper went down very well, Bruce was completely at ease in fielding the ensuing questions and discussion, and nobody questioned his conclusion.

Sadly, the conference proceedings were never published as it was originally intended, and Bruce always felt rather bitter about this and perhaps took it rather personally. Perhaps for this reason he never had the confidence to publish it elsewhere as I continued to urge, so sadly this important work will now never see the light of day.

My next mosaic example is completely different, far less well known but in its way far more important even than the 'Alexander Mosaic' – indeed, to my mind one of the most extraordinary works of art from the ancient world. This concerns the remarkable Maryamin Mosaic of the late fourth century which was in the Hama Museum in Syria, which Bruce first brought to my attention some years ago shortly after his visit there (I believe it is now in safe storage). It was found in the village of Maryamin south-west of Hama, probably forming the centrepiece of a *triclinium* in a villa. The mosaic is unique for a number of reasons. To begin with it is quite literally a 'snapshot' of an actual event: a live musical performance, something I have never known in any mosaic from the ancient world where images are usually formulaic, often staid. A wooden stage or dais is visible in the foreground, upon which six female musicians perform with (from left to right) clappers, an organ, a double flute, metal sounding bows, a cithara and castanets. The castanet player is presumably dancing and appears to be singing; indeed the entire scene conveys movement. The performers are gorgeously and elegantly – even flamboyantly – dressed, in richly embroidered robes: an all-girl band. The mosaic workmanship is of particularly high quality, with small tesserae permitting fine detail of both costumes and instruments to be shown, as well as fine gradations of skin tones and shading. The mosaic had been published (in *Mosaïques de Syrie*, Janine Balty, Brussels 1977), but was not widely known.

But, being a musician himself, it was the musical aspects that particularly caught Bruce's attention. In the first place Bruce pointed out the two *erotes* (winged gods) working the bellows of the organ, clearly demonstrating that this is a bellows organ, not a water organ. The earliest bellows organs are eighteenth century, whereas all earlier organs were water organs. Hence, the Maryamin Mosaic is one of the more important historical sources concerning the history of the development of keyboard instruments. Indeed, the mosaic contains probably the most detailed representation of an ancient organ to have survived, allowing for accurate reconstruction. But more than anything else it was the organist herself that excited Bruce. For Bruce pointed out that she appears to be playing with both hands, suggesting the development of harmony and polyphony some eight centuries before their rise in the Western musical tradition – surely one of the most remarkable documents in the history of music.

There is an interesting footnote to the history of this mosaic: it was to appear on exhibition in London. Between 2009 and 2011 the Royal Academy were planning a major exhibition of Syrian art and archaeology to take place in autumn 2013: one of their 'blockbusters', the biggest assemblage of Syrian art treasures ever gathered together under one roof with objects from all over Europe and North America, but with most of course coming from Syria itself. As one of the curators of this planned exhibition, I was a part of a visiting Academy delegation to Syria in 2011 to discuss loans. The Syrian authorities agreed, within reason, to nearly all our requests for their greatest art treasures to come to London – including the Maryamin Mosaic.

As a spin-off from the planned exhibition, I discussed Bruce's observations of the mosaic with one of the major figures in early music in the world, the Catalan-Spanish conductor, musician and musicologist

Jordi Savall. Jordi was completely taken by the mosaic and was enthused at the suggestion of re-creating the actual event depicted on it in a live performance in London, with replica instruments!

Alas, history has taken its course, and at the end of 2011 the planned exhibition was cancelled by the Royal Academy due to the increasingly deadly civil war in Syria, and we never got the mosaic, the exhibition, or the performance. Right up until the end, Bruce and I were discussing a joint article on the mosaic, with the main contribution being Bruce's on the musical aspects, something not previously published. I had published a brief note on the mosaic in the second edition of my *Rome in the East: The Transformation of an Empire*, (Routledge, 2016), pp. 259–60, acknowledging Bruce's ideas on the musical aspects.

There are many more such examples of Bruce's scholarship that I could cite, and I am sure yet more that others could cite as well. But these two examples illustrate just how closely and carefully Bruce would scrutinise an object or a work of art and bring his huge knowledge, experience and understanding of people to bear and come up with observations and conclusions that many had missed. With his departure, the scholarly world is the poorer.

# AMATEUR MUSICIAN AND
# PROFESSIONAL GUEST

# It began with Schubert's trout quintet at Isfahan

**Norman MacSween** *is a former diplomat, with postings including in Tehran (Persian language student when Bruce was in Isfahan). Keen amateur musician and piano historian.*

We were never privileged to go on one of Bruce's fabled oriental tours. But over the last twenty years Jane and I were lucky enough to share a number of musical journeys with him, more modest in scale but memorable none the less.

The first house concert I remember Bruce organising took place in Isfahan before the Shah was dethroned. Bruce was living in the house of the Anglican bishop, Hassan Dehqani-Tafti, and I was a junior diplomat in the British Embassy in Tehran. Somehow, with the revolutionary crowds beginning to gather on the streets, we induced a handful of musicians from Tehran, who included a superb Persian double bass player, down to Isfahan to play Schubert's Trout Quintet: an improbable moment of Alpine calm before the storm.

I would not see Bruce again for twenty years. When we met again in London, Bruce somehow conceived the idea that a piano duet ensemble would enable us to give concerts, raise money for charities, and be a passport to travel. We road tested this concept at a musical evening generously hosted by Julian Lush and Sarah Searight in their spacious drawing room in Clapham. And there proved to be sufficient four-hands repertoire to entertain a crowded room, particularly when enlivened by Bruce's commentary: a Bach Prelude and Fugue, a Clementi Sonata, and Schubert's magnificent Variations on an Original Theme in A flat.

An export version of our ensemble was tested in Tunisia in 2007. Our friends Alan Goulty and Lillian Craig Harris were living in perhaps the most gracious British Embassy residence in the Arab world, a beautiful neoclassical villa on the outskirts of Tunis with a spacious garden. We could not find anything more oriental for our programme than Schumann's rarely played *Bilder aus Osten*, but this seemed to go down well with the diplomatic corps of Tunis, who had rallied obligingly to boost Alan and Lillian's charity to support displaced and vulnerable women in Sudan. The piano was one of those British grands still to be found in British ambassadorial residences worldwide; my score still has 'x's marking those notes on the piano, which, despite the obliging piano tuner's repeated remedial visits to regulate, it was prudent to avoid in performance. As well as for the wonderful Roman sites in Tunisia for which, in true Bruce style, we hired a car and driver, this visit was memorable for the lemons. On our last day, we passed a street vendor sitting outside a lemon grove. Bruce insisted on us buying up his entire stock of lemons, which necessitated a visit to the bazaar to buy two extra suitcases to transport them. On our return to the UK, we were to discover just how quickly unwaxed lemons go off, but we still treasure Bruce's recipe for lemon marmalade with vanilla.

Over the last decade music, including our four-hands pieces, would also feature at the birthday parties Bruce was so adept at persuading his friends to host in a string of suitably spectacular locations. A palazzo on a hill overlooking Orvieto, a lochside house near Ullapool in Wester Ross, a seventeenth-century villa in the Veneto: there seemed no end to the possibilities Bruce could conjure up, like Ali Baba, from his address book. His friends came from far and wide. Younger players were enthusiastically added to the gathering. The party would go on for days, with Bruce's wider contacts harnessed to provide ancillary cultural diversions, such as an unforgettable private visit to view the precious manuscript copies of the Scarlatti harpsichord sonatas in the Marciana Library in St Mark's Square in Venice.

These were the big gatherings. But Bruce much relished what was perhaps our most intimate, and unusual, audience, the late great Professor Stephen Hawking. A neighbour of ours in Scotland had been running his team of nurses and carers, and told us she thought Stephen Hawking might enjoy a small concert at his house. So we summoned up our courage and knocked on his door in Cambridge, to find a group of his neighbours and carers assembled in his living room, and of course the famous wheelchair and spectral speaking device. Since we knew that Stephen Hawking loved Wagner, we had cheekily prepared the *Souvenirs de Bayreuth*, an affectionate send-up of Wagnerian themes for four hands by Fauré and Messager. He was kind enough to tell us that our music had had a favourable effect on his neurons. We were invited back, and indeed played at the last birthday he celebrated before his death.

Bruce was of course an able pianist and excellent sightreader. But what was it which brought such joy to our music making with him? It was surely that in his approach to music, Bruce showed the qualities that so evidently governed his life overall – abundant generosity of spirit, a zest for the finer things of this world, a mission to expand the horizons of others to encompass his own wide-ranging tastes. When his cancer was diagnosed, Bruce's reaction was that, such was the importance of music to him, he was determined to make as much of it as he could with his friends for as long as it would be possible. We find it hard to imagine that he is not still doing it.

# Accompanying Bruce: piano wars

**Andrew Campbell-Tiech** *met Bruce some fifteen years ago, around an upright piano at the home of Narguess Farzad and George Collie. Bruce was playing Chopin's C-sharp minor Nocturne (1830, posthumously published) and magnificently fluffed the penultimate bravura passage, shrugging as if to blame the composer. They became fast friends. Bruce discovered Andrew was a lawyer. He often asked Andrew for advice. He never took it.*

The piano duet might strike the casual observer as the very symbol of harmony – of man and his music. Perhaps the form is somewhat cloying, redolent of parlours past, too Victorian. But in a fractured, fractious world, surely a comforting reminder of a gentler, kinder age.

Except playing with Bruce was none of these things. As he took his customary place on the piano stool (of which more below), he would arch his back, his face taut, his focus intense and unyielding. Wannell before el Alamein. And I his Rommel.

*Skirmish*
Music, like warfare, is preceded by ritual. The leader stands. The orchestra falls silent. An oboe emits a loud A.

Ours began like this.

Bruce: 'Dearest Andrew, would you like to play the *primo*?'

Andrew: 'No, of course not. I know my place.'

Bruce: 'Are you sure, because I usually take the *secondo*.' (This was an outright lie, as we both knew. Occasionally Bruce would add dubious weight to it by claiming that Norman MacSween, with whom Bruce played 'to performance level' and who was 'a *true* musician, Andrew', always insisted on the upper part. I ignored this plea to higher authority, as Bruce assumed I would.)

Andrew: 'Yes, I'm sure.'

Bruce: 'Well, I may struggle to sightread it but let us try.' (Another whopper. We had played these self-same parts many, many times before. Incidentally, the 'let us' was a sly reference to 'let us pray', conveying Bruce's undermining belief that only the intervention of the Almighty would transform the forthcoming session into something remotely musical.)

Comincia la comedia.

### First Battle: Territory

Piano stools are necessarily utilitarian. I have a not-unpleasant leather-bound example that can easily accommodate two adults of contemporary girth. Bruce of course never attained modernity. So there was plenty of space for us both.

Except there wasn't.

Bruce would start by extending his left index finger and drawing an imaginary line down from middle C, bisecting the seat. Infuriatingly, he would then ignore this division and push me leftwards such that I ended up perched precariously at the edge. He later consolidated this land grab by reference to an idiosyncrasy of mine (see below).

Territory lost.

### Second Battle: Gesture

The first time I saw this, I was transfixed and stopped playing altogether. In the opening movement of Schubert's Fantasia there is an especially lyrical passage – for the *primo*.

Just before the climax of the poignant phrase, Bruce raised his right forearm above his shoulder and further flexed his wrist towards the ceiling. He then brought both down in an elegant arc and stroked the apposite key.

I'm afraid I started to laugh. This led to a contretemps and a short hiatus. We eventually agreed upon a compromise. Gestures were acceptable, but only where Bruce had previously determined upon a breath (see below).

Ground held.

### Third Battle: Feint

Although quite unable to dance, I nonetheless have a real talent for swaying from side to side. I do this unconsciously. Particularly when playing the piano. This is not necessarily to the advantage of my duet partner. As the haunting theme of the Fantasia reappeared at the conclusion of the fugue, I allegedly lurched so far to my right that Bruce – deliberately in my opinion – fell off the stool. He then used the fact of my assault upon him (as he termed it) as historic justification for the permanently unequal division of sitting space.

Rommel squeezed.

## Fourth Battle: Counting

To his unconstrained delight, Bruce discovered that I can't count. This isn't literally true. Of course I can count. What I have difficulty in doing is counting whilst I am playing. I explain this deficiency by reference to a brain overload, and the reason for that is that I am always sightreading (see below). Anyway, as is obvious, if one pianist is keeping strict time and another is treating it as relative, the result is less Schubert and more Schoenberg. Bruce didn't approve of serialism and the Second Viennese experiment. So with ill-becoming glee, Bruce would count out loud, adopting the tone of a slightly exasperated twentieth-century prep school master. One And Two And Three And Four And. One And Two And Three And Four And.

Rommel in retreat.

## Fifth Battle: Pedalling

Bruce, otherwise and famously a free spirit, was nonetheless a devotee of every dogma attaching to the classical music canon.

By unbreakable convention, the *secondo* pedals. The degree of autonomy this gave me was obviously intolerable.

So Bruce resorted to guerrilla tactics.

*Sotto voce*, I would be instructed to take my foot off the sustaining pedal and sometimes to remove my feet altogether from its vicinity. He would ostentatiously look down to ensure my offending extremities were suitably tucked under the small area of the piano stool still available to me. Chastised and obedient, I would then hear a hiss of 'pedal, pedal!' as a new subject apparently demanded an immediate *volte face*.

Rout.

## Sixth Battle: Reading

Bruce approached a score as he did a rare Persian manuscript, or perhaps the other way round. He meticulously noted each *appoggiatura*, every slur. His modest purpose was to divine and deliver the will of the composer for the edification of mankind.

All this concentration made him an average-to-poor sightreader of the quicker tempo. An allegro would commence andante and often end adagio.

By contrast, I look at a score as I do a brief, or perhaps the other way round. I instinctively discard peripheral verbiage or notation. In short, I am a good sightreader, a half-talent that Bruce dismissed as 'glib'.

The trouble is, just as yesterday's case is ancient history, so I forget that I have ever seen the piece before. I am always sightreading.

Bruce exploited this magnificently.

The same thirteen bars into the second of the Dvořák Legends, he would stop and point out all the subtle markings I had missed yet again, his tone one of patient resignation.

*Sauve qui peut.*

### Seventh Battle: Breathing

Having demonstrated my inability to see what was in front of me, Bruce then pursued a related stratagem that was to prove his most successful, namely his superior, indeed exclusive, understanding of implied notation. Waving at an unremarkable series of bars, he would alight upon one and authoritatively declare that it 'manifestly called for a breath'. In honour thereof, he explained that we should momentarily lift our hands from the keyboard, thus causing a *caesura*.

I had never heard of implied notation. Nor has Google.

This Wannellian *rubato* allowed room for the Gesture, much to my irritation. I also noticed that over the years it expanded to encompass any passage that Bruce might unaccountably find a trifle difficult.

Rommel defeated.

### Olive Branch

As every juror discovers, what is exhausting is the intensity of the case, not its duration. So it was with Bruce. Buoyed by victory and with complete operational and territorial control, he could afford to be magnanimous. The counting out loud became less frequent. He stopped staring accusingly at the pedals. We actually played, in and at the same time. A duet.

Unfortunately, by this stage I was in a state of advanced debilitation, not least because of the extensive physical contortions I had been obliged to adopt in the course of my latest defeat. So these sounds of harmony rarely lasted more than a quarter of an hour. As I rose stiffly to my much abused feet, Bruce would look at me warmly, exclaiming, 'We're getting there, we're getting there.'

### Armistice

Two Sundays before his death, Wannell and Rommel met for the last time. Although diminished in stature and with an involuntary *vibrato* in his left hand, Bruce nevertheless reprised each of the battle formations that had brought him such success for well over a decade. No resistance was offered.

Dominance conceded, we embarked upon the glorious sixth Legend, with its rolling bass and sudden changes of mood and key. The *primo* ends in the major with three solemn chords, played pianissimo:

Bruce looked at me warmly. 'We're getting there, we're getting there.'

# Journeys through life

*Like Bruce,* **Christopher Sykes** *went to Wellington and Oriel College, Oxford, where he read German and French. He then qualified as a chartered accountant before working for the European divisions of various international companies. He went on to learn three further languages, all of which he now uses in his retirement as a guide for the National Trust, when he's not ballroom dancing or bell ringing. He and his wife live in south-west England.*

The first journey I took with Bruce was a musical one. We were both at Wellington College but it was older brother James that I knew, as we had been in the same year. In about 1968 a new Musical Director came, Jared Armstrong, who was an inspiration. He changed the rules of the inter-House Singing Competition from requiring every member of the House to sing a song to allowing any number of singers and to allowing instruments and movement. For my House, I selected a number of songs from *West Side Story*, and used instruments and had various people act out the songs. And this was where I first encountered Bruce. His entry was just four singers, and of course it was a madrigal. He won. I was astonished by his complete abandonment of the idea of its being a House Competition and his focus on its being something musical and beautiful.

The head of the German Department, Peter Willey, organised a Gap Year project called 'Be a Berliner for Three Months'. Bruce and I were two of the twelve participants. (Mr Willey used to explore the castles of the Assassins in northern Persia during the summer in the 1960s. I wonder if Bruce ever thought of him during his own travels?) In Berlin, all the nine boys in the group worked in the main sorting office. Bruce loathed it; it bored him. He would disappear for half an hour or so to the toilet where he would sit and read Horace's *Odes* in the original. One morning he phoned in and, in impeccable German, told the supervisor that sadly Herr Wannell had died in the night so wouldn't be coming in, and no, no further details were available pending investigations. Bruce duly turned up for work for his next shift, quite unconcerned.

Another pastime in Berlin was, after work, to go to a Konditorei-Café with two or three others, where we would compete in who could take the longest to eat a slice of Käsesahnetorte, or similar gateau. Bruce won easily, savouring the flavour of every mouthful for an hour. On one occasion, he noticed a very upright Frau watching him disapprovingly. He proceeded to take the lumps of sugar and eat each one slowly and deliberately till the bowl was empty, while her eyebrows rose ever higher.

He had an art of charming people. Others will tell of the time he hitched a lift back to Oxford from Kidlington. He persuaded the driver, a shepherd, to come a few days later to his room in Oriel and bring a lamb, a Watteau-esque effect for the literary *fête champêtre*, when we all had to read something out. He once apparently wrote to the Duke of Devonshire and asked to see his private collection of drawings. I think he ended up staying at Chatsworth. On a visit to Dorset to my parents' house, he asked me if we could drive down to Cranborne, the seat of the Earl of Salisbury. Faced with the 'Private – No Admittance' signs at the gate, he insisted I drive in. We parked in front of the house and Bruce proceeded to explore the gardens. A butler rushed out protesting that the grounds were not open to the public. Bruce calmly asked to speak to Amelia (or some such name). No one here of that name was the reply. 'This is Cranborne School, isn't it?' says Bruce. The butler became helpful and explained to me how to get there (the school was at Wardour, and very close to my house!) Meanwhile Bruce ignored him and continued exploring.

Bruce and I used to go walking in the Lakes each year with our Berlin friend David Anderson. David would book a tiny National Trust bothy called Bird How in Eskdale. It has 'running water' (a stream runs past the door), an Elsan toilet and fantastic views. It appealed to Bruce's poetic side. He is the only man I know who could make putting Dubbin on hiking boots a moment of poetry. Our long walks over the fells each day revealed just how wiry and tough he was despite his literary airs and apparent lack of exercise. Bites of Kendal Mint Cake were forbidden until a summit had been reached. Back at the bothy, Bruce would produce herbs from his pocket – sorrel, wild sage or thyme – to go with our supper, picked as he had walked along. David and I would bring him back down to earth with the twenty-minute stroll to the pub for beer and dominoes.

Bruce would meet the surprises of life with insouciance. On one occasion at Oxford, he missed our German prose class. His excuse was that he had had to go home to his secluded parents' house, as it had been burgled of its fine art and the police needed to know what had gone, his parents being away at the time. His father had been burgled before and had upgraded the security such that the front door had multiple bolts going through the reinforced door frame into the very wall itself. The burglars had simply removed the entire doorway and the surrounding brickwork to get in, leaving it on the lawn. Shortly afterwards, Bruce missed the German class again. The tutor retorted in exasperation 'What's his excuse this time ? Accused of murder ?!' And so it was. There had been a particularly nasty one a few days earlier and the police had alerted all laundries and laundrettes to look out for bloodstained clothing. After a few hours in the cells, he was released when the forensic results came through.

Bruce loved the eighteenth and nineteenth centuries. He read widely and knew his art. We fellow students were amazed by Bruce's knowledge and command of his subject, when, one week, he was selected by the tutor to read out his work to the class. Bruce picked up a sheaf of papers and proceeded to read his 2,000-word essay, fluently and effortlessly. Those of us who sat behind him could see that the papers were completely blank.

A final journey of Bruce's comes to mind. A few years ago I was at home in my Dorset cottage, once my parents', on a winter's afternoon. There was a knock at the door, and there was Bruce. I invited him in for tea and we caught up on old news for about an hour. He stood up; he had to go; his friend was sat in the car outside. He had made no mention of anyone else throughout. I had naturally assumed that he had learned to drive in the intervening years. I often wonder who that patient friend was!

As someone else wrote to me about him, I liked Bruce very much. He was interesting, funny, and we had a shared interest in many things.

# Bruce would call me '*umm-as-salon*'

**Dalu Jones** *is an independent scholar, traveller and writer. Founder and editor of AARP (Art and Archaeology Research Papers) and associate editor of* International Architect and Environmental Design. *She has curated exhibitions and written on Islamic art and architecture, the relationship between European and Eastern cultures and the history of art collecting in Italy. She has been writing regularly for* Minerva *since 1996.*

The 'salon' was originally in London at Priory Cottage in Islington, my house at the time. It was a meeting point, an international crossroads and a safe harbour for many diverse people.

It was a large house and musical evenings would take place there quite regularly, affording live performances from the best and most celebrated eastern musicians like Mahmud Mirza, Amjad Ali Khan, Zakir Hussein, Kudsi Erguner. Also African musicians like Mohammed al-Amin from the Sudan. The concerts were the brain child of Anderson Bakewell who – among many other pioneering ventures – had founded the Maqam Society to foster Oriental Music in London. This was in the early 1980s, nearly forty years ago. Together, Anderson and I hosted the concerts which were rather informal and well attended by many people of all walks of life and nationalities. Even John Cage made an appearance.

And it was then that Anderson introduced Bruce to me.

Thereafter we would go together to listen to Persian poetry recitations, to gallery openings, to lectures on Islamic art. He soon became a friend of my friends. With those who are musicians he would play music.

Later, when he was travelling abroad almost continuously and I had moved to Italy, Bruce would call me to chat and often ask if I had friends he might meet wherever he happened to be or in the next country he was planning to visit. I did indeed know many generous people scattered around the world and ever-widening circles of common friends were created and shared, be it in Italy, France, Delhi, Hong Kong or even Brussels – we both had Belgian family links and shared a multilingual upbringing.

During his long walking trip from Peshawar to Cairo and then on to Europe he would use telephone booths to call me. He called from the Yemen, from Kenya, from Ismailia, from Cairo. At the end of his adventure, when he had finally landed in Europe, exhausted and unwell, he came to rest in Tuscany where I still live in a simple house among olive trees. It is a solitary place and we both thought he could recover here, gather strength and begin work on the book he had been commissioned to write about his quite extraordinary journey.

When he left he gave me the pair of worn out leather sandals he had bought in Ethiopia.

Once – in Florence – he also gave me some rare incense from the Hadramaut. We burnt it over a long evening in the fireplace of the house of a fellow traveller who had some of her own incense from Arabia, but not nearly as precious and all pervading.

Other times he just came to visit when he was on his way to meet his many other friends in Italy. We would explore the lovely towns nearby – in Sovana we had a momentous lunch with local delicacies to complete the visit of Romanesque churches and Etruscan tombs. Italian gardens were admired as was the Cistercian abbey of Sant Antimo where Gregorian chanting was still practised by Spanish monks he could exchange notes with.

He brought back from his journeys tales of distant lands and ongoing – though not always quite accurate – malicious gossip about people high and low, secrets pried open in the corridors of fashionable palaces or ferreted out from the lanes of international market places.

Often and best, he would talk of music heard and shared with friends and of musicians singing and playing *dhrupad* or *qawwali* songs in Kabul, or by a bridge in Isfahan or at dusk in an Indian garden.

Music was his trade and the key to his soul.

# Elusive, implausible

**Joe Roberts** *is an Indophile who has written three books and numerous articles about the Subcontinent. He is fascinated by Indian art, an interest he shared with Bruce. He lives in Bath with his wife and family.*

I first met Bruce in York at Lisa Chaney's house. We were breaking a journey from Northumberland back to Bath and we had two Bengali friends with us. This would have been the late 1990s. Lisa had invited Bruce to meet us. He came carrying a rabab, a kind of Afghan lute with twenty-one strings. He seemed impressed that I knew what it was. I was far more impressed when he started to play the rabab and my Indian friends recognised what he was playing, a fragment of Raga Malkauns. Bruce explained to us that the snatch he had played referred to the snakes around Lord Shiva's neck. All this happened in the first ten minutes of our acquaintance. I realised there and then that he was an extraordinary person.

Over the next two decades, Bruce would often stay with us in Bath. We felt we knew him well but there was something mysterious, elusive, almost implausible about him. He could pop up at random like a fictional character. Eating in the same Lebanese restaurant, visiting the same exhibition, at the same performance of North African music in the Union Chapel.

We met once in the Lodhi Gardens in Delhi a couple of years ago. I'd brought a picnic and Bruce decided we should eat it inside one of the Lodhi tombs, out of the heat. We hadn't eaten much at all before an attendant told us eating in the tombs was prohibited. I was sure it would be but it was typical of Bruce to want such a stylish lunch venue. He was, of course, the best and most knowledgeable guide to the Lodhi tombs one could hope for.

Later during the same visit to Delhi I went to meet the writer Nilanjana Roy at the Hazrat Nizamuddin Aulia Dargah where, on Thursday evenings, *qawaalis* – said to be descendants of Amir Khusrau, 'the Parrot of India' – clap and chant their ecstatic choruses. Across the crowded shrine I suddenly spotted Bruce. He was deep in conversation with the Pir, the spiritual master of the shrine, speaking in fluent Urdu. I made my way over and Bruce, still speaking Urdu, introduced me. Needless to say, the conversation was entirely lost on me. When I asked Bruce what they were discussing he told me they were comparing Novalis' *Hymnen an die Nacht* to medieval Persian mysticism. The truth is I couldn't always tell when Bruce was pulling my leg. I suspect he wasn't.

# Bruce comes to the 'rescue'

**Lucinda Bredin** *is editor of* Bonhams Magazine *(and the auction house's Global Director of Communications). Lucinda first met Bruce in 2011 in Spitalfields, although her husband, Bruce Palling, had met him in 1989 for lunch to talk about Kabul in a borrowed bedsit in Shepherd's Market. Most of the next decade of friendship was spent on trips to the opera and planning a trip to Iran.*

I had heard all about Bruce, obviously. But when the summons to meet him came back in 2011, it arrived from an unexpected source. After an afternoon session of bashing out headlines for *Bonhams Magazine* with my deputy, Matthew Wilcox – my favourite was 'Dying to meter', to go with an article about the last days of Elizabeth Barratt Browning – Matthew cleared his throat. 'Huh, I hope you aren't doing anything on Tuesday…'. The tone implied a veiled warning. 'Bruce Wannell has asked you to supper. At my house.'

It turned out that Bruce had moved in about a month ago to Sclater Street in Spitalfields, where Matthew lodged, in a wonderful house owned by Gwendolyn Leick. And Bruce had been busy ever since. He had staged a series of recitals with several different string quartets, a couple of salons at which Persian poetry had been read, a spoon-carving workshop – and a number of dinner parties, most of which had been cooked by Matthew.

It seemed on this occasion, the cooking bit had been a bone of contention. Matthew, a chef of rare competence, had prepared a boeuf bourguignon, only for Bruce to declare it 'not quite right'. Bruce had then busily set about 'rescuing it' (his phrase). Matthew spent the evening in a semi-sulk, glaring at his ruined dinner.

Bruce and I hit it off immediately. We had two bonding points. One was Willie Dalrymple, who was always effusive in acknowledging the role of Bruce's translations in his books, although maybe not the effect on his household. The other was our teeth. At that point, Bruce was not the suave, groomed, figure he became. In this incarnation, he looked like a particularly shifty extra from *Mutiny on the Bounty* with an odd pigtail-y haircut, possibly self-administered, and without his full complement of teeth. My hair had been professionally cut, but I had suffered a recent mishap when I fainted against a radiator with disastrous results. Within minutes, Bruce made me feel as if my dentistry was an enhancement, an idiosyncratic quirk that lent a pleasing asymmetry to my face. I was utterly won over.

The 'teeth issue' faded, but by contrast Willie Dalrymple became a leitmotif between Bruce and myself. I'd asked Willie to write an article about the Qajar ruler, Fath-Ali Shah for *Bonhams Magazine*. Time ticked on ... and on. Things were getting so late that there was a danger that the sale to which the article was related would have happened before the magazine was published. The front and back sections were already plated up and rolling... and so praise sweet Jesus, when the piece arrived, it was marvellous. Willie had bestowed a narrative, with a rich sweep of historical context, full of dramatic elan, gossip, and murder of every variety, upon a collection of rather rustic paintings that certainly didn't deserve such elevating treatment. Air punch, I thought. Oven-ready copy. Let's shove in the odd comma and bung it off to press.

I hadn't, however, reckoned with Bruce. The WhatsApp arrived at 3 a.m. Bruce was staying with Willie and Olivia and had caught sight of the piece. Rather like Matthew Wilcox's dinner, he felt it only fair to come to the 'rescue' with a bit of cold water and a few unwelcome facts. 'Good morning, Lucinda. Willie sleeps late, so I am unable to discuss this with him. I believe you have to rush to the printers so I'll keep my suggestions brief. White egret's feathers? When Ker Porter has just described them as black? Point 2: Even if an autocrat, Fath 'Ali (please correct spelling throughout) was a Muslim, which would have made it legally impossible to have more than four wives concurrently – let alone 158. Point 3: Fath 'Ali sending this portrait around the country in fresco and rock relief needs rephrasing – I don't think Qajar technology was up to transporting mountains and cliff-faces and whole walls. 4. Georgia I believe was bequeathed to Russia by one of its eighteenth-century kings precisely to *save* it from Persia. Finally, "one of the greatest artistic revivals"? Dear Lucinda, I think advertising overkill. Love Bruce.'

Huh, the presses ground to a halt.

In February, when we were staying with Willie and Olivia in Delhi, I read them Bruce's text. While we were all laughing, I thought yes, Bruce could be infuriating, and at times, extremely inconvenient. But he was usually, well, often, right.

# Somewhere between Spitfire pilot and steampunk

*After a spectacularly brief career in the Diplomatic Service and a regrettably longer one in the law,* **Peter Barker** *is now enjoying the sunny uplands of retirement, grandparenthood and more time with his camera: www.peterbarker.org*

I first met Bruce in Isfahan in 1979. We lost and found one another a few times over the years and then made firm contact when he came to live in York. He occasionally came to stay with us in Beverley and one day he suggested that I should go over and pick him up on my motorcycle, an ageing but beautiful Moto Guzzi which had caught his eye. I agreed but told him that he would need warm and sturdy clothes for the ride.

Come the day, I parked the bike outside his place on Holgate Road. I was only halfway up the path when the door was thrown open and there stood Bruce. He looked magnificent – in some sort of leather battledress tunic, voluminous tweed pants tucked into blindingly polished riding boots, sheepskin gloves clutched in one hand and an ancient pair of goggles in the other. The look was somewhere between Spitfire pilot and steampunk.

We had a fine time that day and the ride was the first of a number that we took over the years round the East Yorkshire Wolds, Holderness and Lincolnshire. We went out to the tip of Spurn Point one day when it was still accessible to a two-wheeler and stopped in a greasy spoon café on the way. A radio was playing some sort of pop and Bruce made them turn it off and then gave the little boy who served us ten pence for being so 'well behaved' as Bruce put it. Another time we rode out to the Lincolnshire coast to see some friends of his. It was a beautiful day but I had to be back for a parents' evening at my daughter's school. This clashed with Bruce's plan to organise a samphire collecting party on the dunes. I caught the last ten minutes of the parents' evening.

217

One day we rode out to Kirkham Priory where Bruce bumped into some member of the landed gentry with whom a distant connection inevitably emerged. Bruce was always bumping into people. It was part of the fun of being with him. The other party always had that slightly bemused look until they realised that resistance was futile. If I was with Bruce and he was simply going to cross the road for a moment I would always go with him because something interesting was bound to happen on the other side.

I think it was on the way back from Kirkham that Bruce suggested we pop into a nursery so he could pick up one or two plants. Needless to say we emerged from the nursery staggering under the weight of his purchases which we then had to load into the motorcycle's panniers. We managed most of it apart from two large potted bushes. There was only one thing for it. We processed back through York at a stately pace, Bruce holding a bush tucked insecurely under either arm, he almost invisible between the two of them. I thought we might attract the attention of the constabulary that day but we stayed lucky.

He brought romance but also a certain impracticality to the pillion. As a prelude to one ride, Bruce had decided for some reason not to sleep the night before. He was dog-tired and lay down on the kitchen floor of Holgate Road for a short nap before we set off but that didn't help. We had not even left York before he had slumped asleep on the pillion sending the bike yawing towards the centre of the road. This did not bode well. I took back roads but the same thing happened two or three times and we were clearly avoiding disaster by only a hair's breadth. In the end I had to stop, let him have another half-hour's sleep on a roadside bench and then warn him that if there were any more narcoleptic interludes I would have to put him on the bus for safety's sake. Somehow we got home in one piece.

Another time – all these moments are coming back to me as I write – we rode out, this time I think on a pair of bicycles, from Beverley to the village of Etton where Bruce was helping a friend with a bit of research on a book she was writing about the dye indigo. Our goal for the day was to get ourselves inside the rather magnificent old rectory in the village. Bruce decided on a frontal assault. It was a hot day. We ran our fingers through our hair, wiped our sweating brows, marched up the drive and banged on the door. When it opened we seemed to move into a slightly different space/time continuum. With the aplomb which so often left me open-mouthed, Bruce explained that he had come to do some research on the subject of the dye indigo and he would like to have a look around the house. There was a moment's silence and then the owner – to his credit – responded as if he had been expecting us for days. Of course, we would be welcome – we could look wherever we wished (and I swear someone in the background almost curtsied as we swept through). We strode round the house and Bruce dragged out a pencil and piece of paper, consulting me in a stage whisper from time to time on matters indigo, as if I were some sort of visiting expert. By the time we had finished and scampered back down the drive we could hardly contain ourselves. I think he did it just for devilment.

One day we went out to Bridlington in a Russian motorcycle and sidecar I had bought. He loved it – especially as he didn't have to wear a helmet. We rode back to Beverley along Woldgate, an ancient road that runs from the coast back out high over the Wolds. To the left we could see cliffs and sea and to the right the rolling pastureland of the Vale of Pickering. We were in brilliant sunshine interspersed with billowing white cloud. I glanced down at Bruce. His eyes were shut, his face turned blissfully to the sun, his nose raised to catch every scent like an ecstatic pointer. It was a glorious moment.

I moved from Beverley a couple of years ago and sold all the bikes then. Now Bruce is gone. There is no need to be sad since in the end everything is gone. I offer a deep bow of gratitude to the fates which permitted me such a long and rewarding friendship with him.

# The call

**Julie Bland**, *friend of Bruce's from undergraduate high jinks in Oxford, then (one of many) London hosts on Bruce's culture stops between the exotic and York. One of most memorable evenings: an opera singer friend doing Schubert songs in a jazz bar in Loughborough Junction.*

From an unspecified location (usually on his current host's landline or more recently a small mobile phone): 'Julie dearest, I trust I find you and the family well?'

Bruce was always charmingly and genuinely interested in all four children, each having a separate honorary-uncle-type relationship with him. With one he enjoyed a particularly mischievous and subversive relationship, not conducive to parental ease of mind, when we left him *in loco parentis*.

'I'm off to (insert exotic location, often war torn). I'm planning to spend a few days in London to get my visa. There's a rather good concert of a underrated little-known Italian composer X at the Wigmore Hall on Thursday and I'm hoping a few friends will join for drinks there.... Do you know Y, fascinating professor of Z, and A, great friend of B, who I used to do music with in Peshawar... and of course the Cs who you met at that opening we went to in Albemarle Street... D may be there, who's just published a book on early Byzantine mosaics...'

'Bruce would you like a bed here?'

'Well that might work well. I'm going to rehearse some piano duets with E in (other end of London), so I could be with you about seven?'

About 8.30 an immaculate figure rings the bell. Fully coordinated tie, suit, pocket handkerchief and scarf, often with overcoat insouciantly falling from the shoulders.

Always an exquisite present, sourdough from the St John bakery, crystallised orange peel in dark chocolate, and *pièce de résistance*, straw hats made to measure for the daughters, from his hatter friends in York.

After a small plate of food and some wine, bed. Then an extremely early start. Working on the latest translation of tomb inscriptions in medieval Arabic.

'This balcony is the best bit of your house,' Bruce announces definitely. Hard to discern an insult or a compliment.

Then breakfast. Mugs were pure suffering. We had to scramble for a teacup and saucer. We knew that this uber civilised approach was also being provided at the housing association house in York, where he seemed to be imposing a high standard of gracious elegant living.

I wondered if his fellow tenants felt a bit like wild animals with a patient but slightly exasperated lion tamer? We certainly felt that an odour of aesthetic refinement had infused the house, and that we were found wanting, but generally he was humorously tolerant of our failings.

On one occasion we had made an effort at tidying. His comment was, 'I have noticed in my friends' houses, that as their children grow up and leave home, their houses become more... civilised... tidy... but perhaps less lively.'

Sometimes he could be quite demanding. While we were still undergraduates, he came to stay with others in a remote freezing house on the North York moors. Think *Wuthering Heights* with old porcelain hot water bottles. None of us really knew how to cook, and mostly ate chicken in a basket and drank quantities of Bardolino in the pub next door.

We must have made some kind of pudding and run out of cream. So I produced a rather ancient tin of Bird's custard powder. I rather liked the way it went from pale pink to bright yellow as you added milk. Bruce was frankly appalled. He set about constructing a double boiler in the kitchen (*Withnail and I*) and made a tiny quantity of exquisite 'proper custard', which I hadn't even heard of previously.

More recently, we had what we thought of as a rather splendid extension built on the back of our house. It took over a year. Bruce sat at breakfast on his first morning in the glass box and said slightly petulantly, 'Well, you really need to plant something big in this corner so we don't have to look at that,' pointing at our neighbours' bicycle rack.

His warm generosity was unusual, in his delight in bringing his friends together, sharing food, jokes and music.

No note of friendship could be complete without a tribute to his extraordinary grace in the face of pain and death. One of my last memories of him was lying down, enjoying the sound of his friends' voices and the tinkling of glasses, as he lay dying.

# Italy with Bruce

**Helena Gerrish** *is an old friend of Bruce's from Oxford days.*

B ruce's sixty-fifth birthday was celebrated in the Veneto in early
September 2017. We visit the Oratorio di San Giorgio in Padua to
look at the Altichiero frescoes followed by gelati at Caffe Pedrocchi.
At the Villa van Axel, a marvellous music and singing party – piano,
flute, violin – and feasts of cheeses, peppers, Austrian hams, sweet
Italian cakes, prosecco. A tour of the Brion tomb by Carlo Scarpa,
wonderful visit to Villa Maser to see the Veronese frescoes, incredible
al fresco lunch, a rush to Possagno to the Antonio Canova museum
of his plaster cast models, drinks at the Cipriani in Asolo, and a tired
but happy band of followers having supper at the end of a memorable
day. It is 10 p.m. Bruce with that steely glint in his eyes says, 'Would
you mind taking X home, he has such a wonderful collection of Italian
glass – you will never see anything like it, only a few miles away.'
We readily agree and load his friend into the hire car. He of course
speaks no English, we speak no Italian, we have no map, so we turn
left or right whenever he indicates with his hand. At first, we count
the lefts and rights then as the petrol light comes on on the dash we
lose count. Up over mountains we go, through darkly lit villages, past
industrial estates, signs to the Austrian border, wondering whether we
should ring our hotel. The owner, well over eighty and dressed as
Eleonora Duse, warned that we must be back by 11 but the mobile
phone with very little battery has no signal in the mountains. After
an hour we arrive at a town – we don't know where – and the Italian
gestures to stop and suggests through hand signals that we come in to
see 'le vietri'. We shake our heads, say 'too late'. He looks relieved
and says, 'Ciao'.

By now tempers are flaring, we lambast Bruce – how could he have
done this to us, the phone gutters and goes out, we imagine sleeping in
the car (a very small Fiat). Another hour goes by, the petrol light flashes
ominously and eventually we arrive at Asolo at nearing 1 p.m. Eleanor

Duse's son is sitting inside the door and lets us in. We go to bed furious with Bruce, and very annoyed at being taken for such a ride.

The next day the plan is to meet Bruce in Florians in Venice for tea, after he has visited the Bibliotheca Marciana to view manuscripts. We arrive still seething – we chastise Bruce in no uncertain terms – his blue eyes twinkle, his mouth shows the start of a grin, and he says, 'How about a pistachio ice-cream – they really are awfully good here.'

# Bruce in Muscat

**Nicholas Armour** *was a career diplomat, a Foreign Office Arabist. Able to join choirs on every posting, including in war-torn Beirut, he wooed his wife Georgina in the Bach Choir in London. Now retired, singing has become almost a full-time occupation.*

My engagement with Bruce over the decades has been largely musical. We first met through a mutual musical chum when he was at Oxford – I was studying elsewhere. I sang at his sister's funeral and he conducted the choir at my wedding several years later. He was, as we all know, very good at sharing his friends with others and also at capitalising effectively on introductions we gave him. All appreciated the energy he brought to such relationships, if sometimes excessively so. I hope Frances Dodd will write about the classical music they made together in Islamabad on his occasional descents from Afghanistan.

In the early 1990s, Bruce visited us in Muscat, heading piously to the mosque at prayer time, dressed in his *shalwar kameez*. It was not really until this century that we began to see a lot more of each other and to make serious music together. By then, he and I (now widowed) were spending more time in England. Although I had got into the habit, as an amateur baritone, of giving song recitals to friends and family for my important birthdays, it was Bruce who tended to see afternoons of practice as having a public end in view. This certainly helped focus my mind, voice and technique. His love of poetry, in almost any language, ensured that he was usefully strict in getting me to understand properly what I was singing and to pronounce it accurately. I remember well a long discussion over the level of liquidity with which I should sing the 't' in the French word 'tu'. More importantly, he wanted to work on songs that were new to me but which he believed I could sing well and that he liked accompanying. He wanted to get the songs performed correctly, of course, but also with a deep understanding of what both the poet and composer were seeking. His search for that soul within music has been critical in my own musical development: Bruce was a first-rate teacher.

Bruce was also an amazing 'involver'. He never seemed to miss an opportunity to get others to perform with him or to enjoy the delights of listening to his playing, ideally with others. New victims might think they were going to spend twenty minutes playing duets with him but then find themselves released hours later having had a fantastic time. Yes, he was critical, but always as encouragement to achieving greater musical rewards. I shall definitely miss his constructive criticism, always partnered with enthusiastic satisfaction.

Our recitals were occasional and varied. We contributed to a German *lieder* evening in Christchurch, Chelsea, where all the other performers were students. We brought a more mature understanding of the music – and about half the very small audience. The Director of Music had to stand behind Bruce with a bicycle headlight shining on the score. With others for Bruce to accompany as well, we did a wonderful afternoon concert in the Clapham salon of Julian Lush and Sarah Searight, raising money for Medical Aid for Palestinians. His sixtieth birthday musical weekend near Orvieto and his sixty-fifth in the Veneto were truly memorable, not least for the erudition and painstaking attention to meticulous detail that went into the enjoyment for performers and audience alike. We returned to Altivole in April 2019 for a memorial concert weekend for the mother of Giovanna Grube: a remarkable event bringing together the musical and academic pillars – or perhaps vaults – of Bruce's life. Over the winter, we were working up some Duparc songs and with a group of young professional singers, perfecting the Brahms Liebeslieder-walzer for his godson's wedding (subsequently postponed because of Covid 19).

Bruce's most notable achievement, to my mind, was his ability to enthuse others with the joy he exuded and not just through music. That is quite a blessing.

# Bruce has come and gone

**Ian Blois** *was born in Caithness, educated in England, the son of a solicitor-turned-farmer and, apart from eighteen months backpacking in the antipodes and south-east Asia, has spent his life in Scotland as farmer-turned-land agent. He's a vicarious traveller, at home in the company of fine writing, fine art and fine fare and has been married to the artist Clare Blois since 1991.*

I met Bruce in our first year of Wellington College in 1966. Memories of those far off school days are elusive and although we were in the same House only a few images emerge. For the first few terms I think I saw myself as part of the middle-brow sporty set, if only to avoid the boys with superior academic ability. Meanwhile Bruce, who had no interest in sport, but obvious talents for music and languages, which I didn't share, was in generally higher classes than myself so we had little apparent in common. Perhaps we recognised in each other a detachment from the assumed camaraderie of boarding-school boys and a determination to resist College (as it is fawningly known by Old Wellingtonians who remember these things), either dragging us in or spitting us out.

As it was, it was a few terms later that we connected, and oddly it was through sport, which was a required school activity for one or two afternoons each week. For Bruce and myself, we found that squash fitted the bill. Togged up in tracksuits and with borrowed racquets, we filled the designated ninety minutes with a leisurely walk past the playing fields to the squash courts where I recall sitting in a corner, out of sight and out of the autumn wind, chatting about who knows what interspersed with a few games to keep warm. No doubt we put the world to rights and we must have found enough in common to keep in contact.

Bruce went on to Oxford and I to Newcastle to study agriculture for my subsequent life as a farmer and land agent. And that might have been that, but somehow we kept in touch and we met on occasion in Paris, Edinburgh and London and then, when I became more settled

Bruce made his periodic but very welcome visits first in the Borders and latterly in the Black Isle (Highlands). And so down the years to August 2015 which was the last time I saw Bruce. My wife Clare, who is a fine artist and cook, was in France at the time and I thought she would be amused by my day at home with Bruce, so I sent her the following gossipy account of his stay which unsurprisingly featured art, music, history and languages, old and new-found friends and shared food.

*Dear Clare*

*Hope you are getting emails where you are. Bruce has come and gone. A pity you weren't here, but your meatballs, currant crumbles and oatcakes were much appreciated. So a light collation for you…*

*I had agreed to meet Bruce, no, more correctly, Bruce had arranged that I should meet him off the Ullapool bus in Inverness at six on Monday evening. He has spent a week or two staying with friends in Lismore and the Western Isles and would take the ferry from Stornoway back to the mainland. I was happy to stay on in the office, before collecting him and driving home for supper.*

*Just after five o'clock my mobile rings. It's Bruce – Ian, the bus is twenty minutes late leaving, so we won't be in Inverness till around quarter past six. That's OK I will meet you then.*

*At 6.15 I'm heading down Academy Street, slightly held up by the traffic edging past the scaffolding around the burnt-out Mackay's shop. My mobile rings – Ian, I am standing below the classical portico at the bus station. I shall wait here till you arrive. Yes, yes I'll be there in two minutes. I think – please don't enter the building behind you. There isn't time for books. I must get home to feed the dog.*

*And there he is, underneath the portico which fronts the Inverness library, distinguished as always with silk-white hair and trim beard, dressed in a full-length trench coat, which does nothing to hide the rich russet cords tucked neatly into heavy woollen socks, plus-two style over smart but sensible brown leather shoes. It is the shoes which I notice mostly, sprinkled as they are with sand, betraying not a beach holiday, but walks on the machair and the shell-white shores of the Hebrides. The provenance of Hushinish possibly, though he has come from Bhaltos this morning.*

*Sharing shelter from the rain was a man in a blue work shirt bulging over his blue creaseless trousers, his belongings in a small faded-black backpack, a man whose life did not include porticos or plus twos. He was treading a dance of avoidance round the columns, hoping without hope that when his wife arrived to take him home, it should not, could not be thought that he was on the same side or under the same roof or in any way comingling with anyone such as Bruce. In Inverness, only on the Eden Court stage has such effective use been made of false portico props or such doubtful looks cast as were cast not only on the character that is Bruce but, by association, on myself. I joke about Russians with snow on their boots, and bundle Bruce and his Oliver Brown duffel bag into my car.*

*And so the drive home, along the south side of the Beauly Firth, always a joy for me, at the end of a day communing with a screen, the inland sea stretching westwards to the distant hills. Strange how proud one can be of one's locality, as if by choosing to live here one has imparted something extra, something of oneself to the scenery, which of course needs and gets no help from me. But is Bruce noticing? Possibly, though he makes no mention of the passing views, quizzing me instead about where the Frasers might live and whether Gordon would be in tomorrow.*

*Home to feed the dog and time for tea and a drink. As I check that the meatballs have defrosted, Bruce says – Why don't we have this salmon I bought in Lewis? I put the kettle on, turn out some oatcakes on a plate and place a bottle of whisky and two glasses on the table. The meatballs and currant crumble, defrosted by the microwave, will wait as Bruce slices up the salmon and salvages the only lemon in the house, found slightly dessicated at the bottom of the fruit bowl. So I pour the tea and two whiskies which we consume with a half-pound of the most delicious smoked salmon from Uig and your own oaties, while I hear of the visits he has made in the islands, and the friends he has stayed with, many of whom were at his sixtieth birthday three years ago in Ullapool.*

*There was Gordon Adam the radio producer he first met in Peshawar, who played the cello and his Macpherson relations on Lismore, Anderson Bakewell the musicologist and his American wife who own Scarp and who has been the driving force behind setting up the first distillery in Harris. Norman MacSween who played the piano for the dancing at Tanglewood, another musicologist who has completed detailed research into the early piano maker Thomas Tomkison,* but is also known to have worked undercover in Moscow for MI6 during the 1990s (as in the Guardian *headline:* 'Secret service fights to limit the damage, the Russian press identified an MI6 officer in Moscow as Norman MacSween'). *I think Bruce met him in the embassy in Tehran during the 1979 revolution.*

*And we remembered some of the others who were at the party: the publisher Barnaby and his wife Rose in the campervan, the Foreign Office chap and his Egyptian partner, now assistant Ambassador somewhere east of Suez, who emerged at the party slightly damp after swimming in Loch Broom. Henry Noltie from the Royal Botanic Gardens Edinburgh, Dr Guy Johnson and the chaplain who sadly now has terminal cancer and Bruce's cousins from Sussex.*

*But closer to home he had met two delightful young students on the ferry from Stornoway who were returning to Aberdeen from a geology trip – Orrin and Axel. Orrin, he thought lived on the Black Isle and of course I recognised him as our neighbour at Redcastle (whose mother delivered our daughter Katy). And did I know Mary Miers who also lived on the Black Isle and how far is it to Moniack and what he would really like to do was visit the Seaforth Highlanders Museum at Fort George as he had recently learnt that both his grandfather and father had served in that regiment. Indeed he was sporting a wraparound scarf fashioned from the Mackenzie dress kilt his father had worn during the war and adorned with the caber feidh cap badge of the Seaforths.*

*By half past eight Bruce thought he should retire to bed. By half past ten with a few fleeting shuteyes in between, he was ready.*

*Tuesday. So Bruce, what would you like to do today, we could go for a walk in Glen Affric or along the beach at Rosemarkie. Yes – it would be lovely to go for a long walk, we could take the dog. Why don't we do that, go to the Museum at Fort George and then visit Gordon. Maybe we could have lunch at the Kitchen in Inverness. Would you have any ground coffee?*

*We start with a light muesli and coffee breakfast. But he has noticed sage in the garden. Why don't I fry some eggs in sage for both of us? I'll try phoning Gordon first. Why don't we go to the museum this morning, maybe the sun will come out later. Then we can go to Gordon's. Do you know Olivia Fraser? She's Willie's [Dalrymple] wife. I think she is staying at Moniack. I'll give her a call. Olivia, wonderful, no, no I am staying with my friend Ian just ten minutes away, it would be a shame not to come over for just a few minutes, won't stay long, I am sure you are busy with family, we'll just drop in for a coffee. Speak to Ian, he'll know where your house is.*

*So why don't we take the dog for a walk first, go round to Olivia's, then go to Fort George. Have you any butter for the sage? I think, Bruce, we should see Olivia first. She said they were going out.*

*So we drive over to Kingillie House, which is a large rambling house between Achnagairn and Inchmore. It transpires that the Moniack Frasers have bought it between them as a holiday home taking possession three days previously, and a clan of cousins have arrived for the summer. It was hard to know how many, I counted at least ten adults and fifteen youngsters up to their early twenties, wandering in and out, breakfasting on the hoof. I recognised Kit Fraser holding court in the dining-room with his sister Sophia. There was Jean Lindsay who has written a biography of her great grandfather Charles Scott Moncrieff the translator of Proust and was hemming some shapeless pink material with long looping stitches. There was Mary who was very rude about Rory's painting and Olivia Dalrymple and her two sons. Later two others turned up in a taxi. Bruce introduced himself in his Urdu to a young man of obvious Asian heritage, who turned out to be from Cambridge. As we were leaving, old ma Phillipa (she who established the Winery) looking ancient, was escorted in by Alastair, brother of Kit. There was talk of tennis and picnics.*

*Out on the lawn Bruce phones Kathy Fraser – I am just talking to Olivia Fraser over at Kingillie. She tells me you have the most amazing library at Reelig, with the letters and drawings of James Baillie Fraser from his time in India. No, Olivia will explain. I have translated old manuscripts from the Sanskrit for Willie. That would be wonderful, later this afternoon.*

*Bruce, I say, it is now half past twelve so rather than stop at the Kitchen in Inverness, I think we should go straight to Fort George, otherwise we will be late getting back to Reelig. Ah late, what does late mean. We leave Fort George at half past four having enjoyed the excellent coriander and sweet potato soup, walked the ramparts (similar to Montrond, you know) and spotted the dolphins and then spent an hour with the most helpful military historian in his archive room. Sadly it transpired that grandfather Wannell was not a Seaforth Highlander at all but a Gunner. Maybe he just liked wearing a kilt. In the car, Bruce phones Gordon Adam – we are just going to Kathy Fraser's to see the James Fraser archives. We won't stay long. Ian has some meatballs we could bring.*

*So it was late afternoon by the time we pitched up at Reelig, reaching it from the glen road, and winding in past signs to various cottages and chalets, signs purposely not mentioning Reelig House, before arriving at an Adam edifice of fading grandeur (more porticos) and unkempt lawns. We were ushered into their huge living room, into which many years ago they had installed a kitchen island and an Aga, with a wood burning stove in the Adam fireplace, and Raeburns on the wall, a museum indeed of silhouettes, engravings and prints, shelves stacked high with books and a dining table covered in the notebooks and files for Kathy's forthcoming book on the Fraser family.*

*Of course Kathy and Malcolm couldn't have been more welcoming and were soon completely entranced by Bruce. The mug of tea and chocolate biscuits shared on the sofa with two border terriers was most welcome. Then an hour spent leafing through the beautiful sketchbook of James Fraser the traveller and artist who retired to Reelig. It was James who planted the trees in the glen and built the folly and bridge where we love to walk. Oh, said Kathy, but you must take Bruce round the Glen, and of course I must, if only to give poor old Cuilean her walk after a day of false promises.*

*It's nearing 8.00 and dark below the trees when we are back in the car again and Bruce is on the phone – Gordon, we are just leaving Kathy Fraser's, we are going home to Ian's to feed his dog and to pick up the meatballs.*

*When we arrived at North Kessock, Rhona was out rehearsing with the Truly Terrible Orchestra, and Gordon had laid the table with a little light smoked salmon salad starter, and potatoes boiled and ready for the meatballs. A fine meal, finished with your two currant crumbles eked out for three with ice-cream. No wine to be found so whisky it was, followed by four short Vivaldi cello sonatas and a little Hadyn to finish. And so to bed.*

*Early next morning with the 7.55 train to Edinburgh to catch – Ian, if you don't mind, I'll take a few of Clare's oatcakes for the train. So I am now out of oatcakes till you return. And then who should we meet outside the station but Willie (Gilmour) from Culloden, looking and sounding the worse for wear, on his way by bus to give a piano lesson in Fife. Never one to miss a musical opportunity, Bruce determined that they should play duets next time he visits, and off he went having arranged to take an old friend to Glyndebourne the following day.*

*Haste ye back*
*Lots of Love*
*Ian*

As it happened, two days later I met Kathy Fraser out walking her dogs. She was so pleased to have met Bruce and delighted to find someone so enthusiastic and knowledgeable about old India and James Baillie Fraser's watercolours. And on hearing that Bruce had died in January Kathy emailed: 'He was so helpful to me and I am grateful to him for pointing out the extremely important Persian detail I had left out of my book – which I quickly included! Thank you so much for introducing us – it is such a pleasure to have known him.'

Kathy's book (*For the Love of a Highland Home*) is the story of five Fraser brothers sent out into the world in the early nineteenth century in order to make a living for themselves and their family home in Inverness-shire. It is derived from their letters written home over thirty years, from their travels to the Americas and India. The letters have lain in a trunk in Reelig but are now brought to life by Kathy's commentary on the family background and the historical context. Her own writing links the letters so well, matching the source material and, packed with beautiful illustrations, the book is a real joy to read. She self-published the book in November 2015 saying she only wrote it for the family, but in my view it deserves a far wider readership. William Dalrymple provided a glowing foreword.

# We'll take the Bruce route...

**Fiona Frame** and **Kai Price** are married and live in York with their labrador Raven, brought together when Fiona challenged Kai to prove his outdoor survival skills. Kai is a practical Yorkshireman, taxi driver by trade, with a past stint in the British army, but would rather be working on a wood project in his shed. Fiona hails from Scotland and has a PhD in Biological Sciences, but you may be able to find her gorging on gooseberries at the allotment.

Sometime in early 2012 Bruce announced his plans to celebrate his sixtieth birthday in style. We were invited to his Scottish birthday party in Ullapool. 'Marvellous,' we thought, 'we love Scotland.' Then somewhere along the way Bruce planted the seed that perhaps we could drive him there from York, and perhaps stop along the way at a few places. There is the direct route and there is, as we found out, the Bruce route. We left one week before the party and Bruce came armed with his book of Scotland and a list!

The first detour was to visit his friends in the Lake District, the Fitzherberts if I remember correctly. We arrived at a delightful house with excellent hospitality where we were served pheasant casserole and visited the beehives before continuing on our way. Our first night was spent with my mum, Nancy Frame, in Alloway, home of Robert Burns, Scotland's national bard. We went for a walk to see Burns Cottage before we had to catch the ferry from Ardrossan to Arran. We realised during this walk that Bruce didn't have much concern for timekeeping. As we meandered through Rozelle Park, we passed the Maclaurin Art Gallery. I mentioned to Bruce that there was an original Henry Moore statue in the courtyard, but alas when we got there it was missing. Undeterred, Bruce tracked down a willing curator who led him away to the closed-off part of the house for a private showing. We waited on the path outside with one eye on the clock. Somehow, we made it to the ferry on time and, while waiting to embark, Bruce struck up a conversation with a Robert Burns aficionado. They agreed to continue their conversation on the ferry. So, as we crossed to Arran, Bruce could be found enjoying a full recital of 'Tam o' Shanter' (all twenty verses) whilst Kai and I did the traditional thing you do on the Arran ferry: feed chips to the seagulls.

Bruce and Kai met on a computer course in the late '90s and were immediately bonded when they realised that neither of them knew how to switch on a computer, much to the chagrin of the teacher. Later, they were housemates at Holgate Road, enjoying chess by the fire, extravagant cooking and playing cupid to a delightful Japanese girl and German boy (now married). Bruce particularly enjoyed Kai's Yorkshire straight-talking, salty humour and risqué banter and Kai didn't let Bruce get away with any airs and graces. They got into some interesting adventures over the years, whether it was foraging for wild food, talking their way into historical buildings without having to pay or acquiring a large chunk of stone out of a skip to make a feature in the garden. 'Oh, you'll have to carry it Kai, if I did, I'd never play the piano again!'

Anyway, I digress: our destination for the night on Arran was Lochranza at the northern tip of the island, but Bruce had some plans before we could get there. First, we went to visit Brodick Castle, where beautiful furniture and *objets d'art* were carefully cordoned off with velvet ropes; no obstacle to Bruce. Then, we took a circuitous route through the island to find the Machrie Moor Standing Stones. This is where we discovered that Bruce had duped us into a 'Standing Stone Tour of Scotland' – we didn't realise until this point that he wanted to see every standing stone between Arran and Ullapool. And of course, once we had crossed said moor the heavens decided to open. Back in the car and a wee bit drookit (Scots for soaking wet), we headed for our bed for the night. All we had to navigate now was the single-track road with blind hills. Past Balliekine and Thundergay we went, and we were very grateful to find our bed and breakfast and a cosy pub nearby serving hot food and whisky.

The next morning we had to catch our second ferry. All seemed promising – after all the ferry port was in sight of the bed and breakfast. But alas, we had a crisis to contend with – Bruce's missing umbrella. He had kindly lent it to us for a romantic moonlit walk along the beach after dinner. How on earth could it have disappeared? 'Oh, it would be terrible to lose it,' he moaned, 'that umbrella has been with me since Oxford.' Now feeling terribly guilty, we continued our search for the forty-year-old umbrella with renewed fervour. After throwing back a door, out fell the umbrella, which had slipped behind. We grabbed our bags and ran to the ferry, where we caught our breath and were rewarded with a beautiful rainbow.

Next was Lismore where we had very kindly been invited to stay with Hugh MacPherson and Sara Robin. We stopped for a coffee in Lochgilphead en route and Bruce was horrified by the tinny radio being played in the café. His immediate request was for it to be turned off. I learned here why Bruce preferred to bring a picnic of his own design rather than risk a substandard café. He demonstrated this to me one train trip to Edinburgh where out of his bag came a tablecloth, glasses, wine, wooden plates, salad, bread, a bread knife and the *pièce de résistance*, a rabbit terrine! The other passengers put down their Smartphones and settled in to watch this display, suddenly feeling like they should perhaps have brought a glass for their can of McEwan's Export.

An incongruous traffic jam around Oban meant another close shave for the Lismore ferry. Nevertheless, we made it, and were very happy to see Hugh waiting for us on the other side. We stayed in Lismore for a couple of nights and were treated once again to glorious rainbows. Hugh took us out for a fishing trip to catch our dinner. We were the proud hunter-gatherers that day rewarded with five mackerel for our efforts. Hugh and Sara had to do various housekeeping duties the next day because they were also leaving for the party. They had a cunning plan to make sure they could get on with it without having us underfoot: they dropped us off at one end of the island and invited us to walk back. We made friends with the local sheep and tramped our way over the peaceful rolling hills back to the cabin where a delicious meal awaited.

We had to catch an early ferry when we left Lismore and headed for the large Visitor Centre at Eilean Donan Castle, where we hoped for an open café and a full Scottish breakfast. Every time we got in the car Bruce would immediately fall asleep and then jump into action once we reached our destination of *his* choice. Kai likened the trip to driving a sloth around Scotland. 'If it is closed,' Bruce said, 'we will just push on,' oblivious to how many miles we had travelled during his slumber. Thankfully the café was open, the driver was fed, and all was well. We saw some more standing stones and stone circles and stone cairns and I am afraid to say I have forgotten the names and location of them all.

On our way to Ullapool via Shieldaig and Diabaig we stopped at the stunning Gruinard Bay, with white sands and turquoise water, where Bruce acquired a large, unusual green rock that just had to come back to York. He proudly walked up the beach towards us clutching his prize. We met up with some other partygoers at Inverewe Garden, where we enjoyed the tropical palm trees, courtesy of the Gulf Stream, and vibrant blue hydrangeas, and the birthday weekend officially started. This involved a walk at Corrieshalloch gorge, where Bruce walked around the car park with a bottle of whisky, pouring everyone a dram. Bruce's birthday morning started with an early dip in the loch, this time with bathing suits, which couldn't be said for the time Bruce and Kai skinny dipped in the Atlantic Ocean off the Island of Scarp whilst staying with Anderson Bakewell. Bracing!

Two evenings of eating delicious food and drinking exquisite wine with sixty guests followed at the delightful Tanglewood House. The whole thing was meticulously planned and executed by our most meticulous and marvellous friend.

# With Bruce for Hogarth at the Soane

**John Nicoll**

I had always rather assumed that Bruce's magical ability to conjure access, information or even musical or poetic performance out of nothing, in the most improbable of circumstances, had something to do with his affinity for abroad. Born in Australia, half Belgian, half Scottish, fluent in so many languages, living and dead, he always seemed the epitome of multicultural, multiracial humanity and in some sense a standing rebuke to my narrow and limited British sensibility, and sense of how the world was, or might be, ordered. So to see him working his magic in the most British, indeed English, of contexts was a remarkable, discombobulating and very Bruceian cultural experience.

Late November last year; death was already announced and indeed quite widely and sometimes profitably advertised. Returning from a remarkable concert of Persian music at the Queen Elizabeth Hall, the driver of the black cab had refused to take payment on hearing Bruce's laconic account of his condition. He wished to meet a friend in London the following Thursday and asked about a suitable venue. An interesting exhibition would be most appropriate it seemed, so I mentioned the Hogarth Series then showing to enormous approbation at the Soane Museum. An ideal suggestion dear boy. But would there be any tickets? Admission was timed and limited. I checked online and sadly there was no availability next week at all. Unimpressed, Bruce decided to check in person and returned having been assured that admission would be granted if he turned up on Thursday afternoon at 3.30. One doesn't know whether his allegedly imminent, but at that point seemingly improbable, demise was mentioned. We also of course wanted to see the exhibition and he assured us that his invitation was general, so we agreed to meet there at 3.30 on Thursday.

My wife was on time. I had been on a train from the north and was ten minutes late. Outside the museum was a large crowd of disappointed would-be visitors who had failed to secure advance tickets, and a smaller number of luckier and wiser ones who had succeeded, threading their way through the mass and being allowed in one by one through the small entrance door. My wife was in the former group, unsuccessfully trying to ring Bruce, of whom there was no sign, and who failed to answer his phone.

Disappointed, and worrying that some misfortune might have befallen him, we resignedly turned to leave, when looking up at the building what should we see but Bruce signalling frantically to us from one of the first-floor windows.

What to do? If we had been in Iran we might have expected some improbable friend of Bruce's to suddenly materialise with discreet instructions as to how to get in by the back door. But here in Lincoln's Inn Fields? Surrounded by a couple of hundred frustrated middle-class British art lovers?

We had only to ask the question, when Bruce himself emerged like a wraith through the entrance door, slipping between the doorman and some visitors, beckoning, asking where we had been and urging us to come in. Nonplussed and a little embarrassed but accustomed to obeying his instructions in comparable if more exotic cultural contexts we followed him to the door: 'These are my friends,' he announced to the doorman. 'Do they have tickets?' 'No, but they are my friends.' 'This is most embarrassing,' said the doorman as others furnished with timed tickets squeezed past and turned off their mobile phones as instructed. Unembarrassable however, Bruce simply led us through the entrance hall as though he were the museum director with a pair of particularly distinguished guests and in a moment we were lost amongst the crowd of legitimate visitors.

Once inside, of course, Bruce had improbably but inevitably met not only the friend he had an assignation with, but another old friend and historian of the Levant, and all the familiar introductions and connections were made.

Needless to add, perhaps, the exhibition itself was a memorable and moving one, and in retrospect the quintessential Englishness of Hogarth's vision, and Bruce's obvious enjoyment and engagement with it, now seems like a wonderful counterpoint to his almost omnivorous internationalism.

And as I write this I listen to a recording of Mozart's 'Durnitz' Piano Sonata, K 284, and hear Bruce endlessly practising the wonderful penultimate variation of the last movement on our badly tuned piano, just three weeks before he died.

We were in Cyprus when we heard the news of his death and were able to light a candle for him in the Orthodox Cathedral in Larnaca, which is rather appropriately dedicated to St Lazaros, and where the resurrected Lazaros was finally buried, though the tomb is now empty. Bruce might have appreciated that.

# Hampi heroes
*December 2009*

**George Michell** *trained as an architect and has published numerous books on different architectural and art traditions of India. During the 1980s and 1990s he worked with John Fritz at Hampi Vijayanagara. He is one of the founding trustees of the Deccan Heritage Foundation.* **John Fritz** *is an American anthropologically oriented archaeologist who has done field work in the US Southwest. Beginning in the 1980s, together with George Michell, he co-directed a survey of the Hampi Vijayanagara ruins in Deccan, India.*

S adly, we never had the chance to travel to exotic destinations with Bruce, other than the joy of being with him in the Veneto for his sixty-fifth birthday. But we had the enormous pleasure of having Bruce travel with us on a journey to one of the most extraordinary historical sites in India. In December 2009, John celebrated his seventieth birthday with a three-day event that began on the sands of Goa and progressed via a seven-hour train journey to Hospet, the railhead for Hampi Vijayanagara. We were delighted that Bruce accepted our invitation, and together with more than 100 other friends and colleagues joined in the evening fireworks on the beach of the Arabian Sea, the New Year's evening coracle rides on the Tungabhadra river at Hampi, as well as the daily tours that we conducted around the ruins of the great medieval 'City of Victory'. In Hampi village Bruce stayed in simple accommodation, taking rooftop breakfasts with other guests overlooking the temple tower. Observing our close friendships with local friends who assisted in the preparations and events, Bruce labelled them the 'Hampi Heroes', a name that we, and they, have been happy to use ever since.

Other travels that gave us enormous delight were musical rather than physical. Bruce was an excellent pianist and was willing to tolerate George's efforts on the cello and piano. Together they explored the piano-cello and four-hand piano repertory whenever Bruce was down in London and could spare an hour or two. In their last session on 3 December, Bruce and George played arrangements of Bach's organ music, ending with the sublime chorale *Nun Komm der Heiden Heiland*. We left for Goa a few days later not to return until after Bruce had died, and so for us it was a musical send-off.

# An Italian memory
## 1976: Rome, the Trentino and the Veneto

**Anthony Eyre** *first met Bruce through mutual friends in Oxford in the mid-1970s, a friendship cemented by holidays in Italy. Anthony went on to work in publishing, then set up The Letter Press of Cirencester (1986–2017), and has since returned to publishing and freelance book production.*

I met Bruce in Oxford through mutual friends who lived together in Isis House on the river. He inveigled me, unqualified as I was, to join his madrigal group which practised in a gazebo in Merton College gardens. I very quickly became aware of the rarefied air which characterised anything Bruce got involved in, at once gentle and uncompromising. There followed the Venetian Masqued Parties at Isis House.

Bruce then turned up – in the way that he often seemed to – in Rome. He was staying with Carla Gabrieli; and seemed to be enjoying a life of effortless freedom – another fundamental characteristic. I was able to invite them both up to the Dolomites/Trentino where we met up with other Oxford friends. Bruce took to the new cultural landscape of cowbells and polenta without a blink; again, displaying a lifelong ability to fit in, whilst never losing his own personality.

This was once particularly well displayed. We had taken the train following the River Brenta down to Bassano del Grappa. Here Monte Grappa descends dramatically from a height of almost 1,800 metres to the plain of the Veneto. On the Viale dei Martiri, which follows the line of the old city walls, we got a good view of the river as it flows out of a cleft in the mountains and onto the plain. The view included a fine-looking palazzo with gardens overlooking the Brenta: it merited further investigation. Perhaps, Bruce wondered, the view from the river might be more revealing.

We found the garden wall stretched all the way to the water; but we also found an open gate in that wall. Without hesitation Bruce entered the gate and led us up the steps onto a wide-open lawn. A fine view of the palazzo; and an equally good view of its owner. *Ma, come siete entratti?* We explained that the gate was open. The owner led us back, and I assumed that we were about to be ejected.

This is where Bruce exercised his extraordinary charm and ability to make himself 'at home' in the unlikeliest situations. He had obviously already won over the owner, for as I made to go out of the gate the owner called me back, saying he merely needed to close it, and we were welcome to come back to the house. Shortly we found ourselves in a drawing room on the *piano nobile*, enjoying a glass of wine and Bruce deep in a conversation – needless to say in perfect Italian – about how best to collect snails in the wild and prepare them for cooking. A delicate process, apparently, involving a purging diet of lettuce. Later he commented that the walk back to the railway station was both long and uphill and wondered if our host might be driving in that direction. We were duly given a lift.

# A carpet bag of reference books
*Dalmatian Coast*

**Richard Lamborn** *is a retired company director and businessman. He was born in London in 1951, raised in Malawi (formerly Nyasaland) and now lives near York.*

Bruce tells Heather and I that he'll be in Italy in June and why doesn't he pop over to spend some time with us in Croatia. 'Oh, I'm busy,' says Heather, 'but I'll send Richard.'

So I meet Bruce off the ferry in Stari Grad, where he's animatedly talking to a very pretty woman in a café. He has two huge suitcases and a carpet bag full of reference books. After a relaxed lunch, we catch the bus to the house in Jelsa.

After an exceedingly relaxed dinner that evening, B says he absolutely must pop to the mainland the next day as there is a pile of old stones he simply must see. In the meantime, could I just check out how we get to the isle of Lopud, just off Dubrovnik? As a chum of his in the UN's archaeological department tells him there's also some stones there which simply have to be seen, and if we got to this hotel on the isle, mention his chum's name, we'll easily get a room.

B returns from his adventure the following evening and we have an extremely relaxing dinner and plan the trip. Modes of transport are discussed in detail with the aid of local red wine.

Ferry, buses, car. 'What about a motorbike?' suggests B.

Following a bump I had on a motorbike some years earlier, Heather had instigated a two-wheeled embargo but if I was with B, she might not mind too much. So the next day, we hired a bike, barely larger than a moped, and set off.

I must paint a picture here. All our clothes – toothbrushes and a change of pants stuffed into various pockets. B exits the house hefting the carpet bag stuffed with the reference books because one never knows just when an historical point might need to be checked.

Bag looped over his arms, B clutches on to me, and we hurtle along the coast road at a steady 20 kilometres per hour, for about 200 km. It's a lovely run and the views are magnificent, but overtaking cars buffer us and the 'library' sways awkwardly at every bend as B enthusiastically points out sights of interest as we go.

We arrive and get a ferry to Lopud, find the hotelier who rents us a room. That evening, we enjoy a very relaxed dinner and plan essential visits to various ruined churches for the next couple of days. Our host joins us, and with his help we relax a little more. He tells us that the islanders are very pleased by an American couple who rescued an old fortress, converted it into a beautiful house, and would we like to meet them? This is arranged for the following late afternoon – to meet at the hotel bar, where it's easy to relax further.

The following day we 'do' half a dozen ruins, B striding briskly up and down hills sharing vast knowledge while I wheeze gallantly behind. That evening a charming man comes to our table and introduces himself and takes us to his fortress. They have done a truly splendid job of rescue and refurbishment. After the tour we are invited to meet his partner and have a drink. He is a very pleasant man and in the company are a pair of very good-looking young dancers from Brazil. The gin flowed and the conversation rattled along, and B behaved like a very naughty schoolboy with a Saturday pass out. I hadn't enjoyed such an evening for a very long time.

Another day exploring stones covered in flora was followed by a most relaxing fish supper. The trip home was equally hazardous and we diverted to visit a lovely garden B had read about that we simply had to see. Another relaxing lunch too.

I'll remember the trip for a long time. Our next trip was to be a visit to the Bridge at Mostar, but that adventure has been postponed for now.

# Kamaa

**James Wannell**, *elder brother of Bruce, has spent his private-sector career in international trade and has lived outside of the UK for forty years including in the horn of Africa, Asia, Belgium and France.*

Bruce and I met on my return from Syria, the location being the Oriental Club by Bond Street, where I could host him in the style he adored. Not only was this building of interest historically, it housed a treasure of a library of the great travel writers of previous centuries, but also a decent orientalist art collection. The paintings were, by some standards a slightly schmaltzy romantic version of the white European colonialist's view of the East, but I personally found them agreeable, and knew they would appeal to his sensibilities. Lastly the cuisine had been upgraded and was both classic and creative, and respected the origins of the club membership and their interest and origin in the East.

We celebrated our reunion over champagne, something we did every twelve to eighteen months, and caught up on news and respective travel stories. I would always try to bring him something of interest from Aquitaine, sometimes a plant from my gardens that I thought would do well in York, a winter flowering jasmine to brighten up the drabness in that season, a pomegranate seedling that could do well against a south facing sunny garden wall etc. I intimated, on leaving, that I had a one-litre bottle in my carpetbag of eau de vie de prune, home fermented with garden prunes, and cooked by an ambulant distiller who would bring his truck-mounted copper still to the stream at the bottom of the valley every winter. I would age the result in oak casks for a few years until the elixir's rough edges had been smoothed and its original clear colour had turned to amber and lost a few degrees to angels.

My adopted roots in Aquitaine had familiarised me with the various seasons for mushroom hunting – amongst others, morels, cèpes and black truffles. Respectful techniques of extraction, to ensure the probability of finding another crop in the same spot of woodland next year, entailed not uprooting the fungus but rather cutting it at ground level, then crushing the remaining roots into the soil with the heel of your boot to ensure the mycellium would spread and remain in the ground.

I had observed neighbours planting a small orchard of young oak, whose roots had been sprayed with truffle mycellium, on the most unrewarding ground where nothing would grow; twenty years later, their truffle crop brought in a greater sum than their retirement annuity. When dining with Italian friends, I had learned to elegantly avoid the debate on the relative merits of their white truffle compared to the black truffle of south-west France – it was a debate with no winners, albeit market pricing giving a higher value to the *tartuffo bianco*.

So the mission to Syria afforded me the golden opportunity to discover the truffle of the third kind: the sand or desert truffle, Kamaa, in parallel with professional obligations.

In short, the Syrian economy at this time (2007) was in most cases dominated by inefficient and bureaucratic state monopolies, and had shown signs of opening up, thereby creating opportunities. The richest prizes, Telecoms etc had already gone to members of the ruling dynasty. However my client, a corporate multinational, wished us to set up an operation, and as always in this type of country, the formula which gave was a mix of Western expertise and rigour, associated with a well-connected local fixer of sound reputation. In other words, a challenge.

The glowing comments of Theophrastes from about 300 BC inspired me. He described the Fatimid Caliphs of Cairo presenting heaped dishes of this desert truffle during their banquets. Avicenna recommended this delight be fed to the sickly in 1000 AD. Ibn Batuta, the great navigator, wrote of them in his log towards 1300 AD. However the first recorded writings on desert truffles were neo-Sumerians.

The hunting techniques for this tuber, to be found in the arid sandy frontier region on the Syrian–Iraqi border, was like much else in this region, chasing shadows. Bedouin who usually brought them to market through middlemen would typically be out in the desert before sunrise to await that first horizontal light that would, when crouching, illuminate unusual irregularities in the sand and the beginnings of small mounds indicating a sudden hidden growth, just as under decaying leaves in an autumnal Aquitaine forest. Local folklore and the ancient writings held that, as the warm air masses from arrival of mid spring arrived to confront the last cold air fronts of departing winter, thereby provoking storms, lightning and violent rainfall. Where a lightning bolt hit the sand, there in coming days would grow this unique sand truffle.

As my driver left Beirut airport and headed towards the Syrian frontier and the descent into the cotton-rich Bekaa valley, I was glad to have taken the shorter and more frequent air route, with its longer and more interesting road trip to Damascus, where I would meet my local partner. My Egyptian partner had always felt close to this country and had lived through the attempt to combine the two countries into a joint United Arab Republic.

On arrival at the Hotel Meridien, I deferred check-in formalities, and asked to see the chef, whom I knew to be French, immediately. I explained my search and asked for his advice. He nodded complicitly, seemingly pleased to share an insider's confidence and his native language. 'Just leave your bags here, you must go immediately to the central street market as they are closing, and it is the end of the season, but I know there are some. You will take my driver and car, he knows the way; come, I will introduce you!' Once more, the generosity of strangers, when a shared interest is discovered during a trip.

Moments later, we arrived in the central market, and as the stallholders started to close in the fading daylight I asked them for this prized treat. Not having Bruce's admirable fluency in Middle East languages, I had sought from the chef any other local term used; he had volunteered 'potato champignon' as a name recognised by market sellers. Finally, at the back of a vegetable stall, under a dusty hessian sack was the last remaining kilo of this legendary tuber; my pulse raced at the sight of the brown nobbly growth the size of a newborn's fist – I buried my face in the rustic heap and smelt the moist sand and unmistakeable earthy perfume.

My challenge henceforth was to keep this prized delicacy in optimal conditions the following twelve days before I landed back in Aquitaine – not an ideal cargo during a complex road trip with varying humidity and temperature conditions.

Some days later, I was invited for lunch at a former hill station behind Lattakia where, during the French presence, people would retreat from the coastal heat. As in many parts of the Near and Middle East, one of the prized delicacies was spring lamb grilled over charcoal and brought to the table still sizzling. As my dish arrived, the restaurant owner drizzled a brownish-red syrup over the lamb adorned with wild herbs. My host poured a glass of raki also for the owner, and we all toasted loudly and joyfully. The syrup combined with the grilled lamb was stunning, both acidic and fruity, a perfect counterbalance to the barbecued meat. I complimented the owner and asked for some details of the sauce. 'Come into the kitchen,' was the invitation translated for me from Arabic. 'My mother makes it from her grandmother's recipe. It is called Dips Homs.' There in the back of the kitchen was a partly veiled old lady, surveying what was obviously her domain. My hosts translated for me, as I was curious about the technique to produce such a delight. After several customary compliments on her recipe, she finally opened up to reveal the inherited wisdom passed from her grandmother. After pressing the pomegranates, it is vital to let the juice settle overnight, as the silt from the bitter skin and pulp will settle to the bottom of the bowl and one can filter off the garnet coloured clear juice. Thereafter, it is a game of reduction over a low heat until the liquid is viscous. Fundamentally there are two types of pomegranate tree: the tropical version that contains a higher degree of natural sugar, and the other that can grow in south European climates, but which may need added sugar.

Drizzled over lamb was that day's discovery, but back home in Aquitaine I extended this to any rich meat such as duck, pork, wild boar or deer. Even a drop or two in a vinaigrette brought an extra dimension. As my pomegranate tree yielded about 200 kilos early every winter, I knew another use for it, but I also knew exactly how much this would please Bruce, as much for the story as the surprising taste.

The certainty of the delight of the intended recipients of this rare mushroom upon my return was a given; my partner who might find inspiration in this ingredient for the final touches to her book on gastronomy, and in my London trip planned immediately after putting my bags down in Aquitaine, my brother Bruce, who would be as thrilled by the story as by the delectation. For him, this would have all the ingredients to please, the classic writings, the apparently unyielding desert capable of producing such delicacy, and the subtle taste itself that would satisfy the palate of the gourmet and gourmand he unabashedly was. Lastly, there was an added trick to be revealed only at the lunch table at my club, where I had planned to host him and deliver the surprises.

Bruce and I had a common childhood and some schooling, but were born on different continents thousands of miles apart. By birth and of mixed family origins, both of us were keen linguists, our paths had separated in the seventies. Mine led me to London and an international career, his to an academic world he revelled in and where he would have continued well into his thirties had the parental benefactors allowed.

The common factor in our respective lives was travel and curiosity in other cultures and traditions. Over the years, living in different countries, mine by choice of professional expatriation and his by materially precarious circumstances and frequently through the underwriting of his friends, we would sometimes meet at airports as a convenient crossroads. During one such meeting at Heathrow over lunch and invariably catching up on travel stories, Bruce on his way out to Persia for the first time, an experience that transformed him, and myself on my way to my second expatriation to Ethiopia for the UN, I teased him – 'You are such a nomad, dear brother,' to which he crisply replied, 'And so, it seems, are you... The only difference is you travel with a corporate Amex gold card.' 'Et tu Brucè,' I retorted as we clinked glasses. He had chosen a rocky road, hugely enriching in cultural and human experience, but precarious and dependent from a material standpoint.

In later years he finally found a home base, very inexpensive digs in a council/charity house in York where he could furnish his room with his four thousand books and a decent collection of oriental rugs, a house that he shared with a revolving cast of ex-cons and some of the more psychologically fragmented elements of York society on early release from various institutions. A small garden gave him an outlet for one of his many other creative talents, and he applied his talent to make something out of nothing, and transformed it, inside and out, into what he could call a home. Such circumstances did not resemble the middle-class comfort that his family surroundings originally gave him the taste for, and this secretly vexed him. However it gave him a form of anchorage that had its importance in lieu of the stability that material success and sentimental partnerships provided to his other family members and friends. The grandeur of friends' hospitality, cuisine, cellars and abodes were his necessary compensation. It was only in this modest dwelling that, as he confided to me, the mask would fall off, and he could truly be himself, not needing for once to sing for his supper or hold court.

Keeping the best till last, I recounted the story of Kamaa. He sat straighter in his chair, eyes agleam, visibly enthused by this account. I warned him that the tuber had not travelled well, and that he should eat this rapidly. Suggesting a Gulf Arab recipe to boil the tuber in camel's milk, and that on nearby Edgware Road there were specialist supermarkets that catered to Middle Easterners who arrived annually to escape the heat and the restrictions of Ramadan, I intimated they would surely provide the milk.

On leaving, I handed over the Kamaa in its brown hessian sack, and reminded him of the picking technique in the forests of Aquitaine – whatever you do keep the shavings of the Kamaa after peeling, chop them up, and grind them into your garden compost with a little sand... and wait for lightning next spring!

The delight on his face at such a new adventure, that connected with his love of gardening, was recompense indeed. On the steps of the club as he left to catch his train back to York, I handed him the bottle of pomegranate molasses, and the elixir at 51degrees, and winked, adding wryly – 'You are still a bad Muslim!'

# Journey back to the violin

**Katherine Schofield** *is a historian of Mughal India and Hindustani music at King's College London. Through stories about alluring courtesans, legendary maestros, and captivated patrons, she writes on sovereignty and selfhood, affection and desire, sympathy and loss, and power, worldly and strange. Her recent publications include* Tellings and Texts *(Open Book, 2015) with Francesca Orsini, and* Monsoon Feelings *(Niyogi, 2018) with Margrit Pernau and Imke Rajamani. Katherine is a keen podcaster, and her* Histories of the Ephemeral *series is available on Soundcloud, iTunes, and Googleplay.*

Praise full of music and music full of praise be to the One who provides for the voiceless, and from the workshop of whose blessing... breathed into me a soul as music is blown into the reed flute, and the melodies of Israfil the Trumpeter on the Last Day were blown into Adam's body... Praise be to the One who blessed man's darkened body with luminous breath and voice... In the beginning the soul entered the body through the music of the angels, and in the end it will come to life again through the beautiful sound of the Last Trumpet.

Ziauddin, *Hayy al-Arwah* (Indian music treatise c.1785–8), my translation, checked by Bruce

A few days after Bruce died, my husband Paul brought home a gorgeous new recording of Australian violinist Richard Tognetti playing Beethoven and Mozart sonatas with fortepianist Erin Helyard. The album opens with Mozart's delicate Sonata no. 21 in E minor (K304). 'Which composer is this, do you think?' Paul said to our nine-year-old son, expecting at best 'Mozart' but more likely a bored shrug. 'It's the one Mozart wrote for his mother while she was dying because he was sad,' Alexander replied. Thoroughly startled, Paul turned to me: 'How does he know that?' Because, I explained, it was the sonata that Bruce and I had performed together at his birthday soirée in York last August. And it was also one of the pieces he and I had played together for his friends in London the last time I saw him, nine days before he died.

Bruce and I should have met years before we eventually did in 2014. I knew *of* him, of course – the man who did such exquisite Persian translations for William Dalrymple's revelatory book *White Mughals*, which appeared just as I was finishing my PhD on Persian sources for Hindustani music during the time of the Mughal emperor Aurangzeb (r.1658–1707). *White Mughals* was an inspiration to a young historian of late Mughal India; what a story! I was, however, briefly annoyed at Mr Dalrymple's assertion that no-one but a 'handful of elderly Hyderabadi Islamic scholars' could read Indian Persian manuscripts. 'Hello,' I said to the imaginary Dalrymple in my head, 'Here we are!' But also, what about your friend Bruce?

What about Bruce? Over the intervening years, I had a strong feeling several times that I should try to get in touch with him, but what with one thing or another it was over a decade before I finally met him at the memorial conference for Simon Digby at SOAS in 2014. I wasn't even meant to be presenting: I was a ring-in for the absent Azfar Moin, who was down to speak about Islamic millenarianism in Mughal India. Instead, I talked about the ways in which Indian classical music in the Mughal empire was believed to be suffused with supernatural power due to the connections music lovers drew between acoustical mathematics and astrology. Essentially, as the ancient Greeks did, the Mughals believed that the movements of the seven notes of the scale through twelve semitonal positions in the octave directly channelled the movement of the seven celestial bodies through the twelve houses of the zodiac.

The theory is as obscure as it sounds without being able to demonstrate it practically. So at one point I broke away from the podium and said 'I'm sorry I don't have my violin with me, otherwise I could show you properly', and proceeded to pretend the long table on the stage was the fingerboard of a stringed instrument, and divided it into halves, thirds and quarters to show the octave, the fifth and the fourth above the open string.

At the next coffee break, this extremely dapper, rather timeless gentleman with intelligent blue eyes and a lovely smile rustled up to me and introduced himself with enthusiasm as Bruce Wannell. He'd loved my paper and wanted to talk more. 'Oh my goodness,' I said, blushing with embarrassment, 'I have always wanted to meet you; we have so many scholarly interests in common – Persian sources, late

Mughal history...' 'Oh yes!' he replied – 'but you play the violin! I play the piano. Do you still play?'

Ah... well that's a tale, and a rather sorry one. I don't remember if I told him the whole truth then, but I certainly would have said, as I did to everyone back then, that I had been very good once, professional in fact, but I hadn't played the violin at all for nearly ten years. Busy academic career, bad back, a baby in 2010.

The truth is that my relationship with my musical instruments has always been difficult. At sixteen, I went to the conservatoire to study, not the violin, but the viola. When I arrived, I discovered that I was no better than middling; but I worked very hard, and at the age of nineteen secured a temporary job as a viola player in a professional orchestra – the summit of my ability and my ambition. Very quickly I worked out that it was not for me. It took a long time to admit it to myself, but I found playing in an orchestral string section boring, as well as unbearably stressful. I wasn't psychologically ready for it; I developed crippling performance nerves that lasted for years. When I went back to the conservatoire, I cried in every lesson for two years.

But at least I now knew what I did *not* want to do with my life. It was in those years that I stepped sideways into Indian classical music, where I found my lasting home as a historian. It was a relief to shed my ill-fitting professional performer's carapace, and to slip smoothly and gratefully into amateur status. I kept playing viola for a while, but after I came back from my first long stint of research in India for my PhD in 2001, I couldn't bear the ravages wrought by lack of practice, so I switched back to violin; it was easier. And then I gradually stopped playing it too. The day I met Bruce, the only remaining musical thing I had been doing for the last four years was singing my child to sleep.

'We must play together! Let's make a date.' My heart sank. 'I don't really play anymore. But,' I said, trying to make up for my reluctance to indulge this lovely man whom I admired so much, 'I'm permanent faculty in the Music Department at King's College London on the Strand. If you like, next time you're down, I can book the Steinway and we can have a bash. As long as you realise I'm incredibly rusty, and it will probably be very embarrassing.'

The first time we played together was horrible, at least for me – the gentleman that he was, Bruce never gave away how gruesome it must have been for him. After a decade of lying idle, somehow, miraculously, my violin strings had not snapped, but the instrument's voice was croaky under my ill-accustomed hands. Having ascertained that I could no longer play either in tune or particularly fast, we stuck with Bach slow movements for the morning. Bruce was a stickler for precision and musicality, but he was endlessly patient with me and very encouraging. By the end I'd actually managed to make a decent fist of the Andante of the B minor Sonata (the double stopping in the Adagio had made me want to crawl into a hole). Afterwards, Bruce refused to let me buy him lunch, but instead shared his rather strange but delicious sandwiches with me.

I slunk home with flushed cheeks, assuming that this excruciating shambles would be a one-off and no-one need ever know. But Bruce clearly thought I needed tough love. From that point onwards, every few months I would get a phone call: 'Katherine, my dear! I am coming down on such and such and can you book the piano again. Let's practise Beethoven this time'; 'I'm playing Handel trio sonatas with George Michell and we need a violinist.' Bruce would never take no for an answer; or perhaps it is more true to say that I found it impossible to say no to him. And gradually, with a great deal of help from muscle memory, my intonation and bow control began to return. Fast movements crept back onto our agenda. It began to feel *good*.

But then Bruce started suggesting we play for other people. 'I'm having a soirée at a friend's house in York for charity. Do come. I'd like us to play Beethoven Opus 12 No. 2.' Hating to disappoint him, I would say yes, but try to rein him in from whole Beethoven sonatas to just playing slow movements. After the first of these soirées (my husband Paul, always the diplomat, said I sounded like 'someone who had been good *once*') I privately vowed to resist all further requests to play in front of people. Gradually, Bruce wore this vow away.

It was about six months after I first met Bruce that I met William Dalrymple for the first time, at an event in Delhi in 2015. It transpired that we were now both working on late Mughal book projects that dovetailed neatly with each other – and that Bruce was working with him again on translations. From then onwards, I kept meeting both of them more often, as our musical and late Mughal interests began to intertwine. I would locate and send photographs of Shah-Alam-period manuscripts to Willie for Bruce to look at, and they would send interesting snippets back to me. And I began inviting Bruce to stay with us at our home in Cambridge, our music mixing for the first time with Persian texts. In the daytime we would work on manuscripts, he very much in the role of *ustad* to my *shagird*. We both commiserated with each other on the difficulties of deciphering scrappy manuscripts in *shikasta* script, and he taught me the advanced idiosyncrasies of Mughal Persian literature.

What I remember most, though, were the evenings we spent *en famille* after the work was done, when Paul prepared lavish multicourse dinners for us all. Bruce of course reciprocated with delicious meals of his own at his house in York; he continued to feed the five thousand right up until the last month of his life. Whenever he came to stay in Cambridge, he always brought us something beautiful for our house – a jug handmade by a friend or a candle holder or a North African bowl, a jar of his delicious homemade marmalade or a piece of French cheese – along with the most interesting, witty, and wide-ranging conversation. And then, before dinner and after dinner (wine-warm), I'd get out my violin and he'd sit at our large upright piano and we would play Beethoven, Mozart and Bach sonatas while my husband and son sat and listened over the potato peelings or the remains of pudding.

But one thing I especially loved about Bruce was that he liked my son, Alexander, and my son liked him back. Bruce didn't really get family life – he'd often ask me to come to things at short notice that were just impossible because of family events or school runs. But he treated Alexander like he would a grown-up friend, perhaps a younger friend who needed kindness but also training. Bruce always called him Sikandar, which is how Alexander is rendered in Iran and India, and sent us all cheery postcards from his adventures abroad.

Alexander and I both went up to York for Bruce's sixty-eighth birthday festivities last August. Bruce and I spent three happy days rehearsing Mozart Sonata no. 21 in various friends' sitting rooms, while Alexander sat and wrote a story on the sofa. When we performed the Mozart at his party, for the first time in twenty years it felt like a piece of music was fully under my fingers. Finally, I was able to express through the strings of my instrument, born aloft on Bruce's sensitively rippling keys, the grief and love Mozart felt on hearing of his mother's death. My journey back to the violin was no longer painful; it was complete. As we finished, Alexander decided he too wanted to make a public contribution for Bruce's birthday, and read out part of the story he had been writing that day.

It is entirely thanks to Bruce's relentless persistence over the years that, in time, my violin playing came back to me; but his presence in our lives was also a gift to my husband and my son. When I heard Bruce had cancer, I was determined to go and see him, and play music with him, as often as I could until the end. My dad prayed for him. Paul, a biomedical scientist, sent him helpful medical advice by text but was unable to see him. Alexander and I managed to play music with him once more in York in January. But only I was able to be there at Bruce's last soirée in London. He was visibly thinner and weaker, but he was surrounded by loving friends, and his love for playing with others was undimmed. The slow movement of Beethoven's Opus 21 No. 2 now slipped from our fingers and floated like silk on water through the winter afternoon sunlight. As I bent to hug him on leaving, I gave him a jar of marmalade that Alexander had made especially for him. He whispered into my ear: 'Promise me that you will play the Beethoven slow movement at my funeral.' I smiled and kissed him, never imagining it would be the last time.

I never got the chance to play the Beethoven, dear Bruce, but I will play it for your friends at the first opportunity, whenever we are able to meet again. And in lockdown, I am working up the Bach D minor solo violin Partita that I told you I'd come up and play for you when I heard you were in hospital. I hope you got to taste Alexander's marmalade before you left, and I am glad you got my last text, even though you were unable to reply.

This evening we lit a candle in the window for you Bruce, welcoming you home out of the dark.

# Learning from a master at work

**Sina Fakhroddin Ghaffari** *is an Iranian-Kurdish percussionist and has been playing the classical Persian drum tombak since the age of seven. He lived in India for sixteen years, studying North Indian classical music (Hindustani Music). He has BA, MA, MPhil in the same field and is currently working towards his PhD.*

It was an evening in December 2018, I was at the Iranian cultural centre in New Delhi, attending a lecture by Dr Katherine Schofield, a music professor at King's College London. After the lecture I could not help but notice the man speaking in fluent Persian. William Dalrymple was there and he introduced me to Bruce. I invited him to an upcoming concert later that month. An instrumental trio with me on tombak, Behdad Babaie on sehtar and Ardeshir Kamkar on kamancheh. The detailed questions he asked me about the musicians, which instruments we were going to play, and telling me about his favorite dastgah and gusheh of Persian classical music surprised me. I hope it will not be too loud he said. That was enough for me to realise that this man understood the intricacies of Persian music. Persian music, like Indian music, is chamber music in nature and was played at intimate gatherings. Over-amplification is not in the nature of the music. The concert was at Oddbird, a small performance space which seats 150 people max, so it would be an intimate setting, I told him. Was he a musician? Maybe, or maybe he studied Persian music in Iran, which is why he is so fluent in Persian and knows so much about the music? Could he be friends with Jean During, a French ethnomusicologist who spent many years in Iran and researched on Persian classical music. These questions remained in my mind. I felt it would be too much to ask him all these questions as we had only just met.

I got in touch with Bruce a few days before the concert to make sure he was coming and to tell him that I had kept a ticket for him, to which he responded, 'I have already booked four tickets, I am coming with some friends.' He had invited Dr Schofield as well, and I was looking forward to seeing her there. I was really inspired by her lecture earlier that month, but she was busy and could not make it. Our concert was followed by a bonfire, more music and dinner with him and a few others at William's farm. Too bad William wasn't there himself. This was the beginning of many more meetings with Bruce. We mostly talked about the music, literature, history and architecture of Iran, India and Central Asia.

On 23 February 2019, we decided to go for a one-day trip to Govardhan and Vridavan. Bruce was staying at William's place. I think they were working on some Persian and Arabic text in relation to William's upcoming book on the East India Company, *The Anarchy*. Bruce and I, along with another friend, headed out of Delhi early in the morning. This was a leisure trip for Bruce but he also wanted to visit some temples and look at some paintings. This was an opportunity for me, a learning experience, watching him collecting data on the eighteenth-century paintings we observed in the Govardhan temples and the Mughal-built Hindu temples, some of which also exist in Vridavan.

Bruce suggested we take the small roads through the villages rather than taking the main highway. We went past some small villages, made a few stops here and there and met up with some villagers. Bruce was asking questions about their livelihood, their family and children. We stopped at a point to ask if there were any chai shops close by so we could get some chai. The guy responded, *Chaiwalla? Chaiwalla kyon? Hum banaeingi* ('Chai shop? Why chai shop? We will make you chai.') I was not surprised at all. Indian hospitality was not new to me. We were invited home for chai and lunch, village-style curry and rice, with fresh veggies and curd, it was amazing. The family had two daughters; we were concerned to hear that they were planning to marry off their fourteen-year-old daughter. Living in the city, we hear these stories, that it is still common for underaged girls to be married off, but meeting them in real life and speaking with them is another experience altogether. Honestly speaking it made me feel sick in my stomach. Bruce told them they should send their daughter to school and college, to which the father responded, that he could only afford to send one kid to school. His older daughter works in a Delhi-based company as a computer technician. He said they would do the marriage ceremony now and get her married to a boy from another village who is twenty-two years old, but that she would leave for the other village and live with the boy's family only after she was eighteen.

We came across a group of women who were stacking dried cow dung, which they use in the winter for burning. They would pile them up in conical or square shapes and then seal it with some wet dung to protect them and keep the structure together. They were making some sort of drawings on it, various geometrical shapes. I remember exactly how Bruce explained to us about these shapes and how in different parts of Central Asia the villagers do this, and how the shapes are different and have different meanings in each area, some religious and some to do with keeping evil away from their farms and houses. This reminded me of the villages in Iran. Though many villages now have access to gas pipelines and electricity, they still stack cow dung for winter use. We got into a conversation with the women about these shapes and what it meant to them. I was more of a translator in the conversation, translating back and forth from Hindi to English. This was so fascinating for me, observing Bruce, learning from a master at work.

We finally made it to Govardhan and went to the temples and studied the paintings on the walls and the ceilings. I remember Bruce and I talking about the instruments that were in the paintings, *veenas* and frame drums that looked like *daf* to me. Notica was making notes and getting them crosschecked with Bruce. After spending a couple of hours at the temples, we headed back to the car to drive to Vridavan. On the way to the car we were stopped by a group of monkeys and had to give them some of the bananas we had bought for the journey.

In Vridavan we visited a few temples, including the famous Govind Dev temple, a monumental Mughal temple which was apparently destroyed by Aurangzeb, another Mughal ruler of India. One builds, the other destroys. Bruce spoke of some of his friends who used to visit this holy city often. He also told us about his earlier visits and took us to one of his favourite sweet shops. We headed back in the evening and arrived in Delhi around midnight.

Bruce and I organised many nights of food and music along with poetry, log-fires and wine in the winter nights on the rooftop of my south-Delhi apartment and sometimes at William's farm. I cooked *qorme-sabzi* for him a few times, it was one of his favourite Persian dishes. I received a lot of love and affection from Bruce like everyone else around him. He was amazingly well versed in Persian literature and also knew a lot about Persian music which led us to endless conversations. I feel like he was a mentor to me because in a very short time I learnt a lot from him and I think he would have been someone I could have looked to as a guru, maybe even a spiritual guru for me in my own way. I couldn't have enough of his company; he was like a spring, a never-ending flow of knowledge on the subjects of my passion: music, literature and history.

I asked his advice on my decision to move from India to Europe, to continue my studies and do a PhD. He gave me a lot of good advice. I was feeling the need to change, to make a change in my life as a musician. I felt the music scene in Delhi was stagnating and not pushing me in the direction of growth, either in academia or performance. Our conversations were so insightful and inspiring to me that I had to record some of it, with his permission of course. In one of our conversations he expressed his disappointment at the level of *qawwali* at the Nizamuddin shrine, where the young *qawwals* have no deep knowledge of ragas and the text:

> *Look at what has happened to Qawwali in this country, I mean… if you go to Nizamuddin, it is so bad… it is ugly, it is too loud, people don't listen properly, it is over-amplified and the knowledge of the text and the knowledge of the ragas has gone right down.*

Our meetings continued well into February 2019. Bruce was going to travel to Pondicherry in March and I would leave for Iran by the time he was back to Delhi. He was going to travel to Iran in April so we knew we would meet again.

We met at the end of April 2019. He had brought a group from England, all of whom were cultural people including the head of the British Museum, Sir Richard Lambert. I arranged a small performance for Bruce and his guests with me and two of the finest and most well-known musicians of Iran, Hamidreza Nourbakhsh, a vocalist and Behdad Babaie, a *sehtar* player. Bruce had already heard Behdad play in Delhi at our December concert and they were both looking forward to meeting again. The gathering was supposed to be in Alamut Castle in a walnut garden. We were both very excited to create another special evening filled with music and poetry. He messaged me two weeks after they had received their visas: *'Let's hope Iran will be green & fertile, & the nightingales singing in the walnut trees @ Alamut'*. Unfortunately, because of bad weather and storms, we could not go to Alamut and the plan was shifted to a hotel room in Zanjan. We drove from Tehran to Zanjan and spent the night there. While we were performing, Bruce translated the poems of Hafiz and Rumi for everyone, the texts of the songs that Hamid sung.

After dinner, Bruce and I went for a short walk, talking about my plans to move to the UK. I had been accepted to King's College to do my PhD. in music performance under the supervision of none other than Dr Scholfield. He gave me around £100 which I refused, saying that I had not arranged tonight's performance for monetary exchange, I just wanted to meet him and his friends. He said, take this *'Sina jān'*, as he used to call me, and then he told me in Farsi *'London lāzemet mishe'*, which means you will need it in London. Now, of course, £100 is not much money in London but this is an Iranian custom. Our elders give us money as a blessing and as the custom goes, we are not supposed to spend that money but keep it, which I still do. It is kept with notes I have received from my dad and grandfather. He was a true master, an orientalist who had a vast knowledge about Iran's history, literature and social customs. Next morning, we had breakfast and I said goodbye to Bruce. I was travelling to Europe two weeks after and we were thinking of meeting in Paris, but that never happened.

On 15 November 2019 I received a text message from our beloved Bruce:

*Dorud bar baradar-e azizam Fakhreddin, va salam az Najaf-e Iraq*

*Tour avordam inja, ba in-ke waz'am khub nist : saratan-e pancreas daram, kheili pishraft kard, hala chand mah faqat baqi manda : in khabar 5 ruz pish az safar barayam resid*

*Omidvaram forsat khwahim dasht, ta ham-digar-ra dobara bebinim*

*Ba taqdim-e mehr*

*Bruce*

My dear brother Fakhreddin, greetings from Najaf – Iraq. I have brought a tour with me here, though I am not in a good condition, 5 days before my trip, I received the news that I have advanced pancreatic cancer, I only have a few months left. I hope we can meet again.

With love

Bruce

We were in touch until December 2019. William told me he was going to visit us in Delhi in February. Bruce filled many people's hearts with love and affection, and we all miss him dearly.

# DRAGOMAN BRUCE

# Bruce the host

**Gwendolyn Leick** *was born in Austria in 1951, studied Assyriology at Karl Franzens University in Graz and at SOAS in London. She lectured in Biblical Hebrew at Cardiff University, Anthropology at Glamorgan and Richmond, the American University in London and finally History and Theory at Chelsea College of Art and Design. Publications include* The Babylonians: An Introduction, Sex and Eroticism in Mesopotamian Literature, Who's Who in the Ancient Near East, Mesopotamia: The Invention of the City, Tombs of the Great Leaders *and* Gertrude Mabel May. *She first met Bruce in York (circa 1995?) at a training seminar for tour lecturers organised by Martin Randall for his travel company.*

The Proto-Indo-European root *ghos-ti* means 'stranger, guest and host' and refers to someone 'with whom one has reciprocal duties of hospitality'. In such an arrangement the guest owes the host hospitality on the basis that this role can be reversed on a subsequent visit. It was one of the many astonishing qualities of Bruce that, given the limitations of his own domestic situation which precluded a quid pro quo, he made himself the sort of guest who becomes a host, combining two separate roles in a performance so accomplished that the host would happily relinquish any attempt at control. I have never been to Bruce's lodgings in York, not for lack of any invitation on his part but simply because one of us was away when the other would have been there or the other way round. Bruce had more reasons to visit London than I had to visit York and so I had plenty of occasions to experience Bruce's hosting when he chose to stay at my former house in Shoreditch, while waiting for a visa application to some Central or East Asian country or when returning from his excursions and wanting to distribute his spoils to friends in London before returning north.

Bruce arrived as a caravan of one, laden with shoulder bags, satchels, sacks and cases, bunches of flowers, books spilling from his jackets and overcoats. At times he would summon my boys to help him carry this gear from or to Liverpool Street, at times he arrived with a comely young man whom he had persuaded or who had offered spontaneously to lighten his load. As soon as he had arrived Bruce would be on the phone to tell his London friends that he was currently staying *with my friend Gwendolyn and Charlemagne her husband at Sclater Street in the East End*, inviting them to join us for breakfast, lunch, tea or dinner or arranging meetings at concerts, exhibitions, parks or other people's flats. As our household was fluid anyway and the place large enough, and as his friends were never dull it was easy enough to accommodate Bruce's sociability and his desire to be the perfect host. He was the perfect host who also had the effect of civilising the household he stayed in, at least our household. His gracious manners even rubbed off on the East End teenage sons of mine, and their friends. We all became more civilised, more courteous to each other without even being much aware of the fact. Bruce not only filled the house with flowers, he presented us with lovely bits of porcelain or textiles he had picked up on his travels, with rugs and books and CDs not only because he was outrageously generous given his hand-to-mouth existence but because he loved having beautiful things around him. It pleased him better to drink his tea from a fragile cup and if there were only mugs he would pick up nice old cups in Brick Lane market on a Sunday morning.

Bruce's greatest delight when staying with friends was to arrange musical evenings. My house, not being very civilised, lacked pianos or harpsichords for him to play himself but it did have the advantage of having a couple of larger rooms for performances of Eastern music, where only rugs and cushions were needed for the musicians who brought their own instruments. The most memorable event was an evening of Persian music, partly because of the implausible number of bodies we manage to squeeze into my bedroom, which Bruce declared to be the perfect venue for the performance, and partly for the chaos of shoes, which he insisted everybody take off, all over the staircase. Then followed a feast commensurate to the occasion for we had cooked all day beforehand with some of Bruce's Iranian friends and could have fed twice as many guests, so vastly did they overestimate the appetite of Londoners.

Bruce loved bringing people together. The more incongruous the mix the more he enjoyed the spontaneous affinities that could result. Since I have a similar disposition our combined efforts could be delightfully unpredictable.

I never travelled anywhere with Bruce but on a London bus or a London tube. But as we were, for a while, in a similar line of business, that of the cultural tour guide, we could talk shop about our punters or guests, as Bruce the perennial host would call them, swapping tips and recommendations on certain sites and local guides. It was clear that Bruce was far more committed to the idea of creating improvised moments of magic than I was. He could do so partly because he spoke Arabic and Farsi and Pashtun and was familiar with local custom, but more because he was so committed to his mission to civilise. By this I mean the furtherance of mutual delight and the forbearance of animosities, which he undertook by letting people see, taste, hear and feel the world that he showed them as an extraordinary and wonderful place and to make them feel privy to that knowledge. He did not cast himself in the role of the one who wields control, the one who holds the keys, as he abhorred the bullying exercise of power in any form, but simply wished to share his own delight with anyone willing to be enchanted.

# His Flemish was camp, singing, poetic, old-fashioned and over the top

**Sylvie Franquet** *travels and travels, mainly in the Middle East, Iran and southern Europe, trying to find mythology in the landscape, in the trees and in the ruins. As an artist she unpicks needlepoints and re-sews them with colours and words, changing their gaze and connecting them with the mythology encountered on her travels, and with dreams of a kinder future.*

I always met Bruce by chance, whether it was at garden parties in London or on the road in Iran. When we first met, he asked me in French where I was from. I told him I was from Bruges, in Belgium, and to my surprise he continued in Flemish. It turned out we had a few languages in common: French, English, Arabic, a bit of Farsi and as I had just discovered, my own language. It was a game Bruce played each time, enjoying my confusion. From then on, whenever I saw him coming towards me, my head would spin gently as I tried to guess which language we would say hello in. I often got it wrong, and Bruce's elegant flow in whatever language then left me a bit lost for words.

His Flemish was camp, singing and poetic, old-fashioned and over the top. It very much reminded me of the way my friends and I spoke when we were seventeen or eighteen, going through a phase when we adored, idolised, the Dutch writer Nescio. And as I write this, I think of one of Nescio's stories 'Den Uitvreter' (a title which cannot be adequately, or with enough love, translated into English), which has the best first line of any story: 'Except for the man who thought Sarphati Street the most beautiful spot in Europe, I have never known a more wondrous guy than "den Uitvreter".' And that goes so well with what I think of Bruce...

# Butter

**Rose Baring** *is a publisher and psychotherapist, who first met Bruce in his Afghanaid days.*

I never tried it, but if you'd put a buttercup under Bruce's chin, I think you'd have needed sunglasses. When he came to stay with us for the weekend, I would search around for the best unsalted butter I could find, because I knew how much pleasure it would give him. Not that he needed any help in the pleasure department. Was there ever a man who knew how to inhale the last mote of enjoyment from an experience better than Bruce? It was one of the things that I most admired about him.

I can think of numerous times when I watched him putting an unseemly sized helping of butter on his plate. The quantity never ceased to surprise me. Can he *really* be going to eat all that? Looking at it with a slight smile playing on his lips and a look of intense concentration, he would scoop up enough for a good slice of sourdough… and dispatch it all down his throat with the first bite. While most people spread a thin layer of butter and a somewhat thicker layer of marmalade, he considered butter to be more important than that, an equal partner, bride to the marmalade's groom. On the last day of our trip with him in Iran, we were almost late for the airport because the hotel happened to offer a glorious combination of traditionally made flatbread (complete with little pebbles), farm butter and honeycomb. The airplane would have to wait, until his Majesty had had his fill.

But the best breakfast of all was one we had eaten on the Turkmen Sahra in the north-east of the country a few days before.

The sun was setting as we sailed through the undulating grasslands of this vast nomadic plain to our home for the next two nights – a Turkman yurt in a small village. Bruce was in his element. His carpet bag melded with the textiles of the interior, and within minutes he had found a corner for himself and hung his shawl and elegant pyjamas from a couple of tent pegs above his bedroll. By the time Barnaby and I had rid ourselves of the dust of the day's journey, lying on our backs staring up through the round window at the apex of the yurt, Bruce had summoned up the region's premier Turkman songster. After dinner we were transported to the wide steppe which extends for thousands of miles in all directions. The Turkman and his two sons, dressed in *khalats* and magnificent sheepskin hats, played their hearts out. With the crazy strumming of the *dutar*, the insistent drums and a wild throat singing, they brought whistling winds and bruising courtships, cruel battles and tender love affairs into the small house next to the yurt. Bruce's knowledge, his interest and his ability to converse with them in a mix of Farsi and Turkic encouraged them to soar. It was a *tour de force*, large enough to fill a major auditorium, played to an audience of five.

The following morning, we woke to the sounds of animals – cows, chickens, goats and sheep. Breakfast was laid out on the ground and included produce from them all: eggs, several different breads and jams… and THREE different kinds of butter: a sheep's butter, a cow's butter and a clarified goat butter, served from its hairy goatskin churn, which looked and tasted like soft butterscotch. Flavoured with brown sugar made from mulberry juice, it needed nothing more than a bit of flat bread as a spoon. For the rest of our journey, as we retraced our steps in our minds, Bruce would settle softly on the memory of that breakfast and the Turkman woman who had created it. Wasn't she beautiful, he would say? And that mulberry butter? And a small sigh would escape his smiling lips.

# Bruce as dragoman

**Antony Wynn** *is an old Iran hand, recently turned to taking small private groups to the country, much helped by Bruce's advice on the subject.*

D ragoman (from the Turkish *tercüman* – interpreter): guide and mentor to European travellers in the Ottoman Empire.

There were two views about Bruce as a dragoman; one could be either enthralled or wearied by the minutely detailed knowledge he had of every building that you visited. If he liked his clients he would take enormous trouble to show them some hidden treasure unknown to the local guide, but if he bored of them he would abandon them at the end of the allotted hour and, like Mr and Mrs Ramsbottom in *Albert and the Lion*, would 'seek further amusement' elsewhere for himself with a local dervish or musician. Favoured clients would be invited to join him.

Three years ago, I was bringing a group into the one and only hotel in Kerman (in south-eastern Iran), a once grand but now fading edifice. As we were checking in we heard a piano playing deep in the recesses of the large and sprawling lobby. The piano is not an Iranian instrument, nor are there many of them, least of all in post-Islamic-revolution provincial hotels, but here was someone playing more than passable Bach. There, with nobody else to listen to him, was Bruce, lost in musical bliss. But not for long, because the very fierce lady receptionist in her black wimple came beetling up. 'Stop playing that non-Islamic music this instant,' she barked. Now Bruce had been competing with some raucously hideous music from a wedding party outside and was having none of this. 'Ah, so you would say that racket outside is Islamic, would you?' This was Bruce at his archest best, but he nevertheless thought it better on this occasion to retreat.

He was escorting a single European lady client *d'un certain âge* on a long trip round Iran. I asked him whether he did not find it a strain to be stuck with a stranger for such a long time, particularly on long stretches of road. 'Not at all,' he said. 'She has taken a shine to the rather handsome driver. He drives with his hand on her knee and she

has an arm round his neck. They don't speak and I just stretch out on the
back seat and leave them to it.'

# Reminding locals of good, forgotten traditions

**Reza Mir**

B ruce was a unique person and you did not really realise this if you had not travelled with him. Of course, everyone who met him even for the first time was fascinated with his character but there is a Persian saying that if you really want to know someone, travel with him/her as a travel companion. As tour guide and tour manager, I had the honour to travel with him twice.

*Knowledgeable lecturer*
Bruce was truly a scholar, something that unfortunately we do not usually see these days. Unlike many lecturers that I travel with, who are specialists in one specific area, Bruce belonged to a generation of scholars who had a holistic approach to a culture, in this case Iran and Persian Studies. When you talk to the new generation of lecturers and scholars, they are so drowned in one subject and forget about other simple elements of the culture so that you think they are from Mars. For example, one scholar is focused on glazed tiles of fourteenth-century north-eastern Iran and knows nothing about the Achaemenid period or Hafiz poetry. Bruce's vast knowledge of different cultures and particularly Persian culture was amazing. He was not only an expert in Persian literature and poetry and a great translator of Persian literary works, but he had an in-depth knowledge of Indian painting and architecture. He had a fantastic understanding and knowledge of Persian cinema as much as he knew about and appreciated Persian cuisine. The way he compared elements of different cultures and how they have influenced each other was amazing. Like a Sufi, he related apparently unrelated things and their relevance to each other. The way that styles of architecture or words have travelled from one culture or language to another was fantastic and as a traveller you always felt that the puzzle of your culture was becoming more complete after his interpretation.

## *Real traveller, true explorer*

Bruce was a serious traveller in a unique way. I have travelled with more than eighty tour leaders, lecturers and colleagues, but travelling with Bruce was without doubt something special. He tried to find something new in every town or city we travelled to and in every site we visited, though he and I had been there many times before. He looked at the historical, cultural buildings and sites as live atmospheres and he used different fantastic techniques to give life to them and make them more meaningful and at the same time interesting. I have so many examples for this, but will take just one: when we visited the seventeenth-century Ali Qapou Palace in Esfahan. For those who may not be familiar with this palace, there is a hall on the top floor called the music room, where the Shah and his companions would listen to music. Bruce knew two traditional *tar* players in Esfahan and he asked them to come all the way to the top floor of the palace to play some traditional Persian music exclusively for our group, so that our tour members or I'd better say travel companions, in his world, could enjoy quality traditional music where it would originally have been heard. This arrangement was not easy, especially on a busy day in a place with many visitors.

He understood and appreciated art and culture in its entirety and working with him was not always easy, because like a Sufi sometimes time and place were not of major importance to him and meaning and understanding were the main goals! Once, we lost him in the bazaar in Kerman and after looking for him for an hour I found him busy talking to an interesting old man in a dusty corner. He appreciated local culture and loved talking to local people and listening to them. He looked at travelling as exploring new things in new places. When you travelled with him, especially in historical, traditional atmospheres like bazaars or historical monuments, you were like an explorer and you forgot you were in the twenty-first century. He was so good at storytelling and performing lectures in an interesting way that group members lost track of time and traces of place. I'll never forget how he started talking about and interpreting a twelfth-century inscription over the entrance to a caravanserai and then talked about how travellers stayed in caravanserais. At the end of the lecture, group members felt they were travellers travelling in a twelfth-century caravan.

## *Great teacher*

Many people are knowledgeable, but they do not talk about it or share their knowledge. Bruce loved sharing what he knew with others. I'll never forget the time he spent teaching the hotel lobby pianist at Homa Hotel in Shiraz how to play a difficult piece of music by Schubert after a long, long day touring Persepolis. The young pianist always appreciated his teachings and his fantastic talent in music. Bruce enjoyed it when people appreciated what he had taught them. He always reminded the locals of good, forgotten traditions. As an example, he believed that the authentic healthy Persian food culture had been terribly eroded by modernism and laziness and other reasons that he very interestingly describes in his article (see page 182).

So he always liked to teach and remind the managers of different restaurants about the authentic Persian ways of processing and cooking food. He believed that *Sabzi* or a selection of fresh herbs, should be served in Iranian restaurants and homes instead of Caesar Salad which is not something authentic. He insisted that tour members should experience and taste things in authentic style. So his first request in every restaurant was 'Do you have *Sabzi*?' Or when we went to Esfahan we lived like authentic Esfahanis. So, unlike all other tour groups we walked from our hotel all the way to the seventeenth-century royal square and then we travelled in time and walked all the way to the twelfth-century Seljuk square and we had lunch in a very popular busy restaurant famous for its specialty – Esfahani Biryani. There are only two confectioners in Esfahan who still bake a particular kind of cookie which was a specialty in the seventeenth-century Safavid period. He took a taxi or asked our local guide to go to New Julfa on the other side of the town just to buy some, so that he could explain about the local specialties in Esfahan. In short, Bruce lived in the moment and enjoyed the moment. I end my words with a line by Sohrab Sepehri, a contemporary Persian poet:

Life is a series of successive drenchings.
Life is taking a dip in the basin of **This Moment**.

God bless dear Bruce.

# Before the gate of the legation
*Tehran, 24 April 2016*

**Richard Lambert** *is chairman of the British Museum and of Bloomsbury Publishing, and a former editor of the* Financial Times. *He and Harriet joined Bruce and other friends on tours of Iran in 2016 and 2019.*

The last day of a glorious Iranian tour, led by Bruce. Through some obscure connection, Harriet and I have been invited to lunch at the British Embassy, which means we won't be travelling around with the group this morning.

Somewhat tentatively, we share this news with Bruce. His response is immediate, and enthusiastic. 'But that's wonderful! The gardens are magnificent! We will all go over for tea! You must tell them that Anne (one of our number) longs to see the wistaria that her father had told her about when she was a child.' Anne's father had worked for Anglo-Iranian oil, BP as was, and had spent lots of time in the country.

Harriet and I confer privately. Which would be likely to cause us more embarrassment – following Bruce's instruction, or ignoring it? The answer is easy. We resolve to pop the question over lunch.

The gardens are indeed lovely, although the wistaria isn't out. Showing an uncharacteristic degree of imagination, the Foreign Office has decided that just about the only members of staff that should be kept on the payroll during the recent embassy shutdown would be the gardeners, and their work is everywhere visible in an estate of a scale and richness appropriate to the great power that Britain once had been.

We dine in the sunshine on a terrace with the *chargé d'affaires* – there are still not full diplomatic relations between the two countries – along with his wife and another seasoned diplomat, who is full of insights and fascinating gossip. We drink a glass or two of wine, which is bliss. Then Harriet makes her pitch.

'By all means come for tea!' says the *chargé* happily. 'My wife and I won't be able to join you – we have another engagement – but our colleague will show you round. How many of you will there be?'

Harriet: 'Gulp. About fifteen.'

Years of diplomatic training pay off. The *chargé* barely blinks. To our immense relief, it's all agreed.

At the appointed hour, Bruce and the group stand outside the massive steel doors of the embassy compound. He knocks confidently on the door. Nothing. And again. Nothing. After a little while, though, the doors swing open by a yard or so to let someone out onto the street. And here is where we see Bruce at his finest. Like an eel, he wriggles through the rapidly closing doors. And disappears.

The group waits outside, nervously. Lost without our leader, in a strange city and an unfamiliar setting. What are we going to do? What's going to happen to us? Will we ever see our hotel again? But our discomfort only lasts for five minutes. The great doors swing wide open. There is the *chargé* and his wife, who have evidently decided to skip their other engagement. Bruce is alongside, and the three of them appear to have been the best of friends forever. We all troop in and have a lovely time.

# A stranger closer than a friend

**Dori Dana-Haeri** *is eternally grateful to my friend Bruce – a true scholar – who showed me aspects of my country that I didn't know existed. Being involved in finance and business, our journey together was a memorable interlude fifty-two years after I left Persia. I live and love the moments often.*

I was lucky to meet Bruce and fortunate to travel through Iran with him.

I arranged the trip with eight friends and Bruce as scholar, educator and guide. He designed a trip taking us from Shiraz through to Tehran, stopping in places that no ordinary tourist would know about.

As we travelled through enchanting sites I realised that Bruce's command of Farsi was far superior to most educated Iranians, and his knowledge of the country, its amazing architecture, its art, craft and calligraphy, and most of all its poetry, was unique. Throughout the journey in our little bus, he shared with us his knowledge, and amazing stories about his past experiences. He continuously surprised us by showing us often ignored sites and valuable objects that could've been missed easily. Bruce made this journey the most unforgettable visit to my ancient country and made me aware that I was more foreign to it than him. Everywhere we stopped he knew friends and acquaintances – and if he didn't, he quickly made new ones – they all loved him.

I have many highlights but one that comes to mind and seemed particularly impossible to achieve without him was our visit to *Ali qapu* – the palace of Shah Abbas in Isfahan. There, suddenly, out of nowhere, he had assembled a musical ensemble – to play in the music room – exactly where the sixteenth-century Shah would have heard his musicians! Other visitors to the place were welcomed by Bruce, who made everyone sit around the musicians and hold court.

We became great friends and I miss him terribly. My only regret is not to have written down every word he uttered during our trip. Our world is certainly poorer without him.

# With Bruce to the Hadramaut
## *Yemen, 2008*

**Sally Sampson**, *ex magistrate and publisher's reader, travelled widely when helping her late husband Anthony with research on his books, and shared his passionate interest in the Middle East and Iran. She met Bruce through Eastern Approaches, and became a friend.*

I first met Bruce in January 2008 on an unforgettable tour of Yemen with Eastern Approaches. Tears come to my eyes when I think of that glorious Bruce-led adventure – and when I read about what is happening now in that beautiful, magical country.

There were about twenty of us on the tour, some in their eighties! We flew to Sana'a and on our first night in the hotel we met a small group of Belgian tourists and chatted with them; they were planning to follow the same route as the one in our schedule over the desert down into the Hadramaut. We wished them *bon voyage*. A few days later we were in Taiz celebrating the wedding anniversary of a couple of our travelling companions when Bruce appeared with an unusually solemn face. He had just heard the news, via Warwick Ball in Scotland, that those nice Belgian tourists had been shot dead by bandits on the road to Hadramaut. The celebrations stopped, and Bruce rushed to his room to consult with Warwick over the phone. After what seemed like a long time, he assembled us and announced that Warwick would be happy to fly any of us back to the UK immediately. The response was unanimous: 'No thanks! We are going on with Bruce!' And so we did. Bruce organised armoured cars, bristling with guns, to drive us along the roads, and where there was sandy desert bedouins escorted us, knives between their teeth and mobile phones in their hands. Our drivers were delightful, friendly men, with bulges in their cheeks from chewing qat. Bruce was in command, in his element, waving us through the various police control stations along the way. His Arabic was perfect.

We reached the Hadramaut unscathed and booked into a picturesque hotel with a blue swimming pool, where we all relaxed. Bruce, dapper in his usual big straw hat, donned a sarong instead of trousers and urged our male companions to do the same; they did so with alacrity. Spirits lifted. Meanwhile we had anxious messages from back home, where relatives had heard about the Belgians. 'Of course, we're OK,' was the reply.

The rest of our journey was less dramatic but still extraordinary. Wherever we went, Bruce took us to places which were off the itinerary, like a private harem in Shibam or the sprawling, smelly fish market in Hodeida where we all got lost. Everywhere we went, with the help of our wonderful Yemeni guide Mounir, Bruce made friends with locals of every class and age group. We always ate in local restaurants, sitting on decorative carpets and eating delicious grilled chicken. Children were always welcome to join us, intrigued by our funny clothes and hats. Bruce's outfits were never creased, and his colourful elegance was much admired by the locals. He had style!

In the following years, I saw Bruce off and on in London at occasions where he always shone – for example at his reading of Hafez's poems at the Iran Society or a piano and song recital at the Lushes' house. And in 2016 I was lucky to go to Iran with him on another unforgettable trip, in which his deep knowledge of the country and its culture, poetry and people was inspirational. As usual, he was supremely elegant in his attire, and a joy to listen to as he mellifluously explained the calligraphy in the mosques of Isfahan.

But it's the Yemeni journey and the fun we all had with that uniquely courageous, eccentric and lovable guide that I will remember best.

# The signature of the calligrapher
*Istanbul, 2018*

**Canan Alioğlu** *is a professional tour guide who lives in Istanbul. It was through her vocation that she had the privilege of meeting Bruce.*

In the autumn of 2018, our common friend Gwendolyn Leick announced that a close friend of hers would soon be in Istanbul and would contact me.

We made an appointment to meet with Bruce in the Galata area, where he was staying. His wish was to visit a private museum, where he had never been before, at the far end of the Bosphorus.

Before we took the scheduled passenger ferry, he told me that a lady from the UK had asked him to purchase some replicas of Ottoman fountain taps. As we were by coincidence in the area of hardware shops, this was sorted easily. We were in luck that day. Many replicas even in different colours and shapes were presented to us in specialised shops and he knew exactly what he was asked to take home. As we did not know each other, I was a little bit nervous although I was an experienced professional tour guide. This time it was not work, but all the same, I wanted it to work out well, because it was a friend's request I wanted to oblige.

The cruise was pleasant although the sky was quite grey. Our chat switched from English to German and we started to get to know each other. At our final destination, Sarıyer, we had delicious fish for lunch and much to my surprise, and contradicting the Turkish hospitality, he didn't let me pay the bill.

Later, we visited the Sadberk Hanım Museum, which has a memorable ethnographic and a chronologically perfectly designed archaeological collection. He fell in love with the displays there. I have been there so many times with small groups, but his passion for the fine textiles and his naive admiration of the textile objects on display was new for me.

Afterwards, I suggested we add a not-so-well-known new museum nearby to our programme, the former summer residence of the Koç family, the pioneers of private collections in Turkey. Nowadays the building houses the complete collection of Anatolian kelims that belonged to Josephine Powell. This 'discovery' was unforgettable for both of us.

By the end of the day, I felt so privileged to have met him.

A couple of days later, we arranged to meet at the Süleymaniye Mosque in the afternoon after prayer time. The mosque complex went through a proper restoration some years ago and looked quite shiny by daylight. He was especially interested and focused on the descriptions of Evliya Çelebi, a seventeenth-century Ottoman traveller. We sat in the mosque for a long while. As we were leaving through the main gate, he pointed at the signature of the calligrapher, which I was not aware of before then.

We visited the whole complex, immersed as it was in delightful late afternoon sunlight, and then went into a bookshop. There were recently printed old classical books like the *Masnavi* on the shelves and I was surprised how Bruce so easily read and translated Persian and Arabic.

Before we called it a day, we had some pumpkin dessert and black tea right across from the mosque. I was then stung by a bee (unexpected at that time of year) and he accompanied me to a pharmacy nearby and offered to take me home. He was such a polite gentleman...

Afterwards we exchanged some emails regarding the Süleymaniye Mosque, and I tried to get him more precise information on seventeenth-century mosque details.

In his emails and WhatsApp messages, Bruce shared his passion for classical music. At his birthday, he sent me a video of himself playing the piano. The music and the roses in the background were magnificent.

After a long time, a friend of his, Pandora McCormick, came to Istanbul and we met with her in the old town. In the meantime, some of my good friends who heard about Bruce through my detailed accounts, were curious about him and he soon become a hero, a myth in their minds.

And then the very upsetting message with a painful tone that arrived one day from Baghdad. This was his last journey.

I feel so happy to have met him even for a short while. It was a very deep experience and I learned so much about my hometown in the one and a half days I spent with him.

Bruce and I really liked each other, and his last message bears witness to our mutual feelings.

Thank you Bruce, you touched me with your soul. After all your travels, tours and expeditions, I bid you farewell on your eternal journey.

# Bruce on tour

**Amelia Stewart** *is a traveller, storyteller and guide. She worked with Bruce on tours to Iran – www.ameliastewart.net*

Most of the world is happily unaware of the Abassi Hotel in Esfahan. Yet without warning Bruce suddenly emerged from it one late afternoon in the spring of 2009. I had been taking a small group around the country and we just happened to be there.

Bruce was at his most effusive. He had, he said, arranged a concert for that evening and exclaimed that I and my charges, none of whom he had met, must attend. Bruce in insistent mode was always irresistible.

So we did. I do not recall how I persuaded our state-appointed guide to sanction this. Still less what I told my group. But by 10 p.m. we had been admitted through the side door of a private house and were led in a crocodile to seats at the back of a long, low living room in the middle of which Bruce was sitting crosslegged on a cushion. He was resplendent in a dark velvet cape. He had a book stand in front of him. By his side was a beautiful young man with a *daf*. Then another with a *setar*. Bruce began to conduct, his eyes closed. It was hypnotic. Hafez followed, then more music. And tea. Hours later we stumbled out into the night. A guest asked me, 'Who was that extraordinary man?'

A lengthy political hiatus curtailed my Iran tours but in 2014 a window briefly opened. Bruce got in touch to propose working on tours together. A number of 'business' meetings in London followed, their location chosen by Bruce. These included a tea house offering *pastel de nata*, a bus stop en route to a lecture on the Pahlavi dynasty, a Polish restaurant in Hammersmith, and a dust-filled library in Lambeth. The only thing all had in common was that they were hellishly difficult to get to.

No matter how determined I was to keep to the agenda, conversation inevitably strayed into scurrilous gossip. And then suddenly Bruce would start dictating wondrous itineraries that spanned the length and breadth of Iran, occasionally lapsing into Farsi which left me hopelessly lost.

Throughout my world, news of Bruce had spread. It seemed *everyone* wanted to travel with him. As did I. I had never before – or since – longed to be my own guest.

His contacts and connections were so vast that he was able to conjure magical moments with ease. Soon came reports of midnight poetry readings in moonlit gardens, private classical musical concerts in the Ali Qapu palace, wildflower walks in Pasargadae and once, an extraordinary horse show at Kuhpaya in the desert (with a group of fifteen in tow). Pre-departure, we would carefully go through the tour and I would give him log books to complete – these were ostensibly a due diligence process and helpful for me to improve services and the like, and I made it clear that he wasn't to write anything that might land us in court...These log books were dutifully filled in with scant attention paid to the instruction, and returned along with bulging envelopes detailing every *rial* spent with every receipt collected. For obvious reasons I've kept them under lock and key and what pleasure they've now brought leafing through them again.

Bruce was a perfectionist. He went out of his way to look after his discerning guests, for whom he sought to give 'some vivid, exceptional and authentic experiences to lift the tour out of the mediocrity of mass tourism'. From insisting I acquire the best glass tea sets for the bus journeys to making sure there was plenty of money for a never-ending supply of Iranian pastries to 'lift spirits' when required, he generously and instinctively lent his own passion and love for the country to those in his charge.

There was always time for tea, baklava and a poetry reading, followed by a discussion on 'intangible cultural assets and identity.' In his words his groups were 'demanding, disciplined, acute, cultured, knowledgeable, enthusiastic, and therefore took longer than most really to look and puzzle out what they were seeing.' He so delighted in many of the sites that still maintained their 'wow' factor but mourned the 'UGLIFICATION of the land by concrete, breeze block and bad bricks/ steel girder construction that spread a grey Stalinist pall of pollution over the country that was too depressing.'

With feigned malice he would pass on group comments to me, particularly on the nature of whatever hotel they happened to be staying in. It was 'commercial traveller/Death of a Salesman level, and not particularly central.' Or in his words: 'the hotel was a Pakistani wedding hall in Slough; tasteless but central.' His pet hatreds were blaring MUZAK and errant drivers – often so incompetent they would 'find themselves and us lost on some Kafkaesque highway.' His charity on my behalf was endless (as his receipts showed). Disarmingly he would often list all the flowers in bloom at the time. Another note suggests his delight when he found a piano in a hotel lobby that turned to utter despair: '...but I wasn't allowed to play.' Then, 'later on I had coffee with the pianist and we played.' An entry timed at 12:03 a.m. reads: 'Wrote 42 postcards in room.' His last reads differently today: 'Almost more than riots and extremist charcuterie, I dread the new Istanbul airport: could you advise me how to negotiate the transfer between arrival and departure gates?' Now, as then, I have no advice. But I thank him for the question and all that preceded it.

# Dragoman extraordinaire

*For twenty-two years* **Warwick Ball** *was director of Eastern Approaches, a special-interest travel company that offered small group tours of cultural and historical interest in most countries between the Mediterranean and China, many conducted by Bruce Wannell, the company's most popular tour lecturer.*

Of course everybody – just everybody! – knew Bruce even if they had never met him. I first actually met Bruce at the wedding of a mutual friend, an old Afghan connection of long standing, in Derbyshire in 2000: he came over ('made an entrance' would describe it more accurately), jacket artistically draped on his shoulders, and introduced himself to us; he might have had a sunflower in his lapel or an ostrich feather behind his ear, I don't know, but there was something about him that made an instant impression. Of course I'd already heard of him: I first heard Bruce's name being mentioned in British Embassy circles in Kabul in 1981; I cannot recall in what connection, but it was the then Oriental Secretary at the Embassy who mentioned him (and whom I next encountered at Bruce's sixty-sixth birthday celebrations in Yorkshire in 2018, a friend of Bruce's still). And others had talked about him since (well, everybody knew Bruce). There was much of mutual interest – Afghanistan of course, but much else as well.

I was still in the early stages of setting up a tour-operating business, Eastern Approaches, specialising in art treasure and cultural tours in the East, and looking for people with specialist knowledge to conduct them, so we remained in touch. In the end Bruce became one of my most regular tour lecturers with a large and loyal following, conducting tours for ten years from 2004 until Eastern Approaches closed in 2014. The tours he led included Sudan, Iran, Ethiopia, Pakistan, Yemen, Tunisia, India, Armenia, Uzbekistan, Turkmenistan, Tanzania and Andalusia, many of them several times over. Not only did he display an in-depth and deeply personal knowledge of the countries covered, but a knowledge of all the languages there as well (with the possible exception of Armenian, for which he can be forgiven) – not to mention many personal contacts in those countries, ranging from musicians to maharajahs, whom he would regularly pull out of a hat to the astonishment of both myself and clientele alike. Well, he knew *everyone*.

In fact, it was Bruce's knowledge of languages and his ability to switch from one to the other in the blink of an eyelid that never failed to impress. Speaking Arabic to an ambassador saved one tour from coming within an inch of disaster (more of that below), I heard him speak Persian to an Iranian publisher who spoke impeccable public-school English and a range of European languages to an international clientele who came on the tours: French, German, Italian. I recall introducing Bruce to a Greek client in Heathrow who had just flown in from New York to join the tour to Armenia that he was conducting – and he immediately greeted her in Greek!

To be honest Bruce was a 'Marmite' person, but fortunately for Eastern Approaches it was about 90% in favour, and he quickly gained a devoted following from people who would repeatedly book on a tour solely on the basis that Bruce was leading it. But it was Bruce's extraordinary knack of snatching victory from the jaws of defeat – utter disaster in some cases – that I remember. This happened on the very first tour that he conducted for Eastern Approaches, to the Nubian remains of northern Sudan, in 2004.

We had a group of fourteen ready to go, visas had been authorised from the Khartoum end a month before departure and the necessary supporting documentation sent to the embassy in London. Passports had accordingly been sitting in the consulate for several weeks awaiting the promised visas, but the visas failed to be issued, despite continued confirmation from Khartoum. In desperation, Bruce and myself travelled to London to visit the embassy in the hope that a personal appearance, flourishing documentation from Khartoum, would prevail. It was a Friday, and the group were due to fly out on the Saturday. We were at the door of the embassy the moment it opened at 9 a.m.: still no visas. We waited and waited: still nothing. Just before 12 o'clock the embassy was due to close for the Friday prayers and there was still nothing. My finger was hovering despairingly over the tour 'cancel' button (as it were), when Bruce suddenly let out an unexpected bombshell:

'I think I'll go out and pray with the Ambassador.'

I said 'Er, okay.' This was a surprising aspect of Bruce of which I had been completely unaware.

Half an hour later, a smiling Bruce returned to announce that the visas were being issued. The tour went ahead by the skin of its teeth, and in the end it was one of the most successful tours that we'd operated. It is probably best expressed in the clients' own words:

> I thought the Nubian journey was a great success and can't be too grateful to Bruce for securing the visas, and his care, commitment & companionship along the way.

> First, thank you for arranging this holiday which was quite fabulous, not just because of what we saw and learnt, but also because we discovered to our great delight that we were not too old to endure the rigours of camping (we actually enjoyed it!), to climb vertical cliff faces and to have one's wife sold off to an ancient Arab on the banks of the Nile – the price wasn't high enough so happily I still have her. It would have been difficult to find more pleasing travelling companions, but your tours do seem to attract that kind of person... We did of course benefit enormously from having personally conducted tours from nearly all the resident professorial archaeologists – Bruce Wannell's ability to buy their willing cooperation with broken boxes of Fortnum and Masons biscuits had to be experienced to be believed. As to Bruce Wannell himself... well, again words fail me. An almost encyclopaedic knowledge, a magnificent linguist, and a delightful travelling companion. I don't think you could run this holiday without [such] a fluent Arabic speaker.

And there was much more in the same vein.

On a tour through northern Ethiopia in 2008, all was going well until crossing Lake Tana by motor launch. Suddenly, halfway across the engine died and refused to restart. There was no radio and no mobile phone coverage, the shore was over two hours away at normal speed and a lightning storm was blowing up in the west. After four hours the two-man crew of the launch managed somehow to limp the boat over to Dek Island, which they reached at 9 p.m. – failing to meet their waiting Land Cruisers on the opposite shore ready to take them on to Gondar for the night. In Bruce's own words:

> Villagers were roused, I gave a lecture by moonlight while the coffee ceremony was prepared, a sheep introduced, discreetly slaughtered, roast at the bonfire and eaten before we dossed down on the ground or sat around the fire as the wind blew cold. Relief boats were sent during the night and took us at dawn to Gorgora for a breakfast enlivened by Isabel's lemon

marmalade. Eighty-seven-year-old Sonya – whom we managed to lodge in a private house in the nearby village – said it was the best night of the trip!

As did many others! Three of the ladies on that trip (who style themselves 'the Brodie girls') still get together every year at a different location in the UK to recall being marooned on an island in Lake Tana with Bruce – and other occasions of travel.

A potentially more disastrous 'shipwreck' occurred on a tour along the old trade ports of Tanzania in 2011. While the group were visiting the island of Zanzibar, the regular ferry to the island from the mainland capsized with large loss of life. Because of this, the private boat that had been chartered to take Bruce and the group back to the mainland the following day was not available, and an inadequate and much smaller boat was put on for them instead. After a storm-tossed, eight-and-a-half-hour crossing, the boat 'careened' onto a beach on the mainland, way off target and after dark, with the group having to wade ashore through surf. Fortunately, Bruce was able to make contact by mobile phone with the hotel where they were meant to land and get them to send cars to their rescue. But while awaiting the cavalry, Bruce entertained the group by launching into an account of how the *very place* where they had landed just happened to be the exact spot (it might not have been, but nobody knew nor cared) where the Ming Chinese fleet of 'treasure ships', commanded by Admiral Zheng He, had landed in 1432 and taken giraffes on board, later to march them in triumph through the streets of Peking. In the words of one (doubtless relieved) customer:

> Bruce, as usual, was an excellent guide though he did go a little silent crossing from Zanzibar. His ability to engage any member of the local populace in conversation, thus learning all sorts of titbits of information for us, is really a huge plus and his knowledge of the historical aspects of the tour must be second to none. His supply of crystallised ginger was also much appreciated. His greatest achievement was near Kilwa when he converted a group of very severe and unsmiling Muslim fundamentalists in a madrassa into happy, smiling, welcoming sweeties, with an account of Ibn Battuta on their island.

What a diplomat he would have made!

On another occasion, a tour in northern India in February 2009 with a group of twelve, a sudden massive snowstorm on departure had thrown Heathrow into utter chaos, with flight cancellations everywhere – including the British Airways flight to India that our group were booked on. Disappointed customers were simply offered a refund or given a form with a helpline number to call the following day, but Bruce refused to be put off. He first packed the group off to the café in the terminal, and then spent several hours arguing tenaciously with BA representatives, who initially offered to take the group a week later but eventually, conceding to Bruce's persistence, booked the group onto another airline's flight to India the same day.

There were many other such occasions when Bruce's quick (or persistent) thinking saved the day, such as the tour through Yemen in 2008 when a Belgian tour group was ambushed in Hadhramaut and several of its members killed. Instead of turning back, Bruce managed to persuade the security forces to accompany them on an alternative route through the mountains to their destination in Mareb.

But of all countries it was in Iran and Pakistan, where Bruce had lived and worked, that he shone most.

> Just returned from a very successful trip to Iran. I have to say I thought Bruce Wannell was Exceptional, a really Brilliant guide and he made the whole difference to our experience. I can't say I am keen on group travel but I would never have seen or learnt so much if we had gone on our own.

> Bruce, well, what can you say? What an extraordinary man and what a brilliant travelling companion. He was born into the wrong century. We benefited from his wide circle of friends and acquaintances, from a ninety-four-year-old retired Pakistani Colonel at Mustuq who formed an immediate amorous attachment to one member of the party, to the president of the Muslim League on the last night in Islamabad which afforded us a fascinating and frightening glimpse into the current political and international situation. … What with Portuguese marmalade and other goodies which kept appearing out of his baggage which seemed to have a Mary Poppins capacity, he kept us well fed and happy.

The very last tour that Bruce conducted for Eastern Approaches was an Edwin Lutyens themed tour in northern India in October 2014, the last year of our full operation. No visa cliff-hangers, no snow, no shipwrecks, just 'full of interest, and unexpected highlights as ever' in the words of one of Bruce's regular followers, such as an unexpected diversion to have tea with the Maharajah of Patiala (whom of course Bruce knew!) 'travelling with old friends and good company.'

As well as an ability to get along with anybody from well-head attendants to maharajahs, Bruce had an unusual affinity with children – unusual in that few men (at least British men) can relate easily with children. Whenever visiting us he made a point of treating our children as equals, never talking down or patronising, a friendship with them that continued after they'd grown. We wonder if Bruce had intimations of mortality when he visited us about two years before his death when he remarked rather wistfully that there was nothing that would be left behind after him, no children, no published works...

Well, the above accounts – a tiny fraction of what could be quoted – speak of the huge affection that Bruce has left behind: 'knowledgeable and informative... also very caring, efficient and great fun,' 'encyclopaedic knowledge, a magnificent linguist, and a delightful travelling companion,' 'charming man with a great sense of humour,' 'miracle working,' 'an extraordinary man and what a brilliant travelling companion.' A loss to travellers the world over, but a lasting legacy.

# Persian picnics
## Northern Iran, March 2016

**Barnaby Rogerson** *was also a tour guide. Unlike Bruce, he has published far too much, speaks no languages and apart from being able to dance has absolutely no musical skills.*

The Koran Museum in the holy shrine of Mashhad is tucked away in a distant corner of this vast and ever-expanding pilgrimage complex. Perhaps not that many Western tourists find it. We were certainly the only visitors that day and had spent such a long time admiring the exhibits and excitedly talking about them, that we were joined by a chador-clad curator, clearly delighted to find such enthusiastic visitors. Bruce was in his element, chatting about how the colour codes used by calligraphers had been inherited from the craft traditions of Manichean scribes, and identifying the earliest examples of demotic commentaries (Chagatai, Sindi, Sistani and Dari) that swirled around the purposely wide margins of the page, so that the dark ink of the central block of the Koran remained untouched. We listened to talk about the early love affair between Arabic script and paper, which as early as the eighth century was favoured, for unlike parchment it could not be erased and corrected. Bruce also pointed out a failure in a transcription that he had just spotted. More curators arrived but instead of looking cross and affronted, were delighted by the acute observation of this visiting scholar. So much so that we were whisked upstairs to have tea with the director in his turban and camelhair cloak, and then taken off to see a new gallery filled with the original watercolours of Mahmoud Farshchian. I was vaguely concerned that my request to take photographs might be considered disrespectful, but the smiles grew broader as we specified scenes that I was especially interested in, such as the event of Ghadir Khumm, where the Prophet Muhammad stands shoulder to shoulder with his young cousin, Imam Ali. Mahmoud Farshchian lives in the USA but gifted many of his original paintings to the shrine, a lifelong tribute of thanks for having his withered hand healed here as a boy.

It was our first morning in Iran, and Mashhad was our base for a couple of days, as we acclimatised and explored the north-east of Iran. The distances were vast, and some of the journeys were clearly experimental, but to be seeing things in Iran that Bruce had never yet seen was a privilege in itself. Our second day took us towards the Afghan border but was broken by a two-mile walk so that we could arrive at an isolated Seljuk caravanserai having understood something of the landscape. Our trip to discover the secret encampment of Nadir Shah (where his treasure had been stored and where he was murdered by his own bodyguard) was accompanied by a thunderstorm that swept a river of mud, speckled with vast boulders, across the road. Like all Bruce missions there was an inscription to be identified, up a narrow mountain gorge, carved into the living rock and which took us through a nomad encampment where he picked up a charming young guide. He was delighted to find that the inscription, like Nadir Shah himself, was vast and imposing, but essentially Turkic with Persian embellishments.

I had first met Bruce thirty years before. He was in disgrace (for spending too much time with Afghan musicians and not enough monitoring Western aid workers) so I was already prejudiced in his favour. After two years as the Peshawar based Director of Afghanaid (1985–87) he had been summoned home to attend a conference where he would be deposed. He seemed unnaturally cheerful about his fate and scooped me off to have lunch with him in Soho. He was funny, fantastically indiscreet about the reality on the ground (vodka-sozzled Russians and kiff-sozzled *mujahideen* engaged in furious shootouts while Pakistani intelligence, KHAD and opium smugglers cut protection deals). He was already waging his personal *jihad* against canned music and on behalf of pepper grinders. I also noticed that, unlike all the other returning aid workers, he did not need to advertise his travels with a Chitrali cap whilst in London but sported a broad-brimmed brown felt one.

Our last morning in Mashhad was enlivened by a game of social chess. Bruce was determined not to be shown the forty-minute propaganda documentary that is usually screened to all Western visitors to the Imam's shrine. A much longer series of interviews culminated with one with a beardless Hazara cleric from Afghanistan, who smiled as he looked us in the eye and delivered a crushingly strong handshake whilst welcoming us with an American accent. Bruce had imaginatively embroidered my importance as a commentator on Islam in Britain. I was thrilled by all the diplomacy. And of all my friends, I could at least be certain that Bruce had read my books. So we ended up in the company of an articulate young guide, who worked as an embryologist in Tehran but came to the shrine once a month to work as a volunteer. He did not profess to understand what happened here but had witnessed too many medical miracles to stay away. He was also plainly enchanted by the diversity of the pilgrims, and did nothing to keep us away from a mad old woman giving us sweets and blessings, or screen us from the sight of a breastfeeding mother quietly reading the Koran, and happily introduced us to an Arab Catholic priest from Hama on a much needed break from the civil war in Syria. It proved to be a wonderful immersion into the lived world of Shiite Islam, from which I doubt I will ever fully recover.

A feature of this exploration of northern Iran was our shared delight in the perfect picnic lunch. It should be late enough in the day for you to be hungry, should be bathed in dappled shade with an uplifting view and should be sourced from local foods acquired during the day's travel. Salad leaves and herbs, fresh white cheese, sliced and dressed vegetables, freshly baked bread (covered in small stones) and watermelon were the principal notes. If nothing of interest could be acquired we went without, propped up by handfuls of dried fruit and nuts that Bruce had acquired in the markets. These had been decanted into a collection of small linen sacks which Bruce remained in complete control of, like an old-fashioned housekeeper.

We decided not to talk shop during the picnic, for my wife and the three professional guides we were travelling with had listened to more than enough about Safavids and Sassanids, Ilkhanids and Abbasids, Timurids and Qajars during the chatty Bruce-and-Barnaby history walks. I remember that our second picnic was dominated by stories about the other Bruces we had encountered: Bruce Clark – *The Times* correspondent in Moscow, Bruce Palling – the wine-loving, south-east Asian journalist turned travel agent, Bruce Condé, who ran the post office for the last Imam of Yemen before ending up an impoverished member of the Derkawi Sufi lodge in Tangier, and Bruce Chatwin – the art-dealer turned travel-writer.

The picnic held outside Qazvin, right beside a chuckling rill in a meadow surrounded by an orchard of ripening cherries and overlooked by snow-clad mountains, was decorated by a posy of wildflowers gathered by Rose, including borage and thyme. While tea was brewed, we were served almonds and dried white mulberries with our slices of melon. I had already interviewed Reza, our chess-playing tour manager from Shiraz (whose great grandfather had been killed by a lion when crossing the desert), Beni from Tehran (who looked like Dürer's depiction of Christ but showed a personal reverence for Pink Floyd in a daily succession of new Pink Floyd T-shirts), Muhammad from Khuzestan (whose grandfather's estate of palm orchards had been totally devastated by the Iraqi invasion) and compiled a quiz for Reza's ten-year-old son (our honorary fourth guide) based on our shared interest in Tintin.

Now it was Bruce's turn and so I interviewed him about the years before I had met him. His time at Oriel had also allowed for an extra year in Paris. So after the four-year-long lotus-eating life of an Oxford student of modern languages was finished, Bruce spent two years in Italy (1975–1977) where a typical 'working' week was subdivided between madrigals, two days of tutoring and researching the History of the Great Rebellion and doing something for 'Voice of Daily America'. This was followed by a year in Berlin, labelled by Bruce 'Max Planck Educational Research' though his memories of this period were overwhelmed by his elder sister's suicide. Bruce remembered that she left behind two letters and for the first time he 'watched the carapace of strength drain from the face of my father.' Artemis Cooper then provided Bruce with a useful introduction to Paul Gosht who invited him to teach English in Isfahan through the British Council. This happy task lasted for two years (autumn 1978 to summer 1980) and seems to have been on an ad hoc basis. Every third month, Bruce would cross a Persian frontier, and travel into Afghanistan, Pakistan or India for a bit, then return to the Iranian frontier and collect a fresh three-month tourist visa.

In retrospect it was this period of his life that turned Bruce from a linguist to an Orientalist. For it was in Isfahan that he taught himself Persian and learned to travel cheaply and with such confidence. It also coincided with the bloody events of the Iranian revolution followed by roadblocks manned by Revolutionary Guards infected by the general anti-Western paranoia of the times. The murder of a Persian friend, executed by a shot to the back of the head outside a prison wall, was a sign that it was time to leave. In the hands of a more callous individual, or a more ambitious writer, it would have made the perfect dark narrative of real experience against which to set a first travel book. But in other conversations, at other times, I felt that these two experiences (the death of his sister, followed by the death of this friend in Isfahan) were veiled, the tragic gateway which he crossed to become a man. I sometimes wonder what would have happened if the Civil Service exam which Bruce sat on his return from Isfahan had sent him off to serve in the British Council, instead of deciding that he could best serve his country in the Inland Revenue. The rest of his life I thought I knew enough about. So I put my notebook down and accepted another cup of tea before the post-picnic siesta.

My wife had taken some tapestry with her on this journey across Iran. She had pounced on some hanks of Persian silk in a market and was using them to complete the shell-strewn beach design on a pair of slippers for her youngest daughter. She has an equable temperament and a gentle way of observing people with interest but without judgement. She made very few demands but joined in on everything. So she became the favourite person in the vehicle of six men. When she expressed a passing interest in a thin blue hairbell-like tulip seen through the window, our vehicle immediately halted and was driven rapidly in reverse, with all eyes concentrated on helping her locate the flower.

We were soon all strolling around in the meadow of a pretty highland valley. An entrenching tool was located from a compartment in the boot and excavations were begun so that she could possess both flower and bulb. Just at this moment, a farmer came roaring down the hill in a military-looking camouflage jacket and a thick black beard. If this was England, we would have been in for a voluble roasting. We were sprawled over his land, drinking tea and stealing wildflowers from out of the meadow. But it was Iran and we were with Bruce. The fierce-looking farmer welcomed us hospitably to his land, shook hands with everyone, refused our tea but took us off on a walk through the meadow, plucking edible meadow flowers and salad weeds for our next picnic. Bruce's eyes brimmed with delight and we carried on down to the riverbed, where an old labourer hidden in the reeds was clearing an irrigation ditch with a mattock. He revealed himself to be the seventy-five-year-old father of the farmer, and joined in the chatter about medicinal flowers, recommending that you harvest hollyhock flowers in early summer to make a tea which is especially good for sore throats. He also invited us to take tea with him in the summer on a beautiful little balcony that had been built over a lone tool shed to catch the cool of the evening breeze. But with an eloquent hand gesture he dismissed us as there was work at hand that needed his attention. We were enchanted at the idea of returning to this useful pavilion, whose season of use was at a time of rest, after the harvest was in. On our walk back, I heard Bruce extract the entire family history from Hassan the bearded farmer. He had a brother who taught metallurgy at the local university, but he himself had turned his back on his own academic career (nautical navigation) to help his father on the land. They had beehives but did not feed the bees sugar, preferring to extract a smaller yield of exquisite honey which was shared out amongst their cousins. If there is an Arcadia, we had found it. And to prove it, a couple of miles later Bruce stopped our vehicles so that I could walk alone over the summit of a hill and discover for myself the view of the sacred crater lake of Takht-e Soleyman, enclosed in its ancient fortress walls. As I descended, a vast herd of goats escorted by two shepherds (their panniers carried by a little mule train) filled the foreground with animation and the twinkling of bells.

Later that evening we talked about the wonderful relationship that seemed to exist between Hassan and his old father. It was not the same for Bruce, who adored his Belgian mother, musical and artistic, but seemed almost incapable of talking about his English father with any affection. I felt my questions were prodding too close to a wound and so chattered away about some of my own family dynamic. Like Bruce I am a third child, with two brothers, a sister, a military father and a beautiful mother. Bruce later picked up the unspoken thread of this conversation, but there was no longer any of the usual fluency, wit, or twinkly humour in his voice. He told me of his father's emigration to Australia after the war, all buoyant and confident, with their piano travelling with them in the hold, but how he had failed to make a success of it, and three years later (burdened with another child) his mother had been forced to travel steerage-class back to Britain. I thought it told well on his father, that he had managed to pick himself up and work his way up through the Argentine meat trade into Unilever and The City – earning enough to buy a house in Surrey and pack his four children off to top-notch boarding schools such as Wellington.

There was a long silence.

Bruce had been brought up to understand that he came from typical upper-middle-class stock; that his grandfather had been a colonial administrator (in somewhere like Malaya) and that his father had served in the Seaforth Highlanders rising to become a major on Montgomery's staff. His father had met his Belgian mother at the end of the war. When he came home from work, she made certain that the house was filled with music and the smell of good food, and that the children spoke French as well as English. It sounded rather idyllic.

Halfway through his youth, Bruce unravelled a slightly different tale. His father, William James Wannell, had signed up to be a regular soldier-clerk in the Royal Ordnance Corps in 1935, aged eighteen. He was following in the footsteps of his own father Ben who worked on the railway line that supplied the big ordnance munitions base at Didcot. Ben was a passionate supporter of the Labour Party and had been a founding member of the local football club in Chippenham. Bruce's father served with the BEF in France and experienced the battle of Dunkirk. He rose rapidly through the ranks and in 1941 was put forward for officer training. During the war years he had sired two young children with his childhood sweetheart, but decided to abandon this young family in Chippenham in order to begin a new life with Bruce's mother. For twenty-five years he managed to keep his two families apart. It is an everyday story of an early marriage, divorce and separation and there is no evil in this, apart from the lonely, fatherless childhood inflicted on the first two children. I think Bruce's discovery of this other family, and this other identity, like some plot from a Wessex novel by Hardy, completed his lifelong distaste for his father. His love for his mother never wavered, she was the source of all the good things in his life: music, language, food and a lifelong delight in literature. It almost certainly confirmed Bruce in his decision to become the cultural absolutist: music before money, poetry before pornography, cooking before convenience, creativity before consumerism, conversation rather than the television screen. I loved him for it, and for that effervescent sense of humour that deflated any attempt to codify these passions into a creed.

After Bruce's death I had the opportunity to speak to his half-brother Christopher Wannell. He confirmed that it was Bruce who alone had made the effort to track down this other family. It was Bruce (resplendent in a tweed suit and a Bohemian pigtail) who had proudly ridden the antique Wannell-family fire-engine alongside his niece Heather at her Wiltshire wedding. I felt proud of Bruce.

# From godfather to friend
## Paris, 2000

*Written in alternate paragraphs by* **William** *and* **Alec Harragin**. *William is Bruce's godson and became his close friend and legal heir. Alec and William are twin brothers. They went on to get an A\* in their French exams (thanks Bruce). They now both work in property and live in London.*

It was the week after the Millennium. My twin brother and I were sixteen and had spent New Year getting up to mischief as we hoped to do for the remainder of our Christmas holidays. My father, however, had other plans. He had organised a trip (even he couldn't bring himself to call it a holiday) with my estranged godfather to escort us around Paris for the purpose of improving our French ahead of school exams and for our wider 'life experience'. It is fair to say my brother and I were not overly thrilled by the prospect.

We met Bruce at Waterloo Station. He approached us looking like something out of a Le Carré novel, vintage brown suitcase to boot. Our outstretched hands were met by a *bisou* on both cheeks and the warmest of embraces. 'Come along boys. I have bought us some patisseries from a charming baker on Brick Lane which we can take with our coffee on the train. You wait until we get to Paris though... Do you know Stohrer on the Rue Montorgueil?' My brother and I exchanged glances before boarding the Eurostar, tripping over ourselves to keep up with our new tour guide. Of course, we instantly adored him. Everyone does.

My first experience of Paris was of walking down a very busy road not on a pavement, as a normal person would do, but along the central reservation in single file with our suitcases in tow. According to Bruce, this was how Paris ought to be approached. It really was quite dangerous. I had to duck a couple of wing mirrors. The beeping from the passing traffic told me this was not normal – even for Parisians.

I remember it being bitterly cold. So cold I took to wearing a pair of tights under my jeans. I am not sure where I acquired the tights. It can't have been Bruce. When it got too cold we would pop into a bar and nurse a cognac. This of course made us feel very urbane. We would mimic Bruce as he smelt the liquor, rolling it around his glass, taking long sips. Warmed, we would sit back into our chairs and listen to him as he imparted wisdom like an imam.

We walked everywhere, Bruce's boundless energy far superior even to our spritely legs. Left Bank, Marais, Montmartre, Pigalle. And the walks in between the places were just as much an education as the places themselves. Bruce would point out an architectural detail, or stop for some delicacy or chat to a Parisian. There was one memorable encounter with an Iranian market trader. Bruce conversed first in French asking where the man was from. He then switched to fluent Farsi much to the man's amazement. They then talked for a further few minutes after which Bruce switched to the regional dialect from the man's ancestral home. By this point the man's eyes were popping out of his head. They were strangers mere moments ago but they left embracing and quoting Hafez. I'm sure everyone has a similar tale of Bruce.

Our trip was packed full of museums, art galleries, Moroccan tea houses and musical soirées. A day trip to Chartres Cathedral, a freezing picnic in Père Lachaise, an evening at an arthouse cinema and a night at the Opéra Garnier. We met friends of his in both bohemian bedsits and Haussmann mansions.

As you can imagine, Bruce was the tour guide par excellence. In fact I cannot think of anyone I would rather discover a new city with. One might have had the impression that, just as we approached the trip with some apprehension, Bruce may not have been overly excited by the thought of escorting two hormonal teenagers around a city he knew so' well. This couldn't be further from the truth and Bruce approached the task with much zeal. What was immediately obvious was that Bruce was not going to talk down to us. He was going to put us on his footing and assume that our knowledge matched his own. This was incredibly refreshing and certainly a break from our teachers at the time. It was also respectful and whilst it is fair to say my brother and I didn't understand a lot of what our polymath guide was saying, we wanted to and that was I think what Bruce was trying to impart. A desire to seek out knowledge and the aesthetic.

Many years later Bruce told me that it was this trip when our relationship changed from godfather and godson to friends. Age was certainly not a barrier to friendship for Bruce and why should it be. It is well quoted that a walk about Paris will provide lessons in history, beauty, and the point of life. But it also provided me with one of the most rewarding friendships of my life. I will miss him dearly.

# If he was kidnapped I should not pay his ransom

**Heather Wannell** *is Bruce's niece and is a practising private client lawyer. She shared her love of the arts and especially music with Bruce, and although they always threatened to play a duet together, sadly they never achieved this ambition.*

Every family loves a mystery and mine is no exception. We'd heard exotic tales of Bruce's travels from 'mad' Auntie Joan Snelling, but sadly we had never met him. Dad's dad had always sought to keep his two families apart. We were products of his first marriage to Margery Gendle; from that marriage was daughter Jennifer who still lives in the family home in Chippenham, and us – otherwise known as 'the lot from Swindon' (see the Beverly Hillbillies for further information!). Bruce was from the second marriage to Andrée, and, being the intrepid sort, had always tried to find us. One day he happened upon someone who knew us, and we were put in touch.

He came to visit us in Wootton Bassett (it wasn't 'Royal' then), about twenty-three years ago. My parents were Mayor of the town and at a function, so I took Bruce around whilst they were out. I was struck by the similarities to us, his high cheek bones and facial features, and the 'Wannell Walk' – just like my Dad, Chris, and my brother Martin. He also had a fabulous sense of humour and was truly a 'Windy Wannell', just like the rest of us!

We visited a couple of old churches and discovered we both had a passion for music. He listened intently as I played my classical guitar. We also both spoke French and German. He visited the pub with Dad and my Dad's best friend who was the local funfair proprietor and they all got on famously. I recall that he sent the shelf-stackers in the local supermarket into apoplexy when he asked for Gentlemen's Relish – they had never heard of that! We had a great few days together and then Bruce migrated to warmer climes. He kept in touch with me as we had so much in common, and I relayed the tales of his travels to Dad. We met up in York on a few occasions, and when I married Charlie we were both honoured that Bruce came to the wedding. We treasure the photo of Bruce, resplendent in a wonderful country tweed suit, sitting on our vintage fire engine riding to the reception. We were deeply touched when he said that he truly felt part of the family that day.

In the years since our marriage, we have met with Bruce in York when we visit my husband's family, and I have seen how he always brings out the best in people, immediately putting them at their ease, and status, connection and, dare I say, class, have never been a barrier to him – unlike Dad's dad who was a terrible snob! I find it hard to call Dad's dad 'grandfather' since that is a title one earns through respect, and he did not earn it.

My secretary will never forget the day that Bruce rang me to tell me that he was going somewhere particularly dangerous, and that he had put me down as his next of kin, and if he was kidnapped I should not pay his ransom! I am very sad that, due to Dad's dad, I was deprived of my lovely uncle for as long as I was, but rather than being angry about what is lost, I celebrate the fact that I was blessed with knowing him for the time that I did. That is certainly the way in which Bruce would have looked at things, and thus the way that I should too.

# LITERARY PARTNERSHIP

**William Dalrymple** *is a writer and historian based in New Delhi. He worked with Bruce Wannell for twenty years, between 1999 and 2019, on* The Company Quartet – The Anarchy, White Mughals, Return of a King *and* The Last Mughal *– between 1999 and 2019. The quartet was completed just four months before Bruce's death, when Bruce was still well enough to attend the book launch.*

'What a world is lost when someone dies!' wrote Bruce in September 2013, on hearing of the death of his father. He was, characteristically, on the road, in Asia. The news reached him in Istanbul, where he was on his way to see the Whirling Dervishes. 'That day,' he wrote, 'we went to hear the Mevlevi sama' which seemed to dissolve and reintegrate into a greater flow with its slow whirling white skirts and outstretched arms.'

That evening Bruce scribbled in a letter that he regretted not having put down on paper anything about his strained relationship with his father, or their partial reconciliation towards the end, and he urged me not to make the same mistake: 'A good memoir is no conjuring against death,' he wrote, 'but it does save something from the "wreck of time".' And then he added, with his usual generosity and skill for fishing out just the right compliment: 'It makes me envy all the more your art of making these past worlds live again in your writing.'

Bruce never did write his memoirs, although he tried many times. And I never managed to get him to sit down for the long series of interviews about his life, a project we had long planned, and which he, characteristically, kept putting off. During his last weeks we set a date finally to do it in early February 2020. It was another deadline he missed, and as usual it was because he had set off on a long journey. This time, though, it was one from which he will never return.

So, despite living with Bruce for probably as long as anyone has ever spent under the same roof as him, there remain many, many attics and basements of his life I have never explored and know nothing of; and there are many questions that remain unanswered. But here is what I remember.

My life with Bruce Aziz Wannell really began on a bright summer day in Chiswick in 1999 when he came over to discuss working on some translations. I had invited Bruce to lunch; he stayed, characteristically, on and off, for twenty years.

He was a little late, I remember. He had just been to a concert, and arrived in high spirits, striding jauntily up the yard, past the roses, gravel crunching under foot. As ever, he cut a dapper and supremely elegant figure in a brightly striped blazer that looked as if it had just escaped from a Jerome K. Jerome story. He was bearing, as usual, a small, rare piece of culinary exotica. Over the years we came to take for granted his albino truffles, the Algerian foie gras, the tiny tins of Iranian caviar, or the small, crisp Kurdish radishes which we were strictly instructed to eat raw, with a little sea salt. On this occasion it was, if I remember correctly, a sweet Afghan mulberry preparation, of which he was especially fond.

We had first met, briefly, five years earlier in Islamabad, in February 1994. I was there to interview Benazir Bhutto and met him at dinner one night at the house of my cousin, Anthony Fitzherbert. Anthony was then involved in an FAO project to reintroduce silk farming into Nuristan, and he travelled regularly around the Hindu Kush on foot, speaking perfect Dari and encouraging the farmers to plant mulberries rather than the opium poppy. Both men had much in common; moreover, there was a grand piano in the house next door. So twice a week Bruce used to pop over for dinner with Anthony, after an evening playing his beloved Schubert, Debussy and Chopin.

Anthony was one of the few men whom Bruce deferred to on matters Afghan: his Dari was almost as polished as that of Bruce and his travels were, if anything, even more extensive. So it was an unusually restrained and maybe even a slightly melancholic Bruce that sat opposite me that night at dinner, dressed as ever in a pristine white salvar kemise.

He was nearing the end of his eight-year stay in Pakistan, and his life there was in the process of falling apart. Recently he had had to leave Peshawar after receiving death-threats of an unspecified nature: 'I am not sure of the exact reason why Bruce moved to Islamabad,' Anthony told me later, 'or who it was who was threatening him. But he did feel threatened and probably genuinely so. It was a dangerous place if you upset certain people and he was not the first friend of mine to receive what are known as "*shab nameh*" – threatening, anonymous "night letters". Living as he was in a sort of "demi-monde" in the old town in Peshawar the reasons could have been many. I do not think he ever told me, and I probably thought it more tactful not to ask.'

Bruce was already planning to return home, and to do so via an ambitious Arabian sea voyage through Somalia, Oman and Yemen. I was then dreaming of something similar: a journey in the footsteps of St Thomas from the Red Sea to Kerala, looking at the roots of Eastern Christianity. So we spent the evening comparing notes on dhows and Somali pirates and made vague plans to meet in the monastic library at St Catherine's Monastery in the Sinai.

In the end my journey turned into something rather more firmly fixed on *terra firma*, a trip from Mount Athos to the Kharga oasis in the far south of Egypt, and Bruce never made it to St Catherine's; but his odyssey homewards grew if anything even more ambitious as he trekked through the war-torn Horn of Africa to the Gulf, and then on into the heart of the Arab world. These two long journeys meant that it was five years before our paths crossed again, at a chance meeting at an *oud* concert in the October Gallery in London. We hugged and chatted, and I ended up asking him to come over and look at a Persian text that I thought would interest him.

During that first lunch in Chiswick, I showed Bruce a large leather-bound volume that I had just bought in the Hyderabad Chowk. It was the *Kitab Tuhfat-ul-Alam* by an eighteenth-century Persian traveller, Abdul Lateef Shushtari. Bruce picked it up, opened it on a chapter describing the writer's impressions of the eighteenth-century East India Company in Calcutta, and began to translate from it as fluently as if he were reading the front page of the *Guardian*:

> Neither men nor women remove pubic hair, accounting comely to leave it in its natural state. And indeed, most European women have no body-hair, and even if it does occur, it is wine-coloured, soft and extremely fine.
>
> By reason of women going unveiled, and the mixed education of boys and girls in one school-house, it is quite the thing to fall in love and both men and women have a passion for poetry and compose love poems. I have heard that well-born girls sometimes fall in love with low-born youths and are covered in scandal which neither threats nor punishment can control, so their fathers are obliged to drive them out of the house; she follows her whims, mingles with whom she fancies; the streets and markets are full of innumerable such once-well-bred girls sitting on the pavements.
>
> Brothels are advertised with pictures of prostitutes hung at the door, the price of one night written up with the furnishings required for revelry... As a result of the number

of prostitutes, *atashak* – a severe veneral disease causing a swelling of the scrotum and testicles – affects people of all classes. Because so many prostitutes are heaped together it spreads from one to another, healthy and infected mixed together, no one holding back – and this is the state of even the Muslims in these parts.

Before we had even started lunch, Bruce had agreed to take the project on. By the time we had polished off his Khurasani mulberries, he had moved in. Bags, which I hadn't even noticed, were unpacked by coffee time. There soon followed the first of the many small enhancements Bruce brought to our diet: 'Willie, you don't happen to have a small glass of grappa?' he asked. 'I find a *soupçon* of it goes so well with mulberries.'

Soon his papers were piling up on the coffee table next door, kept in place by a pair of Mughal Mir-Farsh carpet-weights that had miraculously apparated from his luggage. The sofa bed became his place of residence for the next few months, though in truth he rarely used it as he usually worked all night, and dozed every afternoon, mouth open, head thrown back on an armchair, his snores echoing out into the kitchen.

We soon got used to Bruce's odd working hours. He would often meet his friends for lunch 'in town', then attend a late afternoon concert at the Wigmore Hall or the South Bank, a complex he said he hated but where he nonetheless spent many happy evenings. He would then stride back up the yard just as we were heading for bed, and regale us with his adventures – 'Do you know Ian Bostridge? Exquisite voice. Exquisite man.' 'I can never make up my mind. Which do you think is the greatest Monteverdi aria, "Oblivion Soave" or "Lamento della Ninfa"?' (In those days, prior to my musical education at Bruce's hands, I'm pretty sure I knew neither.)

We had small children at the time, and my youngest son, Adam, was an infant of six months, just beginning to crawl around everywhere. Often, in the early morning, I would stumble blearily downstairs to get him a bottle of milk, to find that Bruce was still up, and having just finished translating some complex passage of Mughal erotica, complete with detailed footnotes of his own observations, was now standing at the Aga in a wide-sleeved kaftan, baking bread and making coffee. The kitchen smelt completely delicious.

On one occasion I had decided I was too wide awake to bother returning to bed and went out to watch the dawn break over the garden. A few minutes later, Bruce appeared with a tray. Amaretti had been crumbled on the cappuccino, while the warm, freshly baked bread had been sliced and divided in four:

'This one has *Bonne Maman* strawberry jam, which I do think is terribly good. This one I made from Hunza apricots sent to me by a friend from his orchards in Baltistan. And on this quarter is jasmine honey from the hives of the Sultan of Oman's niece. Did you know Rashida? Awfully nice woman – and makes the finest honey in the Hadramut. Her bees are trained to gather pollen from the Omani night-flowering jasmine. She had an Irish nanny who taught her to sing the "Rocky Road to Dublin" in Arabic. Shot dead by her husband last year. So sad.' (I'm making up the details here, but it was something along these lines involving a winning combination of a name-drop of Gulf royalty, marital abuse and a tragic denouement.)

The fourth quarter of the bread was topped with a square of chocolate balancing on a great thick slab of pale, unsalted French butter.

'What's this Brucie?'

'Black Lindt 70% Cocoa. Awfully good. My Belgian aunts would always give us the darkest of dark chocolate on baguettes every breakfast.'

From this point on, we began to discover how exotic life in suburban Chiswick could become after a Bruce makeover. Persian musicians would descend on us, and fill the garden with the sound of *sitar* and *daf*. Richard Burton's bronze Bedouin tent turned out to be only a short walk away along the Thames in Mortlake Cemetery. We found ourselves invited to concerts in a warehouse off Brick Lane where the last of the Pontic spike fiddlers would duet with Afghan *rabab* players while *tablas* laid down the *tal* and Persian *ghazals* were sung.

Afterwards, Bruce would produce extraordinary meals of charcoal-grilled goat and great tent flaps of naan. It was then that he would introduce us to his eclectic assortment of friends: bespectacled professors of Persian, elegant French women of a certain age who needed Bruce's help with calligraphy, Foreign Office Arabists and besuited 'civil servants' who were clearly spooks; musicians from Mali who played what looked like dead goats; thin, glamorous Persian emigrés in Chanel and pearls, willowy art historians in velvet pants, all of them eager to meet Bruce's latest protégé – an Afghan singer, a young Ethiopian harpist or perhaps a new Tuareg poet reciting from the Gallimard edition of his work in a blur of indigo.

Brucie was generally an unusually empathetic houseguest, but just occasionally he got it badly wrong. Once, two very camp, stoned and bedraggled friends of his rocked up uninvited by us, but clearly made welcome by Bruce, at my mother-in-law's house. They made their appearance at noon, a full hour before Bruce was invited, solo, for a quiet family Sunday lunch of roast chicken topped by my mother-in-law's patent, very coagulated bread sauce. The two friends, who had apparently just emerged from a nightclub, were psychotropically wide-eyed and giggly and in other circumstances might have been entertaining company; but in the quiet of my in-laws' Sunday morning they seemed quite fantastically raucous and badly behaved, especially when one of them was violently and noisily sick in the downstairs bathroom.

When Bruce swanned up in his silks, all-smiles, late, at 2 p.m., we had to hiss at him to remove his friends immediately before my elderly father-in-law had another coronary. Letters of grovelling apology were quickly written and what Brucie described as a 'guilt cake' was despatched. But the incident was never forgotten, at least by my mother-in-law, who always furrowed her eyebrows at Bruce whenever she saw him thereafter: 'Isn't that the man who brought those two dreadful...'

Amid all the lively dazzle and exotica that became part and parcel of life with Bruce, the translations continued steadily. Bruce, in fact, worked extremely hard, but as his translations were usually done alone and at night one rarely saw him at work; what was visible was the figure flouncing around in boxer shorts and a skimpy kimono at noon the following day. The translations he produced were always beautiful and occasionally quite exquisite.

As unveiled by Bruce, Shushtari's *Tuhfat-ul-Alam* turned out to be one of the most fascinating texts of the period: a strikingly graphic account of eighteenth-century India as perceived by a fastidious and highly intelligent émigré intellectual, who reads like a sort of Persian version of V. S. Naipaul, *avant la lettre*.

It had been written in 1802 when Shushtari was under house arrest in the aftermath of the scandal around which my book, *White Mughals*, was beginning to centre: the passionate love affair between the East India Company Resident at the Court of Hyderabad, James Achilles Kirkpatrick, and a Persian princess, Khair un-Nissa, who was Shushtari's niece. Since the entire Shushtari clan was in disgrace, the book gave a notably jaundiced account of India, which Abdul Lateef regarded with all the *hauteur* that high Persian culture was capable of.

Abdul Lateef's visit to the subcontinent started badly. On arrival, Shushtari recoiled in horror from the sights that greeted him at Masulipatam. According to Bruce's translation he was 'shocked to see men and women naked apart from an exiguous cache-sexe mixing in the streets and markets, as well as out in the country, like beasts or insects. I asked my host "What on earth is this?" "Just the locals," he replied, "They're all like that!" It was my first step in India, but already I regretted coming.'

Shushtari compared his book to 'the flutterings of a uselessly crying bird in the dark cage of India,' remarking that, 'to survive in Hyderabad you need four things: plenty of gold, endless hypocrisy, boundless envy, and the ability to put up with parvenu idol-worshippers who undermine governments and overthrow old families.' Yet for all its sectarian animosity, the *Tuhfat* proved to be an acerbically perceptive account, which brought the faction-ridden world of courtly Hyderabad into sharper focus than any other surviving text.

Over the months which followed, Bruce worked his way steadily and industriously through the other rare Persian-language texts about Hyderabad – the *Tarikh i-Asaf Jahi*, the *Gulzar i-Asfiya* and the *Tarikh i-Yadgar i-Makhan Lal* – that I had brought back from the vaults of my Hyderabadi bookseller friend, Mohammad Bafna.

But it was not just translation. Bruce's depth of knowledge of the most arcane corners of the Muslim world was unparalleled and a single Persian word could lead him to write a footnote that would make far-reaching connections and bring with it a harvest of dazzling insights. About Shustari's cousin, the ambitious Hyderabadi courtier, Mir Alam, Bruce scribbled a spidery footnote which led to this paragraph: 'Muslim chroniclers, by contrast, singled out his qualities of *ferasat*, which is sometimes translated as intuition but which has far greater resonance in Persian, referring to that highly developed sensitivity to body-language that almost amounts to mind-reading, and which was regarded as an essential quality for a Muslim courtier. It is still an admired feature in much social and political life of the Muslim East.' These were subjects about which I knew nothing, and Bruce's deep knowledge and sometimes profound intuitions added immeasurably to the depth of the book.

I had written travelogues before, but this was my first stab at history. Bruce in many ways oversaw the whole project, editing page after page with scholarly severity, filling the margins with spiders-crawl notes, and constantly urging greater clarity and precision. He found it impossible to write narrative non-fiction himself and he eventually had to give back the advance for his own book of travels; but he was a surprisingly severe and demanding editor and guide, and with *White Mughals* he led me forward every step of the way. It was for this reason that in the end I decided to dedicate the entire book to Bruce.

He had transformed the project and it would have been a completely different book without him.

If *White Mughals* brought out Bruce at his best and most industrious, its successor, *The Last Mughal*, highlighted some of his potential limitations as a colleague.

The book was inspired by a discovery I made in the Indian National Archives during the research for *White Mughals*. Rootling around one morning while waiting for Hyderabadi documents to be delivered, I chanced upon a printed catalogue dating from 1921 entitled *The Mutiny Papers*. This was something of a surprise. It is a commonplace of books about the Great Uprising of 1857 – in Britain still thought of as the Indian Mutiny but known in India as the First War of Independence – that they lament the absence of Indian sources and the corresponding need to rely on British material which carries with it not only the British version of events but also British preconceptions about the rebellion. In that sense little had changed since Vincent Smith complained in 1923 'that the story has been chronicled from one side only.'

Yet all this time in the National Archives there existed as detailed a documentation of the four months of the uprising in Delhi as exists for any Indian city at any period of history – great unwieldy mountains of chits, pleas, orders, petitions, complaints, receipts, notes from spies of dubious reliability and letters from eloping lovers, the Urdu and Persian texts all neatly bound in string and boxed up.

What was even more exciting was the street-level nature of much of the material. It contained the petitions and requests of the ordinary citizens of Delhi, exactly the sort of people who usually escape the historian's net: the bird catchers who have had their charpoys stolen by sepoys; the sweetmeat makers who refuse to take their sweets up to the trenches in Qudsia Bagh until they are paid for the last load; Hasni the dancer who uses a British attack on the Idgah to escape from the *serai* where she is staying with her husband and run off with her lover. Then there was Pandit Harichandra who tried to exhort the Hindus of Delhi to leave their shops and join the fight, citing examples from the *Mahabharat*. Or Hafiz Abdurrahman caught grilling beef kebabs during a ban on cow slaughter. Or Chandan the sister of the courtesan Manglu who rushed before the Emperor as her sister had been seized by the cavalryman, Rustam Khan.

As the scale and detail of the material became apparent, and as it became obvious that most of the material had not been accessed since it was catalogued when rediscovered in Calcutta in 1921, the question that became increasingly hard to answer was why no one before had properly worked on this wonderful mass of material. Using the Mutiny Papers, and harvesting their riches for the first time, felt as strange and exciting, and as unlikely, as going to Paris and discovering, unused on the shelves of the Bibliothèque Nationale, the entire records of the French Revolution.

In order properly to access this vast quantity of material, we moved the family out to Delhi in the winter of 2004, and put the children in the British School in the Diplomatic Quarter. The plan was for Bruce to come too, to work on the Persian files from the Red Fort, while Mahmood Farooqui translated those in Urdu from the sepoy camp.

In the autumn of 2004, Bruce flew out on an Ethiopian Airlines flight from Addis Ababa, where he had been walking in the mountains. The small but beautiful farmhouse we had rented had no spare bedrooms, nor a sofa bed, so I arranged for him to stay with the wonderful Persian scholar and historian, Dr Yunus Jaffery, in his Mughal-era courtyard house in the Old City of Shahjahanabad. The two men were kindred spirits and Brucie loved it. He was back in his element – an old Indo-Islamic town – for the first time since he was forced out of Peshawar, and he adored Dr Jaffery, who soon became his *ustad*. The two became firm friends and the whole family took Bruce under their wings, as they showed him the secrets of Shahjahanabad.

And then, quite quickly after his arrival, Brucie fell in love.

I was never introduced to the gentleman in question; Bruce said only that he was a dancer. But he began to turn up later and later at the archives, and when he did, he often fell asleep at his desk, had a long siesta, only to then leap up at teatime and disappear off to see his friend, and dance the night away. Trips also began to be arranged to show the dancer Brucie's favourite places: Orchha, Mandu and a trip to Ladakh, with Simon Digby in tow.

Soon, Bruce reported that he was struggling with the scribal shorthand of the court Persian. Moreover, he said he was unfamiliar with the *shikastah* (literally 'broken-writing') script, which omits many of the diacritical marks and can be ambiguous to anyone who doesn't have some prior idea of the contents. He also said he was unfamiliar with the surprisingly large number of Sanskrit-derived terms and other vernacular words that the Mughal Persian administrative documents contained, in contrast to the less hybrid, literary Persian Bruce was familiar with.

Dr Jaffery was one of the most practised readers of this material and Bruce could have sought his help; but he seemed to be spending less and less time with the Jafferys too. His concentration was slipping, and with it, his interest in the project.

I had flown him out and continued, ever hopeful, to pay his rent; but at the end of several months, Bruce had produced only the thinnest folder of translations, and that in large font, with lots of white space between transliterated passages of the Persian original and his somewhat emaciated renderings of them. Very few made it into the final book.

Bruce was always powered by his enthusiasms and when he was fascinated with something, nothing could restrain him. Equally, when his interest ebbed, there was very little that you could do to bring him back. The moment had passed.

In the winter of 2009, as the latest neo-colonial adventure of Tony Blair and George Bush in Afghanistan began to turn sour, I had the idea of writing a history of Britain's first failed attempt at controlling Afghanistan in 1839. This catastrophic intervention, known in British history books as The First Afghan War, ended with the massacre of the Retreat from Kabul, from which – in legend at least – only one man from the East India Company army, Dr Brydon, made it back alive.

To anyone who knew that bit of Afghan history, newspaper headlines were beginning to look oddly familiar. The war was waged on the basis of doctored intelligence about a virtually non-existent threat. Then, after an easy conquest and the successful installation of a pro-Western puppet ruler, the regime was facing increasingly widespread resistance. History was beginning to repeat itself.

In the course of my initial research I visited many of the places in Afghanistan associated with the war, and wherever I went Bruce's name would crop up, and would open every door. In Kabul, it seemed everyone had a Bruce story and tales from his Peshawar days and his ?1987 ride across Afghanistan had become legendary.

In Herat too, I found he had become an almost mythological figure. He sent me to see his old friend from Peshawar, Jolyon Leslie, who was restoring the ancient dun-coloured Herat Fort, the Qala Ikhtyaruddin. The project was for the Aga Khan, and seemed to be employing more workmen than usually toil in Cecil B. de Mille biblical epics. When I arrived Jolyon's army was moving vast quantities of soil and revealing the Timurid tile decoration which had lain hidden for centuries. They also made other, less welcome discoveries. During my visit, Jolyon's team had had to remove dead Soviet cannon and anti-aircraft emplacements, as well as a massive and still live and dangerous Soviet boobytrap left as a farewell present to the *mujahideen* of Herat who had besieged them. This consisted of a network of live shells connected to an old tank battery at the top of a thirteenth-century hexagonal Timurid tower.

One of Jolyon's principal Afghan assistants had met Bruce in the middle of the Soviet occupation, during his epic ride. He told me how Bruce had heard about some early Timurid tilework on the Soviet side of the besieged city and despite warnings, had calmly crossed the battle lines to inspect it. Wearing the Afghan dress and Pashtun turban he affected at that period, Bruce had apparently disappeared one morning on a donkey. When he did not reappear after a week, they assumed he had been captured by the Soviets and tortured to death as a spy. But ten days later Bruce reappeared, bubbling over with excitement about some previously unknown Sufi verses he believed he had found on the tiles and had been the first to transcribe.

Like everyone else, Jolyon's foreman said he was astonished at how flawless and idiomatic Bruce's Dari was. So when I found a treasure trove of previously untranslated Dari sources for the 1839 war it was clear a new collaboration with Bruce was looming. It had all begun when Dr Ashraf Ghani, now the Afghan President, but then the Chancellor of Kabul University, directed me to a second-hand book dealer who occupied an unpromising-looking stall at Jowy Sheer in the old city. The dealer, it turned out, had bought up many of the private libraries of Afghan noble families as they emigrated during the seventies and eighties. In less than one hour I managed to acquire eight previously unused contemporary Persian-language sources for the First Afghan war, all of them written in Afghanistan during or in the immediate aftermath of the British defeat.

The most colourful was the embittered but witty *Naway Ma'arek*, or *Song of Battles*, written by a tetchy Afghan scholar-official named Mirza Ata Muhammad. This account told the story of the war from the point of view of a dyspeptic official who started off in the service of the British puppet, Shah Shuja, but later became disillusioned with his employer's reliance on infidel support and who wrote with increasing sympathy towards the resistance.

Mirza Ata had a wittier and more immediate turn of phrase than any other writers of the period, and when I showed it to Bruce he took to the text immediately and threw himself into it. Over the next few months he had great fun bringing Mirza Ata's often irritable prose into English as the Mirza talked proudly of Afghanistan as being 'so much more refined than wretched Sindh, where white bread and educated talk are unknown.' Afghanistan, he wrote, was after all a country 'where forty-four different types of grapes grow, and other fruits as well – apples, pomegranates, pears, rhubarb, mulberries, sweet watermelon and musk-melon, apricots, peaches, etc. And ice-water, that cannot be found in all the plains of India. The Indians know neither how to dress nor how to eat – God save me from the fire of their dal and their miserable chapatis!'

The other source I gave to Bruce to translate was perhaps the most revealing of all the Afghan accounts of the 1839 war: the *Waqi'at-i-Shah Shuja*, Shah Shuja's own very colourful and sympathetic memoirs, written in exile in Ludhiana just before the war and brought up to date by one of his followers after his assassination in 1842.

Shuja explains in his introduction that – as Bruce translated it – 'to insightful scholars it is well known that great kings have always recorded the events of their reigns, some writing themselves, with their natural gifts, but most entrusting the writing to skilled historians, so that these pearl-like compositions would remain as a memorial on the pages of passing time. Thus it occurred to this humble petitioner at the court of the Merciful God, to record the battles of his reign so that the historians of Khurasan should know the true account of these events, and thoughtful readers take heed from these examples.'

In rendering these memoirs into English, Bruce was able to translate the hopes and fears of the principal player on the Afghan side in 1839 – a vital addition to the literature. Yet astonishingly, while all these sources are well known to Dari-speaking Afghan historians, not one of these accounts ever seem to have been used in any English-language history of the war, and none were available in English translation until Bruce made them so.

He began working on the texts in York in early 2011 and got more and more excited the more he read. I was back in Delhi, and began to receive an almost daily flood of emails, often dotted with exclamation marks: 'This morning I've been murdering Burnes in the bath – with 2 paramours!' he wrote to me in January 2011. 'Mirza 'Ata likes it gruesome! It all bears uncanny resemblance to modern anti-Soviet or anti-American bazaar gossip. Perhaps that's why it was reprinted in Peshawar so recently.'

He particularly enjoyed trying to capture Shah Shuja's personality: 'I think it's quite important to try and get the tone of Shah Shuja's voice,' he wrote, 'a bit fatuous, self-idealising, stuck in the pomposity of being royal, but not unlikeable, just conceives everything in terms of abject loyalty to his person or heinous betrayal.' He added:

'Good luck with the writing – I wish I had been able to occupy your Delhi broom-cupboard and survive on dal-chapati, so that I could have given you my undivided attention: here in York I have NO SUPPORT SYSTEM AT ALL, and have to do everything myself.'

After what had happened with *The Last Mughal*, I didn't respond to the hint and after a month he nudged again. 'I have a trapped sciatic nerve,' he wrote, 'as well as my index-finger sliced a full centimetre down the middle through nail and flesh while preparing pheasant for lunch – in fact a lot of minor mishaps make work quite painful and have necessitated time at the hospital A&E. I do sometimes feel the lack of anyone to help or support me during this marathon of translating… How I wish we could just sit together in your garden and talk – I have so much enjoyed our conversations and all the unexpected sparks of intuition and enlightenment... I will not bore you with the psychotic druggies who smashed up the kitchen. Suffice to say that there was a lot of clearing up to do. BUT from tomorrow early I get back to your work and send whatever I've finished on Thursday – which should easily cover Ghazni, and I hope more. *Quando fiam uti chelidon ut tacere desinam.*'

Despite the druggies who lived with him in his Council House, he seemed to be making good progress so again I left him to it. But in the autumn, when he flew out to Hong Kong to give some lectures, his spirits had clearly dipped. 'I was feeling pretty suicidal when I left for HK,' he wrote. 'Life seemed to have collapsed in York, the lunatics taking over the asylum, and too much work left uncompleted. Do you still want me to finish translating for you? It seems that you've – quite rightly – steamed on ahead without waiting for the laggard.'

Then Hong Kong went wrong too. The Royal Geographical Society, to try to drum up some interest on Bruce's lecture, had titled his talk in such a way as to imply that all Chinese culture actually emanated not from the Middle Kingdom but from ancient Persia: 'Rupert whatever his name has altered the title of my RGS talk to something stupidly controversial,' he wrote, 'with the result that the papers and TV here are out for my blood. I'd only prepared a puff for an [Iran] guide book, not a *guerre des bouffons* about Chinese culture originating in Iran ... aargh!'

I finally relented and offered to email Bruce a ticket to Delhi. He more or less flew out on the next plane.

Bruce arrived in October 2011, just as the monsoon was giving way to the first chills of the Delhi winter.

We now lived in a farm on the outskirts of Delhi with a large vegetable garden. Here we had made ourselves pretty self-sufficient and kept chickens for eggs, and a family of incestuous goats for milk, and had a bee-hive for honey. Bruce turned down the offer of one of the children's bedrooms and chose to live instead in a large Mughal-style tent which he had erected just outside the back door. Slowly items of furniture began to migrate from the house into the new Bedouin encampment: first some Baluchi carpets, then, in swift succession, a charpoy, some *murrah* cane chairs, an electricity lead, a radiator, various vases of flowers, a desk, and finally a bottle of malt whisky. Once his nomad's palace was fully equipped, he threw himself into the new sources. Some days we did not seem him at all, except when he appeared in a skimpy bathing towel to have a shower.

Bruce was working on two remarkable heroic epic poems – the *Akbarnama*, or *The History of Wazir Akbar Khan*, by Maulana Hamid

Kashmiri and the *Jangnama*, or *History of the War*, by Muhammad Kohistani Ghulami, both of which read like Afghan versions of *The Song of Roland*, and were written in the 1840s to praise the leaders of the Afghan resistance. They seem to be the last survivors of what was probably once a rich seam of epic poetry dedicated to the Afghan victory, much of it passed orally from singer to singer, bard to bard: after all, to the Afghans their victory was a miraculous deliverance, their Trafalgar, Waterloo and Battle of Britain rolled into one.

Bruce loved the fact that both poems had as their villain the British Orientalist and spy, Alexander Burnes, who was usually seen as something of a hero in British accounts. In that sense they presented a mirror, which allowed us, in the words of Alexander Burnes's cousin, Robbie Burns, 'To see ourselves as others see us.' For according to Bruce's rendition of the Afghan epic poets Burnes, far from being the romantic adventurer of Western accounts, was instead the devilishly charming deceiver, the master of flattery and treachery, who corrupted the nobles of Kabul: 'On the outside he seems a man, but inside he is the very devil,' one nobleman warns Dost Mohammad:

> But he of depraved nature and unholy creed
> Had mixed poison into the honey
>
> From London, he had requested much gold and silver
> So that this gold may render his own schemes golden
>
> With dark magic and deceit he dug a pit
> Many a man was seized by the throat and thrown in
>
> There remained not one amongst the Khans of power
> Whom he did not place thus on the devil's path
>
> When he had bound them in chains of gold
> They swore allegiance to him one and all

It is, moreover, a consistent complaint in the Afghan sources that the British have no respect for women, raping and dishonouring wherever they go, and riding 'the steed of their lust unbridled day and night.' The British, in other words, are depicted as treacherous and oppressive women-abusing terrorists. This is not the way we expect Afghans to look at us.

The single known copy of the *Jangnameh* turned up in Parwan in 1951 lacking its front and end pages, and written on East India Company paper apparently looted from the British headquarters. The *Akbarnama*, which also resurfaced in 1951, this time in Peshawar, recounted the deeds of Wazir Akbar Khan, traditionally seen as the leading player in the uprising. When I showed Bruce the printed copy he picked it up and translated the introduction straight off. 'In this book,' he read, 'like Rustam the Great, Akbar's name will be remembered forever. Now this epic has reached completion, it will roam the countries of the world, and adorn the assemblies of the great. From Kabul, it will travel to every gathering, like the spring breeze from garden to garden.'

In time, due in part to Bruce's beautiful renditions of these new Afghan voices, and partly because of the ever-more topical nature of its subject as the Taliban seized ever-more of Afghanistan, the *Akbarnama*'s prediction was realised: to our surprise, Bruce's translations of the poems in *Return of a King* did indeed roam the countries of the world and really did come to adorn the assemblies of the great. Hillary Clinton discussed the book in an email that, thanks to Wikileaks, ended up on the front page of the *New York Times*. *Return of a King* was also read both in Obama's White House and by President Karzai in Kabul, and I received invitations to brief both on the lessons of the history of 1839. We were also encouraged to do an Afghan launch in Kabul in the winter of 2013.

By this stage, Bruce was already back in Afghanistan, transliterating and translating Timurid gravestones for the Aga Khan. He started in his favourite old stomping ground of Herat, where he worked on the inscriptions of the beautiful Sufi shrine, the Gaza Gah, which had been much loved by travellers as diverse as Babur and Robert Byron. Then, shortly before the launch, Bruce moved to Kabul to continue work on the gravestones there.

As usual, Bruce fell on his feet. He was living in DAFA, as a guest of the French archaeological mission, then run by the ebullient and fantastically charming beret-wearing Philippe Marquis, who was famed in Afghanistan not just for his bravery and archaeological prowess, but also for keeping the best table, the best cheeses and the best wine cellar in the country.

Olivia, Adam and I flew in on a chilly, bright November day with high blue skies, just around the time the trees were beginning to turn. Bruce met us at the airport and later that day took us around the newly restored Bagh-i-Babur. We wandered up to the marble Shah Jahan mosque at the top of the garden, through newly planted mulberry and apricot orchards, dotted with the last of the yellow asphodels and ragged pink hollyhocks. Adam was wide-eyed at the sight of a city which resembled one of his beloved war-movies, with its ubiquitous blast walls and gun-toting guards in APCs. But nothing impressed him quite so much as Bruce's polylingualism, which coalition Kabul gave him ample chance to deploy.

'He spoke to us in English,' he remembered, 'and to the gardeners in Dari. He translated the Mughal Persian of Babur's tombstone about the Light Garden of the Angel King, then greeted the Turkish foreign minister, who was also touring the garden, in fluent Turkish. Finally, he took us back to DAFA where he chatted to the different archaeologists in perfect French and Italian. All in the space of about ninety minutes.' At the book launch that evening, on a freezing cold star-lit night in the open courtyard of Rory Stewart's mud fort, within sight of the bullet-strafed ruins of the old British Embassy, Bruce was able to dust off his Arabic, Spanish and German too.

The following day we were all escorted to the great Arg, the citadel of Kabul, for our audience with Karzai. The book had had particular resonance for him as he was a direct descendant of Shah Shuja and had found himself in much the same situation as his forbear. The parallels were striking: Shah Shuja was the chief of the Popalzai tribe in the mid-nineteenth century; Hamid Karzai was the chief of the same tribe today. Shah Shuja's principal opponents were the Ghilzai tribe, who today make up the bulk of the Taliban's foot soldiers.

Karzai cross-questioned us about the lessons of the book, and said that he thought the US was doing to him what the British had done to Shuja. But he would not be anyone's puppet. 'America and Britain deal with us as if we also came through a colonial experience,' he said. 'We did not. We always won in the fights but lost politically. This time I want to make sure we win politically too.'

Karzai was however perhaps most animated when comparing notes with Adam about going to school in India: 'I fell in love with Simla when I was at college there,' he said. 'There was a lovely cinema called the Regal on the Mall by the ice-skating rink. Every Friday I would go and see Peter O'Toole movies and *Goodbye Mr Chips*. That is where I began to develop a lot of respect for Britain.'

We all looked at each other in surprise.

'Not forgetting what they have done to us,' he continued, 'but the Raj has served India very well. I also fell in love with English literature there: I read Thomas Hardy, but my favourite is of course Shelley. I like him verrrry much. I keep reading him, regularly, regularly, once or twice a month. And I love John Betjeman: his poetry and also his talk shows on life in rural Britain. Two lovely books: *Butter Toast and Trains* and *Tennis Whites and Tea Cakes*.'

That evening Bruce threw a small party to celebrate at DAFA. Philippe opened a bottle of chilled Moët & Chandon, which we drank with gooey French brie, Afghan naan and a tin of Scottish shortbread that we had brought for Philippe.

The night ended at the foreign correspondent's hangout, the Gandamak Lodge. There we all had dinner with the historian Nancy Dupree, whom Bruce had got to know in his Peshawar days. Most of the other diners, and almost all those propping up the bar, were shaven-headed, gym-going young men in their twenties and thirties: a scrum of adrenalin-surfing hacks and cameramen who had grown up watching movies like *Salvador* and *The Year of Living Dangerously* and who now filled the bar with their tales of derring-do in Helmand and close shaves in Lashkar Gah.

None of them, however, had half as good a seam of war stories as the raffish silver fox sitting at the corner table in his salvar with the bird-like eighty-six-year-old woman, both of them picking quietly at their steaks. Nancy and Bruce compared notes about Masood and the *mujahideen* of the eighties, and Nancy talked about her current life commuting between her homes in Kabul and Peshawar, sometimes driving herself down the Khyber Pass in her little Renault 5, sometimes by Red Cross flights: 'I am their only frequent flyer,' she told us.

At this point, bursts of automatic gunfire echoed from the street outside. Immediately, all the hardened correspondents dived for cover, ourselves among them. Only Nancy continued unfazed, announcing from her seat, 'I think I'll just finish my chips.'

In 2015, Bruce and I began what would prove to be our final project together. It was to be a history of the East India Company, and was intended to complete the Company Quartet we had collaborated on, describing the transition from the world of the Mughals to the dawn of the British Raj, between the death of Aurangzeb in 1707 and the Great Uprising of 1857.

The central figure of this project was the ill-fated Shah Alam. His life formed an arc linking the Mughal glory days when Delhi ruled all of modern India, Pakistan, Bangladesh and most of Afghanistan, to its lowest nadir during the anarchy which followed the Mughal collapse after 1739. By the end of his life, as the famous doggerel had it, Shah Alam's rule stretched only to Palam, today the site of New Delhi airport.

At the end of 2015, we began by making a series of raids on the Persian manuscripts of the British Library. Here Bruce's old friend Ursula Sims-Williams, and her brilliant assistant, Saqib Baburi, of the Persian department brought out trolley-fulls of old, leather-bound Mughal manuscripts for us to look at. Some were originally from the library of the Red Fort, others from that of the East India Company Fort

William College in Calcutta. Both had ended up rubbing spines and gathering dust together in the same collection under the grey skies of King's Cross.

No one really seemed to have much idea what any of the manuscripts contained. The BL catalogue gave only the briefest description of each and almost none of them had ever been translated. Translating the eighteenth-century Mughal Persian Bruce knew so well is a skill only a handful of scholars now possess, and the late Mughal period is one almost completely ignored by scholars. Bruce had found a Kurdish café which made excellent *gozleme* at the back of the BL, and we decamped there each lunchtime. As Bruce ordered Kurdish delicacies in fluent Eastern Anatolian Turkish, we tried to make up our minds which manuscripts looked most promising, and which we should have copied and set to work translating. In the end our choices came down pretty much to pot luck.

This became apparent in the autumn of 2016 when Bruce moved back into the farm again to begin work on the mountain of photocopies which had just arrived from London. The first manuscript he read through was the *Ibrat-Nâma* or *Book of Admonition* of Fakir Khair ud-Din. This sounded most promising, and was, he wrote in an early note, 'full of metaphorical allusions to the political turmoil of the late eighteenth century, such as the *tûfân-i haul-afzâ*, a typhoon storm which increases a sense of terror, or the Sea of Oman which robs you of your conscious rational mind. For the admonitory purpose of this history is this: by considering these past lives, take heed for your own future.'

Sadly, the text turned out to be focused for much of its length on the reign of Akbar and Jahangir, a full century before the birth of our hero, Shah Alam. This became apparent within a few days, but, as Bruce himself put it, 'I am a bit like [the liner] the *Queen Mary*. Once I'm at full steam, it takes weeks to turn me around.' By the end of that year, Bruce's translation notes were full of gems such as the following:

> (**8 recto**) The 4th regnal year, anecdote of a qalandar visiting the court of Shah Jahan with a large tame lion called La'l Khan, who seizes a naked Yogi and mates with him as with a lioness, leaving him prostrate after an effusive ejaculation, but with no scratch or bite marks.

It was all fabulous stuff, but of absolutely no use to *The Anarchy*. So when Bruce returned the following autumn in October 2017, I did my best to keep the liner more closely on course. With this in mind, the week of Bruce's arrival, I persuaded him to head off to the small

Rajasthani town of Tonk. There, the former Nawab's library was said to contain a previously unstudied and untranslated full-length biography of Shah Alam by Munshi Mohan Lal. There was, however, a good reason why no one had ever studied the manuscript: the library's rules were incredibly strict and forbade the use of laptops, photocopies or cameras. Bruce duly went there, drank endless cups of tea with the librarian, helped him with his English correspondence, attended his family wedding, exercised his charm to the full, and before long had been allowed, against all the rules, discreetly to photograph the whole manuscript on his phone.

Shortly afterwards, on a trip to Pondicherry, Bruce befriended the scholar Jean Deloche of the École Français d'Extrème Orient. He returned bearing copies of a number of eighteenth-century French travel accounts of India – Madec, Gentil and Law – but the real find was Deloche's long-out-of-print critical edition of the *Voyage en Inde du Comte de Modave, 1773–1776*. Modave, it transpired, was an urbane friend and neighbour of Voltaire from Grenoble who had cast a uniquely sophisticated and sardonic eye on the eighteenth-century Indian scene, from the boulevards of Company Calcutta to the ruins of Shah Alam's decaying Shahjahanabad. Moreover, not a word of his book had ever before been translated into English. Bruce knew immediately that he was on to a winner, and emailed a sample passage to me from Pondi:

> The Empire held together while Aurangzeb reigned, and even for some years after he died in the early years of this century. For generally beneficial laws have a certain inner strength which allows them, for a time, to resist the assaults of Anarchy. But at last, about forty years ago, a horrible chaos overtook the Mughal empire: any spark of good that Aurangzeb had done to promote commerce was snuffed out. Ruthlessly ambitious Europeans were no less deadly in these parts. As if Europe and America were too small a theatre of war for them to devour each other, pursuing chimeras of self-interest, undertaking violent and unjust resolutions, they insisted on Asia too as the stage on which to act out their restless injustices.

Bruce's beautifully elegant renditions of Modave, Gentil, Khair ud-Din, Shakir Khan, Munna Lal, and the anonymous *Tarikh-i-Ahmad Shahi* are, I think, some of the very best work he ever did. Indeed, his last three Delhi winters, 2017, 2018 and 2019, were probably his most productive.

As well as his own work, he kept a sharply critical eye on mine and never allowed me to get sloppy. On one occasion, I sent off an article on Qajar Persian painting to a magazine which he believed to be inaccurate. He took it upon himself to ring up the editor, without telling me, and make various corrections before it went to press. Perhaps precisely because it was so easy to dismiss Bruce's scholarship as that of a showy peacock or some willowy dilettante, he was especially rigorous about double-checking every small detail. His translations always contained the exact Persian transliterations of every sentence translated in case the accuracy of his work was ever challenged. Sometimes whole weeks, even months were lost cross-checking obscure points of Mughal court protocol or regalia: who exactly was eligible to carry the Fish Standard, the *mahi maratib*? Which Nawabs were eligible for *alams*? 'Willie, a word in your ear,' he would say. 'Please make sure to double check the details of the battle standard of the third Nawab of Murshidabad. I know you laugh, but these things are very important.'

Equally, he could also be scathing about those who did not meet his own high standards. 'Wanting to massacre Professor X,' he texted me one afternoon. 'He is incapable of giving a correct page reference, so finding the original for his dodgy translation is like wading through a bog! He just doesn't know Persian, at least not in any idiomatic fashion. And as for his Hinglish – Gawd spare us!'

By now, Bruce had got into his routine. When he woke, which would often be in mid-morning, he would eat an elaborate breakfast of café au lait, baguette and a thick slice of white President French butter, topped by Bonne Maman apricot jam and Lindt chocolate. All of this would be specially fetched for him, according to minute written instructions, from a particular patisserie in Khan Market.

He would then get into his white pyjamas and sit on a cane chair in the garden, reading through the BL photocopies of his sources, under the shade of a wide-brimmed Cecil Beaton-style straw hat. He liked a small glass of wine or two at lunch, and would often invite friends to join him. Our guest list and lunch parties always became much grander and more exotic when Brucie was staying. The elegant wives of ex-Sri Lankan Presidents, Iranian drummers, British Museum curators, Aligarh Mughal experts, Cambridge musicologists and celebrated Scottish botanists would all make their way out to the farm to see him. Those who were lucky would be treated to post-prandial readings of Persian poetry, accompanied by his translations, during which he might serve mango and limoncello, one of his favourite summer combinations. These lunches often saw him at his sunniest and, depending on the company, most wheezily giggly.

He would then take a nap, and by 5 p.m. was busy in the kitchen instructing our amazing Bengali cook, Biru, who adored him, on the finer points of making petit-fours or drop scones or crumbling butter shortbread, all of which he loved for tea. This was a meal Bruce took with an Edwardian seriousness, serving it on trays with plates and silver and china teapots. That done, he would then teach Sam Persian for an hour, encouraging him to learn by heart *ghazals* by Hafez, Rudraki and Sa'adi, long before Sam knew enough Persian to understand any of them. Often their meanings would only become apparent much later when, partly under Bruce's direction, he began Persian at Oxford. Sam still knows them all by heart.

There often followed an evening gin and tonic with Olivia, when the two would set the world to rights. Intelligent female company always brought out the most private and empathetic side to Bruce, and Olivia was often privy to confidences I was only much later admitted to, if at all: a broken engagement soon after Oxford; the pain of his rejection by his father, who had named him after his favourite Labrador but showed him rather less affection, and who, at the end, cut him out completely from his will, leaving him nothing except for a pair of old brogues; his brief, unhappy – and most unlikely – period as a London tax-inspector; his much-loved sister's suicide, and the memorial concert of Monteverdi madrigals he had organised in her memory.

Finally, by seven or eight, he was ready to begin work. Unless he had arranged to go to a concert, he would usually skip dinner completely and work all night. Often we would return from Delhi parties long after midnight to see his light burning and Bruce tapping away on the laptop, his half-moon glasses perched at the end of his nose.

His main form of entertainment was to visit the various ruins of Delhi, to go to concerts, and to find pianos to play. He befriended our landlady, who had a lovely grand, and would treat her to evenings of Liszt and Debussy. Somehow Bruce also came into contact with a bespectacled American diplomat from Minnesota who was whispered to be the CIA station chief. The two played Shostakovich duets in a grand mansion under the yellow amaltas blossom of Amrita Shergil Marg, watched over by the American's fearsome Kazakh bodybuilder wife. They made a most unusual threesome.

Bruce loved to drop hints about his friends in the intelligence services, and this was one of the questions I most longed to ask him at the end. We never did get to the bottom of exactly what he was up to in Peshawar, and the question of whether he was actually in MI6 or just a translator and source of information on some outer periphery of that world. After all Bruce, for all his many qualities, made an unlikely James Bond.

Both my boys, Adam and Sam, loved to refill his glass and ask him about this period of his life. Sometimes, if they were lucky, he would tell them stories – of being chased through the plains of Afghanistan by Soviet helicopter gunships while riding pillion on the back of *mujahideen* motorbikes; his regular visits to Peshawar banks to cash aid cheques and deliver suitcases stuffed with bank notes by mule train to the different Afghan groups in the Panjshir Valley; of being invited to lunch by Osama Bin Laden after he tried to get the Peshawar-based aid agencies to stick up for their Afghan staff who were being intimidated by the Pakistani police who would plant opium on them and then lock them up until they paid bribes to secure their release; his dislike of Gulbuddin Hekmatiyar, who he regarded as a vicious barbarian; of the night the ISI (the Pakistan intelligence service) – so Brucie believed – assassinated his friend Juliet Crawley's husband, Dominique Vergos, and how it was he who found the body hanging strung up on the garage door with an assassin's bullet in the rear base of the skull; and the glimpse he had of the silhouette of the shooter disappearing over the compound wall in the moonlight.

This was actually a crucial turning point in contemporary history. It was the moment the Wahhabis of the Pakistani ISI and the Saudi General Intelligence Directorate seem to have broken ranks with the CIA and MI6 and began channelling their funding to only the most extreme Islamist groups among the *mujahideen*. At the time of his assassination – and Bruce was always very clear that it really was an assassination, not a bungled robbery, as the Pakistani police insisted – Vergos was said to be compiling a dossier on the atrocities wrought by the ISI's favourite client, Hekmatiyar. The assassination was therefore the first time the Wahhabis in the intelligence community turned on their Western allies. This was the beginning of the road to 9/11, and all that followed, and bizarrely, there was Bruce, caught blinking in the headlights, right in the middle of it.

We longed to know more. But whenever we pressed him too hard he would just smile enigmatically, give a coy shrug of his shoulders, and say he had to get back to work.

In December 2018, my beloved father's flame was ebbing and we all rushed back to Scotland to sit by his death bed.

Bruce was left in charge of the farm, with a full woodshed and wine cellar, and instructions to help himself. When we returned, a month later, after the funeral, the farm was transformed. Both shed and cellar were completely empty, and the terrace outside Bruce's bedroom had been turned into what were soon referred to as the Hanging Gardens of Bruce. Every pot plant and every palm, every brazier and every Moroccan lamp in the farm had been relocated to Bruce's new open-air boudoir, where in our absence much merriment and many fine concerts of Persian music had been held, illuminated by blazing bonfires as well as the distant light of the stars. The pale moon of the winter solstice had been the occasion for a magnificently boozy celebration. From time to time, I still meet strangers who attended the party that night, and who compliment me on my beautiful roof terrace.

Soon after, Bruce began to complain of stomach pains. He had fallen and cracked his ribs the previous winter, so initially he was convinced it was something to do with that. Bruce could be very stoic about pain and discomfort, but he could also be something of a hypochondriac, and his emails and texts were often full of descriptions of ailments, major and minor. But as the year progressed, he began to get more and more certain that something was wrong. His father had died of pancreatic cancer, and he somehow felt sure it was hereditary. He promised to get checked out after he left Mira Singh Farm for the last time in April 2019, but delayed doing so while taking a last set of tours around various madly dangerous conflict zones in Afghanistan and Iraq. On arrival back in York he sent a note which showed his suspicions:

> Hello dear Willie
>
> As always, it was a bit of a wrench leaving, I'd fallen into such a productive rhythm of long days with occasional escapes
>
> Thank you and Olivia for being so hospitable and such good friends. I left the flat-pack photocopies from the BL on your round table in your study. The Mir-Farsh paperweights, are all on top of a cupboard in Ibby's bedroom, out of the way till I get back: if for any reason I don't, I'd like Samsam al-Daula and Adamski to have one Mir-Farsh each.

He was in surprisingly high spirits that final summer, despite his growing anxiety and pain. He especially loved England in June and July, and my memories of that time of year are full of episodes dashing around the country from Arundel to Arisaig, chauffeuring Bruce to churches or concerts or country houses or operas, or usually, combinations of all the above.

Taking Bruce to the opera at Garsington became, in particular, something of an annual event. As always, he would sing for his supper, filling the journey there with stories of the composer or his music or how the opera came to be written and commissioned. He loved dressing up, and he loved music, just as he adored good company and good food, and outings to Garsington Opera provided all of these pleasures at once. We went twice in the summer of 2019, once to *Pelléas et Mélisande*, for which Brucie dressed up not in a dinner jacket but in a magnificent Afghan *chapan*, and once to the Monteverdi Vespers, which was dress-down, and for which he turned up barefoot, wearing a simple sadhu's *rudraksh* around his neck. In the photos, he is laughing, as happy and relaxed as he had ever been, as if he did not have a care in the world.

But he knew something was badly wrong, and he waited nervously for his NHS appointment. After the launch party for *The Anarchy* in September, he sent a thank you note: 'What a wonderful party,' he wrote, polite as ever, 'Congratulations on the finished *chef d'oeuvre*. I hope it will do really well – & thank you for your very generous acknowledgement. I miss our collaboration, & your company. I leave Saturday for Chechnya & Daghestan. Then into hospital to solve the searing stomach pains that have kept me from sleeping for the last 6 weeks – ulcers or cancer?'

As we all know, it was a particularly fast-acting and vicious version of the latter. On 31 October, I woke in Delhi to find a terrible text:

Hello dear Willie
Pancreatic cancer, far advanced, maybe 10 months left
They've promised pain-control, & a few months of active life
I've been playing baroque chamber music, to forget the pain
I'll be sorry not to be around for our next project – thank you
for stimulating friendship & collaboration over the last 20 years
LB
PS Please keep this to yourself for now

We saw each other a last few times in December. My Company School show, *Forgotten Masters*, was about to open at the Wallace Collection, and I went around it for the first time with him on a bright, wintry Sunday morning, fresh off the plane from Delhi. He had lost a lot of weight, but was as elegant as ever, and appeared for the occasion in a perfectly tailored cashmere coat, topped with an Afghan lambskin *karakul* hat. He was high as a kite on strong doses of opiates, but was as brilliant and charming as ever, translating inscriptions on the paintings and dazzling the Wallace's director, Xavier Bray, with the full beam of his charm and intelligence. Immediately after that, we had a last, long, hugely indulgent Christmas lunch together at his favourite gastro-pub, the Carpenter's Arms. Towards the end of the meal, his face fell as he recited a Persian *ghazal* by Hafez, which he then translated for our benefit:

The night is dark, I am afraid of the waves,
This savage whirlpool terrifies me.
You who walk on the distant shore, light-burdened,
What do you know of my inner state?

I saw him for the last time at the launch of *Forgotten Masters*. Bruce always loved a party, and he looked so happy, with all our mutual friends circling around him. We made plans for him to come and be pampered at the farm in January. We even hatched a plan to go to Dharamasala to see the Dalai Lama's personal physician, which seemed an appropriately Brucie response to any illness. He was sure he would have another six months, and maybe one more glorious English summer full of operas and trips to his favourite abbeys, and he talked about getting tickets to a concert in the Chapter House of York Minster during the York Early Music Festival. But he went downhill fast after that, much faster than anyone had ever imagined. On 21 January he wrote to say he probably would not make it back to India after all:

Dearest Willie,

Yes, the spirit is willing, but the flesh weakens more every day – I shall let you know when the candle is guttering finally, but for the moment, music is the best therapy – of which I've had daily doses here in London. It was good to play Mozart & Beethoven sonatas with Katherine. Henry also came from Edinburgh & we played piano duets: music takes the mind into different places.

Give my love to everyone on the Farm, especially Biru, Bina and Vijay. I miss you all, & must write to Sam & the Memsahib.

Back to York tomorrow, Macmillan cancer-nurses overdue to adjust pain-relief. The medication needs recalibrating, as it's no longer controlling the pain, which is tiring, so I sleep a lot...

Saying goodbye to friends while I am still able to do so with some pleasure & in spite of sleepless nights. The kindness of friends has been beyond anything I could deserve. So heartwarming and comforting – & you one of the very best.

If doctors manage some remission for me, a visit to India might be possible, but for the moment I can't stand or walk. I sleep much of each day. The prognostication or rather haruspication doesn't go beyond 3 months, & I find it difficult to look beyond the end of my nose, let alone next week.

Keep well, dear friend, & good luck.

A big hug

LB

Bruce died less than a week later. His last twenty-four hours were spent in hospital in York. He received so many visitors that he had to be moved to a ward all on his own to avoid disturbing the other patients. Up to his last afternoon, he was still planning a lunch party he wished to hold that weekend. Death ambushed him before he'd decided which of his prize Afghan mulberry puddings he would serve his guests.

May he rest in peace.

As he wrote himself: what a world is lost when someone dies!

# THREE FAREWELLS

# Pots, pottering and *cintamani*

**Isabel Denyer** *is a potter. She lives in Yorkshire.*

'Ahha,' he said, '*cintamani*.' This was Bruce within fifteen minutes of meeting him. He had very recently arrived in Yorkshire having travelled back overland from Afghanistan and was staying in the next village with a mutual friend of ours, Juliet Peck.

He was curious to see my pottery and spotted a plate which at the time was housing all sorts of detritus and 'useful tools' beloved of potters.

Thus started, for me, a fascinating exploration of *cintamani* in all its connotations and incarnations as used on ceramics and textiles. I had unconsciously used the three-dot pattern as a pleasing one over the years, so I was delighted to find that historically there was a connection, not only through Buddhist and other traditions but also representing the Christian trinity.

This first encounter led to much enrichment, as he wanted to know more and more about pots and the process of making them and eventually to meet other potters. He often used to come and help me at ceramic shows and events such as Art in Action. And inevitably the events themselves became an excuse for further explorations, discovering  yurt makers in Herefordshire, taking walks along beaches, seeking out tithe barns, ancient churches and carvings, visiting stately homes (often explored from a slightly different angle from the usual) and beautiful gardens. A journey wasn't just a journey: it would become an opportunity for adventure and seeking. Frequently he would not allow me to look at the map, really because he didn't want me to see how many, many miles out of our way we might be driving in order to see an inscription, a monument, a standing stone, a beautiful object or just to find some interesting food or a shop that he had heard of and had to investigate.

He was very good at spotting pots in dark and dusty corners of potters' workshops or studios and at very graciously persuading the maker that that pot would find a very good home with him, which indeed it did, and his eye was unerring in spotting beautiful things. One such was a magnificent large platter, a second, made by Edward Hughes (sadly deceased), which still has a special place in his garden – a site of much solace and outpouring of loving care at Holgate Road – where the platter is used as a bird bath. Many a moment has been spent just sitting nearby in the 'bus shelter'/arbour and quietly watching the birds having a glorious time splashing about.

Memories and images arise from further afield, such as the magnificent faience tiles on the Friday mosque in Isfahan, the lyrical brickwork and purity of the city's Sheikh Lotfullah mosque, the tiles in the church in Jolfa, the Armenian quarter of Isfahan. From Istanbul come memories of Isnik tiles and ceramics at the Topkapi Palace and Rustem Pasha Mosque, along with explorations of small out-of-the-way mosques and buildings of interest on the periphery of the city. And Sufi music, and dervishes too. And so the stream of memories continues: Persian pots in private collection, Kashan lustre and fritware ceramics, music in the Royal Pavilion, more Sufi music and classical Persian music on the *tar*, the *tombak* and the *oud*.

And in Orissa, a never-to-be-forgotten moment on our way to Puri. We made a diversion, courtesy of our driver, to the village of one of the driver's relatives. We drove down a long dirt track till we got to a cluster of houses nestled in amongst a coconut grove. It was Dandasi, where lived a master painter who mainly depicts Hindu fables. Amongst the pile of paintings that we were looking at I came across a small delicate painting on palm leaf which had been done by the painter's

wife, and to my delight it was a scene of a potters' village with all its associated activities. This was the one for me.

We were asked to return on our way back, by which time the whole extended family had assembled. On the rooftop in the sunset and amongst the coconut palms we were entranced for a couple of hours by the spectacle of Gotipua and Odissi dancers with their full regalia and make up. It was magnificent.

Bruce was a wonderful person to travel with. His breadth of knowledge and many languages opened doors to so many people and places. With his ability to communicate and explain, history, timelines fell into place, along with art, culture and beauty, for which he had an insatiable need. He had a way too of digging out people's better nature and being gracious to peoples of all cultures and walks of life and customs and most especially in connection with anything of beauty.

If one 'got' him and onto his wavelength (and stopped muttering darkly if one's own plans were changed!) and relaxed into his rhythm and off-piste approach, whether it was striding over the moors and getting inspiration for pots from lichen and landscapes or listening to music – Handel, Afghan, lute, Greek, Sudanese, Persian, north African, Bach, sometimes heard intimately in people's drawing rooms, sometimes on rooftops, at the Wigmore Hall or Glyndebourne, wherever possible and in whatever form possible – one could not help but enter into a world of discovery, caught up by his endless curiosity.

His generosity was great. I think of how he lugged heavy, bulky things back on planes including Iranian stone cooking pots, large baskets from Ladakh or shards of pottery and interesting food stuffs. Always he came back with some gift, despite very often being strapped for cash. Another gift was his way of making something as simple as bread, butter and honey into a feast just by the way he presented it. Or I think of chairs he rescued from a skip and gave a new life. He was sometimes accused of being a sponger but he more than sang for his supper in what he gave back, not in monetary terms necessarily but in his sharing of beauty in the little details as well as in the obvious ways, in his appreciation of so much, in the wealth and breadth of discussion with him and in his far-ranging knowledge. He also gave one the freedom to express and be oneself and be listened to which was a great gift.

For me he was also an ambassador for my work, as my pots seem to be all over the world thanks to him, which I find both humbling and rather awe-inspiring. They connect with people through the ages and the world. As Sasha Sunderland said, 'He caressed and cared for his pots,' and loved sharing them with others.

# Moscow, 1971

**George Lemos** *knew Bruce from 1971 to 2020.*

About a brilliant scholar, abundantly productive but excruciatingly taciturn, people quipped that he could be silent in ten languages. Bruce probably had ten languages too but for him people would have to choose a different adjective. A visitor once joked, noticing the etiolated ringing of my telephone (I am he of the miracle by which three days were transmuted into as many years), that it must have been exhausted through use by Bruce.

In their opposite polarities Bruce and the productive scholar evade the invidious distinction between the work and the life. Posterity can have the measure of the scholar, just as it can of figures whose living presence was averred by contemporaries to be even more impressive than their impressive works. But what can it make of someone who was true, however unwittingly, to Plato's strictures against the fixed and published word? The truth seems to have become that 'the current of his feeling failed; he became his admirers.' Bruce more than most people could be all things to all men. But he seems to have been put on a character diet and slimmed down to a hybrid of Anthony Blanche and Lawrence of Arabia with a dash of Artotrogus. He could do with restoration.

I first saw Bruce on 28 December 1971. We were in Moscow – a group of sixth formers and undergraduates. The second thing he said to me, having ascertained that I was a schoolboy classicist reading Horace, was that he had turned to Horace in the cultural isolation one feels in Germany. I remember thinking that this was either very silly or very profound and that I couldn't, however intrigued, tell which. I was intrigued again on New Year's Eve when Bruce was one of only three of us (the other apart from me was Robert Chandler, now well known as a translator from Russian) who peeled off to a cinema to see the Soviet cut of *Andrei Rublev*, even though he couldn't expect to understand a word.

I last saw Bruce on 28 January 2020. We were in the York hospital with Isabel, Lisa and Natasha. He couldn't say much, mumbling apologies for morphine-induced stupor. What to say? The sight of him brought to mind some lines of Rumi and, thinking that he might like the sound of Persian, I started to recite them. But the gesture was unthinking ('Ah! How colourless and formless I am, when shall I see myself just as I am?'); at the politely appreciative mumble from the bed I stopped. What to do next? Perhaps read something aloud. To hand was a recent edition of *Daphnis and Chloe* which I had on me for the train. Bruce didn't know the language but unlike the Moscow projectionist I could do something about it. The pastoral fantasy and the hospital reality were in marked dissonance; but so decades before were the pastoral play put on by the undergraduate Bruce and the roar of the eights week hearties surrounding it. Enter Daphnis; exit Daphnis pursued by a nurse. Bruce roused himself to inform her that his visitor was translating from ancient Greek. She pretended interest with a smile. Her business, deftly and with kindness carried out, was to move Bruce to the physical isolation of a single room to die.

> *Spring has been hesitating and capricious, with many sudden returns to icy gusts after days of warm balmy air – but now it seems definitely arrived and almost turning into summer. Today in the Tiergarten a nightingale suddenly started singing just above me, uninterruptedly for 5 minutes – I had never hoped that in Berlin! When not working, I go sailing with He. on Wannsee or sing madrigals, or lute songs with Hi. who plays very well, or learn Persian with Ma. – I met her at a concert and afterwards we went on to a Persian evening & there she forced me, the only European, to dance Persian folk dances with her. I coped as well as I could with an approximation midway between Cossack and Flamenco with the occasional arm movement taken from allemandes & the odd pas-de-bas – it was exhausting! In revenge I'm getting her to teach me Persian – I feel very obtuse, and as she knows little English and even less Deutsch, we are reduced mostly to grins and gestures, which is no doubt a good foretaste of Isfahan University.*

So Bruce from Berlin in the spring of 1978 taking the first steps of his *anabasis* ('*expedition up from* the coast, esp. into Central Asia'), auspiciously attended by a bulbul. No more need of Horace.

The proclivity to dance had a future for which I was particularly grateful. Five years later Bruce decided that he had to learn the *zeibekiko* and the *hasapiko* to take an active part in a forthcoming evening of *rebetika*. As was his wont, he kept up with his teacher after the show (transfiguring her in report, as was also his wont, into an expert on Hugo Wolf from the admirer which is as much as she confessed to being); because I happened to pick up the etiolated telephone when she returned a call from Bruce, we got talking and not long after got married. Bruce would regularly send Natasha notes of dances he had seen. In the early days they were on the back of postcards; the very latest, last October, now that he had mastered WhatsApp – too late, he was already stricken! – was a video clip of wedding dancing from Chechnya.

The lines from Berlin epitomise Bruce's insatiable appetite for new experience, the desire to be part of everything, the openness to other people. These made him, for me at least, the most agreeable of interlocutors – how often did we sink or, to put it more accurately, raise the sun in talk! But they could and did put him in real danger: an early case was a needless visit to the Notting Hill Carnival in 1976 which ended with Bruce suspended from each limb by four young men who, with calm contempt, ignored the blows of my weak hands and of an umbrella wielded by his sister, Corinne, while a fifth emptied his pockets. But this was nothing beside his experiences a decade later. And he could and did overstep the mark and often did put a foot wrong, literally as Natasha tells me was the case with his attempts to dance and metaphorically when his conversation outran his own copious supplies of knowledge. But, as has been wisely said, 'Of course one can "go too far" and except in directions in which we can go too far there is no interest in going at all; and only those who will risk going too far can possibly find out how far one can go.'

Why Bruce did not go as far as publishing his experiences is still an unsolved mystery for me, because his letters show an obvious capacity for unforced descriptive writing. Here is one sent to us from Faryab province in Afghanistan on 18 October 1987.

> *In the last few days' travelling, you've both been frequently in my thoughts – this mountain valley of Gorziwan is very beautiful and if ever this country is freed, I hope you'll come to the valley. Yesterday I took a day off from work (inspecting schools and clinics – both terms only remotely appropriate to the jolly peasants and mud houses that I actually see) and rode out with a friend to a magnificent waterfall that gushes out of a golden cliff and disappears into a cave at the bottom of the cliff; the ride took us through woodland of tall, widely spaced*

*walnut trees, the leaves already turning yellow and brown and falling into the clear broad streams. Caravans of white and grey donkeys were coming down from the mountain with heavy loads of winter fuel, sweet smelling shrubs and logs of juniper; and the woodsmen in their turbans and chapans and gaiters looked as if they still inhabited a 16c miniature. The madrassas I've visited also seem to be in a different age, the curriculum unchanged for centuries, piles of dusty tomes of canon law and exegesis and traditions presided over by a white-turbaned mowlawi who listens to the young scholars repeat their lessons in groups of three or four – he knows the books by heart and sits serene and apparently half asleep under the rafters – quinces hung to dry and bunches of grapes perfume the room. Very different from some of the party schools I've visited where the main lesson seems to be chanted slogans and revolutionary Islamic songs, full of hatred and an almost fascist rigidity. I wonder whether traditional Islam can survive.*

*It's 2 months that I've been on the road and I'm grateful that my riding accident delayed me, as I heard yesterday that the French journalist I was due to accompany was handed over to the Russians last month by a collaborator. The road is full of pitfalls, robbers, precipices and soon avalanches as well as the ambushes that decimate mujahideen caravans – we had a narrow escape in the Yekpay pass near the border. It's a pity relations with Iran are so bad, otherwise I'd be tempted to go out via Herat.*

The next letter I will quote was written on 25 March 1991 in Peshawar. Its lucidity, untinged by any romantic submission to the Orient, speaks for itself and needs only one gloss: of the word *Zalong*. It derives from *Salon*, as pronounced by Bruce's Berlin landlady ('*umsteigen wir in Salon*', she would say after dinner) and in that pronunciation Bruce and I felt it added an essential element of risibility to self-regarding coteries, particularly of persons enraptured by the Orient. We treated it as a Semitic triliteral z-l-g and formed any required derivatives by dint of the grammatically correct prefixes, infixes and root geminations (to say, e.g. 'He was put into a state of utter Zalonghood').

*Easter greetings, if they reach you in time – otherwise take them as May Day (Magdalen Tower not Kremlin) or Whitsun – none the less warmly felt from the heart for being late, as was ever my bad habit!*

*I enclose a compact disc of what purports to be Ottoman music by Greek composers of Constantinople – an unlikely trouvaille in Peshawar, brought by a tentacle of the Zalong, who uses UN funds to promote Zalongs – the next to be an Afghanerie – perhaps we can have the musicians sawing and puffing away in the Buddhist ruins of Taxila and call it Canti Kushani? I also enclose photo of self as Ottoman thug all shaved skull & chin except for whiskers! This at a candlelit evening of rebab, though the flashlight exposes the fancy dress mercilessly.*

     ...

*I have been encouraged to write a series of 12 documentary dramas for the BBC Pushtu and Persian service to warn locals of the dangers of heroin addiction – this in order to restore some of my battered solvency. The interviews took me into hospitals, prisons, tribal jirgas (like the Manx parliament) and heroin dens and have given me a new view of my host country – the black/drug economy is said to be 2x the official economy, 7 members of the National Assembly are notorious heroin traffickers, and the US pressure to control drugs is only beginning to have an effect now the local addict population is nearing 2 million – much talk of the Colombianisation of Pakistan!*

*As for Sufism which you mention in your Nativity card which has just reached me, from what I see of it here – it seems to be a mixture of theosophy & primal scream therapy & disco dancing + the well-known techniques of sects of fixation on a father figure, restructuring of the personality in group sessions, clique solidarity & an excuse for obstreperous behaviour not normally tolerated in the dour conformism of Islam – all in the cause of self-knowledge, of sensing the 'ground of being' unity which underlies the disparate & fragmented phenomena of ordinary experience – to that extent it is perhaps a sort of 'lived philosophy' and a safety valve on a society which does not leave much room for self-expression or aesthetic experience. I suppose its academic interest is due to the fine thinkers & poets it has managed to inspire – do the Moonies or the Scientologists have anyone to hold a candle to Rumi or Hafez or Suhrawardi or Ibn Arabi? Perhaps the sociological interest is due to its role in social control – after all, I can't remember any college chaplain, not even Fr James Forbes the Benedictine, commanding the sort of loyalty & tail-wagging puppy-like subservience ordinarily awarded to even the most modest Pir. Is it just that Montaigne, Descartes, Voltaire, Renan, Hume, Freud etc. have just not penetrated out here? I've never read Palamas & only skimmed Loyola's exercises – in their own time they no doubt were immensely influential, but did they ever dominate the culture of their century even down to the level of the street & tavern in the way Rumi did? I imagine European culture has always maintained, even in its most Christian phase, an access & escape route to its alternative identity of pagan, rational classicism – hasn't that limited its appeal to mystics?*

*Moreover, the ordinary Christian emphasis on selfless service to our fellow men takes some of the wind out of the sails of 'specialised' mysticism – though the Quran hardly ever mentions belief without also mentioning good works, yet the ritualisation of alms, charity, hospitality, pious endowments etc. seem to leave an empty space for mysticism. Perhaps people are not yet acculturated to an industrial society or to the breakdown of the extended family & take religion and outward piety more seriously here. Certainly religion is abused for political purposes to an extent that would be unthinkable in Cheltenham or London!*

*I finally found a copy of Spiros Vryonis' book on the decline of Hellenism in Anatolia – a depressing story, but also slightly disappointing treatment – in spite of all the detail I was left feeling I wanted to know much more & that I didn't understand the whys and hows. The basic point of the destruction of the autonomous economic base of the church leading to the decay of the community organisation is well made but my Ramadan-befuddled brain couldn't grasp much more. I'm also dipping into Jakobson's* Poetics, *which opens up new avenues for reading Hafez & the Indo-Persian poets & also Russell's* Introduction to Mathematical Philosophy *to clear the brain after too much Quranic Cantillation. George I miss you & Natasha.*

Bruce, we miss you too.

رسیر بوی گلستان بگلستان رفتی

There came the scent of the rose-garden, to the rose-garden
you went

# Bruce's house

*This is an extract from the letter* **Nick Robinson** *left behind for his children to read after his death. Nick predeceased Bruce by six years. As you can tell from this letter, he was a true friend of Bruce, for they were both highly cultured mavericks. As Nicholas Shakespeare has written elsewhere: 'It will surprise none who knew him that Nick succeeded in creating one of Britain's leading independent publishing houses. He was someone who preferred not to fish in the main river. Constable & Robinson reflects his strengths and character, a marvellous mingling of the traditional and the modern. He was an unsnobbish gentleman in the best sense, yielding to no-one in his passion for art and field sports; he also had the beady eye of his Harris hawk for a business deal and a new trend.'*

My friend Bruce Wannell was staying and we were having breakfast – a meal he always used to turn into a feast with small plates of fruit compote and walnuts as well as poached eggs, brown toast and mushrooms in a cream sauce.

Bruce lived for many years in Pakistan and became a Muslim for a while. Breakfast for Bruce is not a hurried meal – ideally it takes a couple of hours and results in long conversations. On this occasion he said, quite suddenly, 'Good manners are the basis of civilisation'.

I thought this was a bit shallow and said so. Civilisation has many foundations (urban development, social hierarchies, the rise of the city and therefore citizens with enough time for leisure – lots of historical stuff like that).

Nettled, he said, 'I will now tell you why and when I have finished you will agree with me.'

When Bruce lived in Islamabad he had a house with a courtyard where vines grew over the doorway and Afghan musicians would come and play in the afternoons. In the mornings he met with refugee leaders and dispensed advice and aid. Some years later, when he returned to England, he was very poor and was meant to be writing a book on his travels. He lived with different friends for a year and then fell on the mercy of the Housing Department of York who provided him with a room in a rundown terraced house near the city centre, which they used to house newly released prisoners and other single men who, for one reason or another, were on what used to be called 'their uppers'.

When he arrived at the house there were four other inhabitants. The house is one of those tall and narrow early nineteenth-century houses which are now much sought after but in fact are rather poky with a room on each floor. You can imagine the atmosphere in a house like this – undecorated, poorly lit, with a dingy overgrown garden at the back full of weeds and a basic and bare commercial kitchen, a shared bathroom with a single light bulb.

Bruce said the atmosphere was awful. The inhabitants didn't talk to each other and occasionally grunted a greeting on the stairs. Meals were all takeaway, eaten in bedsitting-rooms – alone. I asked him what he did. He said simply, 'I cooked'.

He cooked a meal in the unused communal kitchen – more food than he needed for himself – and left the door open. One of the others came in and said how good it smelled. 'Have some,' said Bruce. The man filled a plate and moved to leave with it. Bruce said, 'No, the only thing is we have to eat here – together.' Over the week, the others came in lured by the smell and free food. They ate together round the table.

'The point,' said Bruce, 'is this. If you cannot sit down and eat and converse together in a way that permits you to be considerate to each other, then you have nothing. The great pit that the West has fallen into is the functional meal with people eating what they want, when they want to – grazing from the fridge. They live in their own worlds of sensation and excitement but often fail to share these things or anything else. Sharing our food, our ideas and our opinions together is the basis of civilised life. We have conventions to make this sharing more pleasant for those we share our needs with, whether in one culture we don't eat with our left hands or in another we don't chew with our mouths open, we offer different dishes to others at our table. Good manners are not shallow, they are based on sharing and consideration for others – and these things are the first steps of civilisation.'

# AFTERWORD

# Bruce's last performance

*In a set of marvellously strange Bruce-type circumstances,* **Lisa Chaney** *was 'sent' him a quarter of a century ago by an old friend of his: the man whose secrets were crucial to Lisa's biography of Elizabeth David. Lisa Chaney has also written definitive biographies of J. M. Barrie and Coco Chanel.*

Dear B&R,

I do hope you're surviving purdah, and not succumbing to the virus.

Am looking forward to more meetings, to some answers to questions about our dear, mysterious Bruce's distant past, and to your London Memorial party. Tho' suspect Corona virus may end by postponing it?

Meanwhile, following the Memorial and our after-party here, I began the alarming task of sorting through Bruce's papers. This meant initially culling as much as possible, before it arrives here and I reckon with my promise to write some kind of book for him.

His storage was remarkable, a positive feat. In his circa five by three metres attic room, I'd not realised the extent to which his library was stacked not one, or even two, but three deep. (Lydia Wilson has valiantly taken in hand making a bibliography of his collection, pasting in the bookplates Mark Hearld made for him with her cohorts.) Discovering the layers of books has been instructive in my appreciation of the breadth of Bruce's reading, including the thousands of pages of photocopied scholarly articles and book chapters. If reading choices reflect aspects of the self, each layer of books and articles has been as if peeling back another one of Bruce's.

I wondered how much had become as hidden from his consciousness as it was from public view. But Bruce was a practical, unselfindulgent man, wasn't he? Keenly aware of his past, I think he'd gradually rejected being handicapped by his sorrows. He'd managed them with a mix of deftness and austerity that left him, ultimately, whole. Possible, perhaps because his gift for joy overcame much of the darkness.

In his third, hidden book level, with the distinguished prizes he'd won at school, were many of the core texts of the Western cannon. A number in French, German or Italian are hints at the future linguistic ability I could only marvel at. Almost every book is inscribed, either from a friend or, with date and place acquired, in his own confident hand. Many have notes or letters inserted. He'd also lovingly saved quantities of the birthday cards we all sent him.

Then, there are the yards of old diaries, papers, letters, lying in wait for me in the eaves. Put reading aside for later. Failing this stricture, I begin a small pile of the devotional lines I notice he's written or underlined over the years. Plus the informed, razor-sharp political comment on 'assignments' and 'briefs' I don't yet understand. Is it wishful thinking that it wasn't for brevity alone that a number of people's names are only represented by initials? But while self-revelation is tantalisingly scarce, there are small nuggets, some hilariously self-aware.

Bruce's life is encapsulated in this one small space: his drawing-room-study-bedroom-haven for almost a quarter of a century. His chaise a day bed, each night he laid out a bedroll on his kilims and rugs: this way, closer to sleeping in a nomad's tent. Before anything was moved or taken away, a tribute was owed him. His beautiful room was difficult to photograph, but I tried to capture something of its subtle atmosphere of exotic, contemplative, manly charm.

Sorting went better sitting on the floor on his rugs. His scent still hung on the air, lingered on each scarf – those trademark scarves – and the dashing hats and coats jostling for space on the back of his door. He'd squirrelled away thousands of photographs. Poignant, old family ones and many more, including the lodestone Middle Eastern years. There he is in the mountains, in the Afghan traveller's coat, neck festooned with fox skins, now near me on the chaise, or wrapped in a luxuriously thick silk scarf, here on the chair, or smiling at his companions in Peshawar, standing on the very rug and kilim I now sit on. Time recedes, shrinks and then expands, and I'm there with him in spirit. But really I'm here, alone in his room, of a sudden caught unawares by the weight of his loss.

Surrounded by his books, papers, reams of sheet music, his lovingly collected objects – treasured as aides memoires to places and people – I remember the voracious appetite for travel, for exploration, and of the mind. (Unlike the great traveller Odysseus, Bruce's modesty meant he didn't seek heroic legend status.) Was his questing ultimately about hope, about searching for 'the other'? Not unconnected, was that intense and infectious ability to rejoice in the moment and equally, to relish the future. Remember how devoted he was to the young. (Preferably well-behaved ones.) They were deliciously 'new', yes, but I think it was essentially because they are heralds of the future.

Down the years, Bruce became more his own man, don't you think? In part liberated by parents' deaths. Less need to name drop. Well, a bit less? He grew kinder, more austere, wickedly funnier, less apologetic about who he was, how he lived. Sharing this Housing Association house, recently more by choice than necessity, with the panache and generosity of the suavest salonnier, he welcomed even more guests to his table. At the same time, while his bank balance typically ran perilously close to empty, he was one of the few people I've known who could have given away his last penny.

Instructions: 'When I die you mustn't forget my phone, my address books, the kitchen journals'. Every delicious meal taken with him at No. 46 is in these *Journaux Alimentaires*. We are all there noted, too. Plus details and critique of each skilfully prepared course, a sprinkling of wince-makingly accurate snipes, and the blackest humour. But over and again there is a touching comment on a meal he's given, or received, reminding how deeply commensality moved him. Sitting down to food with friends, the garden, along with music his animating spirits.

For several hours a day, for over three weeks, I'm there. Sometimes: 'thank goodness, I can throw away this wadge of particularly worthy-looking photocopy. Better have a quick check'. And there on page 16, a few lines of revealing comment. 'Oh, damn it, damn it, got to keep!' Fiona and Richard make determined inroads into the towers of books; begin boxing them up for their various destinations. Bruce's life is being dismantled.

When I'm alone his longtime housemate, Mark Speak, brings cups of tea, helps me sort through his clothes, right down to his cashmere socks, and the fine textiles not yet apportioned. Mark talks; I realise how much this gentle pastry chef was Bruce's devoted righthand man in this sometimes-mad ménage. We chuckle over Bruce's peccadillos, his barmier foibles, how utterly infuriating he could be, and marvel at his open-mindedness, his tolerance. Mark reminds me how Bruce put food out at night for the drug addicts who were then their housemates. He'd said, 'They need to eat, they graze at night, like wild animals'. Mark repeats how good to him Bruce had been. I think, Caritas.

My seclusion in this monk's cell, that he didn't regret, was unintended. (Did you notice how unresentful he was of the houses he stayed in, however grand they might be?) But out of it, something came to me about this deeply elusive man, and probably recognised long since by others. I saw the years of dedication to the Sufi texts, the line in an old diary, the underlinings in a manuscript – those words I'd accumulated in my little pile. Words that humbled me before Bruce's long practice of devotion, they described different aspects of the same notion.

Namely, that one need not, indeed should not profess one's beliefs. By every *act* of non-judgement, reticence, of silence, patience, loving kindness, generosity and graciousness, one obviates the need to look obsessively inwards. One's spirit will look after itself because one is *living* belief.

I'm not edging Bruce towards sainthood, God forbid. But these words describe his way of being in recent years, and why he could say to us with such grace, at breakfast here in Cygnet Street, the morning after his diagnosis, 'I have had such a good life, have wonderful, loving friends, I am not afraid to die.' He then chuckled, adding, 'I may end a snivelling wreck but let's hope not.'

His papers were finally ready to bring here and I could begin his piece for your book. But then I was felled by what has almost certainly been Coronavirus so, my apologies for the long preamble. I'm hoping for a few days' grace? I'd like to call it *Bruce's Last Performance*, describing the day Isa (Denyer) and I followed his ambulance to hospital, just four days before he died.

We were put with him in a quiet room, looking out onto tall old trees. For several hours, a steady flow of nurses and doctors came and went: questions, checks, bloods rushed off to the lab, listening to his heart, observing the fluid in his painfully distended abdomen etc. They were very gentle with him as they tried to decide what would serve him best. In between medics we talked a bit, he held our hands. After a few hours, Isa was sad she had to leave; in the early evening Fiona arrived from work.

It was clear that Bruce didn't have much longer. But for the eight hours and more that I was there, I had a prime seat at an unforgettable performance. As soon as the miraculous, now intravenously supplied morphine reduced his excruciating pain, the patient became more himself again.

He lay there, a miracle of dignity and stoicism. The autocrat; wicked wit, minor prince (the bed happened to be raised up as if on a dais), the man who 'got' the various levels of status in an instant and was just as gracious to the most junior nurse. The man who couldn't pass up making a connection or introducing people to one another, having rapidly discovered family origins in a far-off land. 'I must introduce you to so and so', in another far-off land. To cap it all, having clocked their name badges, he amazed and delighted everyone present by breaking into the mother tongue of each foreign medic who entered the room – I counted seven languages in all. In no time, this dying man had conjured an atmosphere of sunny optimism. The medics came to offer Bruce what healing they could, but as they left the room one saw that each of them felt a little healed themselves. Now and again the 'socializing' was too much for Bruce and he closed his eyes.

The Hindu consultant finally came, spoke with him, held his hand and then asked, 'Tell me Bruce, are you afraid of dying?'

Bruce's answer brought everyone in the room to a stilled silence. Moving his hands as in a graceful dance he replied, 'As Shiva, doctor. What is happiness without sadness, life without death? After the winter, the spring, as now, is so beautiful when it comes. I'm not afraid to die.'

The hours had flown by and when Fiona and I finally left him settled in that night, I felt privileged to have been there. The next day Bruce's habitual vitality had plummeted. The following day his strength was ebbing fast. He spoke little, he was in pain, he also smiled. With his body declining, as if by the hour he grew thinner, yet his spirit seemed to take over and his face continued refining. In those days before his death, despite the pain, to me his face had grown beautiful.

All my best wishes
Lisa

Perhaps I should add a PS. My initial apprehension about intruding into Bruce's room was soon dispelled. It had a warm, beneficent feeling. The dear man was both all around me and nowhere. As if with calm good cheer, through all the books, papers, diaries, the letters of his life, he was smiling back at me. Above all, he was excited to be off on the next leg of his journey.